The Lorette Wilmot Library
Nazareth College of Rochester

D1071255

Applied Linguistics and Language Study

General Editor: C. N. Candlin

Strategies in Interlanguage Communication

Edited by
Claus Færch and Gabriele Kasper

London and New York

Longman Group Limited
Longman House, Burnt Mill, Harlow,
Essex CM20 2JE, England
and Associated Companies throughout the world

© Longman Group Limited 1983

Published in the United States of America by
Longman Inc., New York

First published 1983
ISBN 0 582 55373 3

BRITISH LIBRARY CATALOGUING IN PUBLICATION DATA
Strategies in interlanguage communication. —
 (Applied linguistics and language study)
 1. Communication 2. Language and languages
 3. Psycholinguistics
 I. Færch, Claus II. Kasper, Gabriele
 III. Series
 401'.1 P90

LIBRARY OF CONGRESS CATALOGING IN PUBLICATION DATA
Main entry under title:

Strategies in interlanguage communication.
 (Applied linguistics and language study)
 Bibliography: p.
 Includes index.
 1. Interlanguage (Language Learning) — Addresses,
essays, lectures. 2. Communication — Addresses,
essays, lectures. I. Faerch, Claus. II. Kasper,
Gabriele. III. Series.
P53.S87   1982   418   82-13087

Set in 10/12 pt Times New Roman

Printed in Great Britain
by Butler and Tanner Ltd., Frome, Somerset

Acknowledgements

We are grateful to the following for permission to reproduce copyright material:

Julius Groos Verlag for the article 'Strategies of Target Language Learner Communication: Message Adjustment' by Tamás Váradi *International Review of Applied Linguistics* **18/1**, 1980; Language Learning and the authors, Eddie A. Levenston and Shoshana Blum-Kulka for their article 'Universals of Lexical Simplification' *Language Learning* **28/2**, pp 399–415, 1978; The Ontario Institute for Studies in Education and the authors, Elaine Tarone, Andrew Cohen and Guy Dumas for their article 'A Closer Look at Interlanguage Terminology: A Framework for Communication Strategies' *Working Papers in Bilingualism* **9**, 1976; Teachers of English to Speakers of Other Languages and the author, Elaine Tarone for her article from *TESOL Quarterly* **15/3** September 1981.

Contents

Preface

There are a number of reasons why it is especially appropriate now that this collection of papers should appear in the *Applied Linguistics and Language Study* series. Studies in second-language acquisition have come to regard the investigation of learner-learner and learner-native speaker *interaction* in classroom and non-classroom settings as a prime source of research data; ethnographers of language and discourse analysts have similarly turned to such data in their studies of human pragmatic behaviour; language learners' language provides an obvious basis for psycholinguists wishing to investigate learning processes in general and, finally in this list of reasons, we may expect that language teachers and materials designers will draw from these papers some clear indications for the design· and organization of classroom tasks directed at promoting particular types of communication among learners.

The contributions from the Editors are not only themselves examples of pioneering studies, they demonstrate clearly the development and prospects of what has become a major field of activity in applied linguistics. Moreover, from their Introduction to the book as a whole, and their explicit introductions to each of the three Parts, we can see how this field of activity presents a coherent face to both researchers and to practising teachers. Even more importantly, the wealth of examples provided in the collected papers, and the clear indication of the research methodology employed in each study, offer to teachers every opportunity to carry out parallel research into interlanguage strategies in their own classrooms and among their own learners, where, after all, the significant data are created.

Given the explicitness and the clarity of the organization of the book by Dr Faerch and Dr Kasper, I see little point, as General Editor, in reiterating in this Preface what they have already amply provided. A guide to a comprehensive and critical guide would be superfluous. Instead, taking the idea of development and progress in the field which is a strong thread running through this collection, I propose, as an alternative, to provide some discussion on possible *Futures* for research and practice in interlanguage communication studies, thus providing both a framework from which the collection of papers may be read and a point of possible departure for future research and development. In doing this, however, I am conscious that many of the issues and suggestions treated here are themselves alluded to and adumbrated in both the introductions of the Editors and the papers of the contributors.

Strategies of interlanguage communication relate to problems learners face. They represent, in the definition which the Editors have arrived at, 'potentially conscious plans set up by the learner in order to solve problems in communication'. In what follows, I want to take up this matter of *problems* and to widen it from communication *per se* to take in both problems of learning facing the learner and problems of interacting with materials and with instruction; recognizing all the time, however, that communication, learning and instruction interact and influence each other, much as they are shown to do in this collection of papers.

If we are to make sensible statements about learners' problems in communication it would seem axiomatic that we characterize, in as full a way as we can, the constitutive ethnography of those activity types (to use an overarching label) within which the learner is co-participant. At the same time, we need to recognize that such a descriptive task will be complex, if only because the classroom as event may subsume a variety of ethnographically distinct encounters each of which may present multiple and different problems of communication to learners. Furthermore, since second-language learning has as its defining objective the enabling of learners to communicate as freely as possible in the target milieu, we may expect that the encounters learners are involved in in classrooms ought to bear a resemblance to those encounters, however defined, that they may reasonably expect to participate in after instruction. Learner communication problems, then, need to be understood against an ethnographic account of the variety of encounters met with in classrooms, described both in their own terms and against a contrastive account of extra-classroom activity. So much, then, for the need for descriptive adequacy in studies of learner problems in interlanguage communication. What of explanatory adequacy? To an extent, of course, if our classroom ethnographies have stressed the pluralism of encounters in classrooms and shown how each such encounter may stand as a particular realization of some ethnic encounter, displaying thus relationships between classroom and non-classroom settings, this requirement of explanation may be met. The requirement, however, goes further. If we see classroom communication as the creation of all the participants, constitutive of a particular cultural environment and demonstrative of the presence of constraints on the perception and evaluation of utterances by these participants, then our study of learner interlanguage will, at very least, have to take into account the presuppositions and personal communicative goals and intentions of the co-participants. If we are to undertake such studies, as it seems we must, then we cannot do so in some sociological vacuum. We must have as point of departure a social theory in terms of which we can offer explanations of the freedom and circumscription on the allowability of learner contributions (in terms of topics, turns and tasks) and the appropriateness of learner inferential schemata within the social world of the classroom or elsewhere. To come straight to the point, who identifies the problems in communication and in what terms are they to be described? Answering these questions poses, in my view, some serious problems for interlanguage research. Different participant ideologies and social views engender a pluralism of norms against which learner utterances are to be judged; miscommunication, error and pragmatic failure are relative matters. Moreover, the wide variety of alternative models of analysis has the uncomfortable consequence of uncovering divergent 'problems' in communication. Different analyses produce differing results. Indeed for some analysts to talk of alternative models already begs the question of whether any 'top down' analysis can ever hope to capture the participants' eye view, so to speak. At very least we shall have to look to the validation of our methodology and through procedures of triangulation seek to corroborate what otherwise may be a partial point of view, of the participant or of the analyst. Labov's 'observer's paradox' will have to be accommodated, lest we misinterpret what is 'going on'. If problems are cues for strategy, then identifying problems is a necessarily prior activity.

Overcoming problems of communication is not only the motivation for strategic behaviour among learners, it also offers evidence from which we can gain, albeit indirect, insights into learning. As several of the papers argue and illustrate, learner communication strategies offer, as overt behaviours, 'windows' on the covert cognitive behaviour of the learner, giving us clues as to how the learner is thinking and coping. There are two cautionary points to bear in mind, however. The first is that we need to remember that although various communication strategies signal, obviously enough, learner processing, that is not the same as saying that certain communication strategies can be directly keyed, as it were, to those learning strategies rather loosely held at present to be promotive of language acquisition. Secondly, the variation in learner strategy in terms of learner, task and situational characteristics ought to make us even more cautious in making too facile a link between overt and covert behaviours. Differences in communication strategy that we may determine need not necessarily be either promotive or demotive of learning, certainly not in any universalistic sense across learners. It would seem from this, then, that for studies of strategies of interlanguage communication to be of interest to psycholinguists and language teachers rather than merely to ethnographers and discourse analysts, we shall have to set in train some major research programmes which, as some of the papers here suggest, will have to focus on particular learners in particular encounters with the aim of building up a gradual mosaic of experience. Our present state of limited knowledge of second-language acquisition, especially among adults in non-institutional settings, would seem to suggest that this research is both urgent and likely to be of some duration. Moreover, the present focus on performance and production in the study of interlanguage communication will have to be matched by an equal interest in learner interpretive strategy if we are to have a more complete picture of how individual learners adopt particular strategies not only to cope with immediate problems in communication but also to facilitate that interaction which in some associated way, aids and augments their acquisition.

Implicit in what I have said above is the suggestion that communication strategies not only serve to overcome problems learners face but are also used by learners to create the conditions for intake. If this is so, then instruction should presumably take the form of offering problem-posing tasks to learners so that they may in some concerted way co-exercise their communication and their learning strategies in the accomplishment of the tasks. Within a communicative methodology, as the Editors acknowledge in their Introduction, such an emphasis upon a process in which learners are faced with a range of differentiated tasks through

which they can exercise their strategies is a defining characteristic. We arrive, thus, at the third area of problem which I identified at the outset of this Preface, namely that facing instruction
and pedagogy. The problem essentially concerns this concept of
problem-posing tasks: upon what basis are they to be designed
and organized? If we are concerned with producing evidence of
learner communication and interpretive strategy, then, presumably, the tasks will need to be designed to raise obstacles to
learner communication and interpretation as stimuli to such
strategies. The extent of the variation among learners, against a
host of relevant criteria, and the improbability of learning
strategies, at least, being 'taught', would seem to speak against
any attempt to individualize tasks far ahead of time, as it were, in
some staged syllabus. Moreover, such an attempt would be likely
to encourage 'forcing the data' by constructing artificial encounters which lack plausibility and verisimilitude in target communication terms. We risk avoiding presenting learners with the
rich and varied target content data needed to excite learner affect
and to provide examples of that language the learner is engaged
in acquiring. However, let us suppose that we can devise tasks
which retain that authenticity to target in their content data. Here
another and counter-problem arises. It may be that such target
content acts against the state of learning of the learner. It may be
too difficult of access or, less frequently acknowledged, it may
cast the learner in the role of subservient in the discourse such
that the learner cannot authentically exercise those communication strategies which would allow him to create the conditions for
intake. In such a situation, authenticity to target will be at odds
with authenticity to process. What action can be taken? What is
needed, I believe, is an experimental typology of tasks which,
through a programme of action research in classroom and in
other settings can be shown to engender particular kinds of communication and particular kinds of communication strategy
among varying learners. Furthermore, since learners are engaged
in a dynamic process of language acquisition, we shall need to
keep a continuing account of the data stimulated by such tasks,
for particular learners. There will be many variables affecting
such research, some of which I have indicated above. Such a research endeavour, moreover, will have a profound effect upon
curriculum design. It will speak for a communicative curriculum
which replaces a prescriptive syllabus with a negotiated process of
task selection linked to precise recording of learner communica-

tive behaviour and related, however obliquely, to learning strategy.

This Preface has, I hope, indicated that the issues raised by this book are ones which are central not only to applied linguistic research but also to language teaching practice. The papers, many of which have either been written especially for this book or are drawn from sources not easily accessed, all touch upon the problems that I have tried to outline here. More than that, they provide through their argument and their evidence, stimulating sources for discussion and debate. Most happily of all, they offer to teachers researchable questions in the contexts of their own classrooms and a variety of methodologies by means of which this necessary research can be carried out.

Christopher N. Candlin   *Lancaster*
General Editor   *January 1982*

Introduction

It is now more than ten years since the appearance of three articles, each of which emphasized the language of second or foreign language learners (henceforth 'L2 learners'[1]) as a potential source of knowledge about second or foreign language learning[2]: Corder's 'The Significance of Learners' Errors' (1967), Nemser's 'Approximative Systems of Foreign Language Learners' (1971), and Selinker's 'Interlanguage' (1972). During the seventies, the area of 'interlanguage studies', as it has come to be known, expanded rapidly, and different types of interlanguage (IL) were investigated: the language of second and foreign language learners, of migrant workers, of pidgin and creole speakers. Irrespective of which of these types of IL has been in focus, researchers have concentrated on one of the following main areas of interest:

1. the IL as a *linguistic system*, described relative to various types of IL users at different stages of their learning process;
2. the *learning process*, described in terms of the IL development and the means whereby the IL user builds up and extends his IL system;
3. the IL *communication process*, described in terms of the reception/production processes in the IL user and the way he makes use of his IL system for communicative purposes.

Within each of the three areas, a development can be seen during the second half of the decade from descriptions of the IL itself and the learning and communication processes as rooted in the IL user (i.e. the IL seen *in isolation* from the social environment), and towards descriptions which contrast the IL with whatever language the individual is exposed to and which attempt to integrate learning and communication processes within a more comprehensive, interactional framework.

Area (1) can be characterized as *product-oriented*: the researcher aims at a description and classification of observable IL phenomena. Best-known among such descriptions are probably error analyses of the language of L2 learners (cf. the studies quoted in the following bibliographies: Bausch 1976; Sajavaara and Lehtonen 1975; Palmberg 1976, 1977; Rattunde and Weller 1977), which later gave way to more comprehensive descriptions of both erroneous and non-erroneous aspects of IL performance (Zydatiss 1976; Kielhöfer and Börner 1979; Chun 1979; Kasper 1981). A number of researchers have described the input of the IL users in linguistic terms (cf. the contributions by Chaudron and Long in Seliger and Long forthcoming), an approach which brings the product-oriented, linguistic research represented by (1) into close contact with the other two areas.

(2) and (3) can be referred to as *process-oriented*: the researcher is interested in discovering the underlying mechanisms which lead to a certain IL behaviour. The first subtype of process-oriented studies ((2) above) focusses on the *learning* process as it is reflected in IL use. As well-known studies within this area can be quoted analyses of error-causes in L2 learning (most of the works cited above for product descriptions of IL systems also attempt process descriptions of the data) and descriptions of L2 learners' developmental sequences (as discussed and summarized in, e.g. Hatch 1978a; Krashen 1978; Dulay and Burt 1980; Wode 1981). Language learning is frequently described in terms of 'strategies' activated by IL users in developing their IL, cf. Dulay and Burt 1975, pp. 220ff; McLaughlin 1978, pp. 38ff and Færch and Kasper 1980, pp. 61ff for discussions of this point.

In particular within the area of language learning the emergence of analyses of learner input and of the interaction learners participate in has led to a better understanding of the general principles which govern the learning process. Among contributions in this area can be mentioned Hatch (1978b) and Larsen-Freeman (1980) for L2 acquisition, and the articles included in Seliger and Long (forthcoming) for L2 learning in classroom situations.

The second type of process-oriented IL research ((3) above) is aimed at the description and explanation of IL *communication*. Here the area of IL speech production has recently received considerable attention (see e.g. the articles in Dechert and Raupach 1980a, b), whereas the receptive side has been less thoroughly investigated (but cf. Levelt and Flores d'Arcais 1978). The interest in analysing *interactional* aspects of communication, which developed rapidly during the seventies as regards communication in the native language, has also spread to IL communication, and recently a number of studies have appeared which describe the ways in which IL systems are utilized in specific communicative situations between interlocutors who typically do not share an L1. As examples of this can be mentioned Rehbein (1978), in which repair sequences in the foreign language classroom are investigated; Kasper (1981), who describes various pragmatic and discourse functions in the IL of German learners of English in role-play interactions with native speakers of English; and Sajavaara and Lehtonen (1980), which contains a number of descriptions of Finnish learners in discourse with native speakers of English. Related to these studies are analyses of the communicative effect of IL performance on interlocutors ('tolerance investigations'), see, for example, Johansson 1975, 1978; Politzer 1978; Albrechtsen, Henriksen and Færch 1980).

There is a close link between the two types of process-oriented IL research mentioned above: after all, learning takes place *through* communication in informal environments and — perhaps increasingly so during recent years — partly also in the classroom, thanks to the shift to more communication-oriented teaching goals and methods. Thus one particular act of verbal behaviour can have both learning and communication functions for the IL user. However, whether learning and communication occur simultaneously — as is typically the case in first and second-language acquisition — or consecutively — as is typically the case in the traditional foreign language classroom — is quite irrelevant for the distinction *in function* between these two areas: *learning* L2 refers to the processes whereby the learner discovers the rules (pragmatic, semantic, syntactic, phonological) of L2 and gradually comes to master them, thereby developing a continuum of IL systems. *Communicating* in IL refers to the ways the learner uses his IL system in interaction. It is on this latter area that the present volume will focus. But as can be seen from a number of contributions included in the volume, this does not mean that the learning aspect of using IL for communication is altogether left out of consideration.

For reasons we shall go into below, we have restricted the area of IL studies which will be dealt with in this book to the use of *strategies* in IL communication. It would be premature to venture a precise definition of the term *communication strategy* at this place — each of the four articles included in Part One offers its own way of defining the area, just as the articles which make up

the rest of the book contribute in various ways to a better understanding of 'communication strategies'. The best we can do here
is give a broad characterization of communication strategies which
will hold true for most of the contributions included. In order to
do so, we have to introduce a distinction between two different
types of IL use, which occur side by side in a great variety of IL
discourses. First, there is the possibility for learners to use their
ILs productively and receptively without experiencing any problems in planning and executing their utterances, or in taking in
their interlocutors' speech. This 'unproblematic' IL use is seen
from the learner's point of view and thus focusses on the production and reception *process*: whether the result is 'native-like',
'learner-specific', 'erroneous', is a completely different matter.
Secondly, the learner might *not* find it possible to use his IL in an
'unproblematic' way, for reasons which will be discussed by various contributors to this volume. In this case, he will have recourse to *strategies* in order to cope with such problems. One can
therefore maintain a distinction between *strategic* and *non-
strategic* IL use. Describing *communication strategies* in IL communication is the same as describing the strategic use of IL
systems.

The choice or even the availability of certain communication
strategies will be influenced by a variety of factors. Of these factors, the context in which the learner has learned his IL seems
particularly powerful. A number of studies have demonstrated
that various areas of learners' IL systems (morphology, lexis,
pragmatic and discourse structures) reflect specific features of the
original learning context. For example, learners who acquire their
L2 under unfavourable social and interactional conditions in non-
pedagogic contexts have been shown not to develop their IL
above the level of a pidginized system (cf. Schumann 1978;
Heidelberger Forschungsprojekt 1977). It has further been
shown that L2 learning under classroom conditions produces specific communication patterns in the learners' IL performance
(Kasper 1981, 1982). If IL systems and communication patterns,
then, reflect the original learning environment, it seems reasonable to assume that the ways learners cope with communication
problems are determined by these contexts as well.

Apart from the (past or present) *learning* context, the present
communication context will also influence preferences for certain
communication strategies. The learner's communicative experience and his assessment of the situation will determine his choice

of communication strategies. It will be an important task for future research to establish a typology of communication strategies in terms of their potential success in varying types of discourse.

A better knowledge about the variables which influence the use of communication strategies and their communicative effects has clear implications for foreign or second-language teaching. Ever since the shift from foreign language courses which centred on the *formal* aspects of language — no matter whether they were taught by explicit rule formulation or by a direct or audiolingual method — to *functionally* oriented syllabuses aimed at communicative competence as the overall teaching goal (cf. the discussions of this in, e.g. Piepho 1974; Wilkins 1976; Johnson and Morrow 1978; Widdowson 1978; Breen and Candlin 1980; Johnson 1982), a lot of effort in foreign language pedagogy has been devoted to structuring foreign language courses according to notions, communicative intentions, speech acts, situations and topics, thereby substituting the traditional 'grammatical' by a 'pragmatic' selection and grading of teaching content (cf. the extensive work initiated by the Council of Europe, e.g. van Ek 1975, 1976; Conseil de la Coopération Culturelle 1976; Europarat 1980; see also the practical applications of a 'functional' approach in Candlin, Bruton and Leather 1974; Abbs, Sexton *et al* 1978; Piepho and Bredella 1978; Johnson and Morrow 1979). Unfortunately, the problems involved in classifying these pragmatic aspects of language use in a theoretically justified and practically relevant way are far from being solved (cf. Knapp-Potthoff 1977; Edmondson 1981 for a detailed criticism). Moreover, no one has yet succeeded in matching in more than an ad hoc way systems of pragmatic categories with the linguistic means by which they can be realized, and we doubt that this can ever be achieved (but see Leech 1980 for some suggestions). However, even if these difficulties were overcome, and the concept of communicative competence as a teaching goal was better founded, operationalized and teachable, learners would first and foremost be communicatively competent in those areas of interaction which were included in the syllabus they followed. Whether this knowledge could then be extended to new communicative tasks would depend on the individual learner's capacity for using this knowledge in a creative way. Even though much pain has been taken to analyse learners' communicative needs and to relate these to teaching goals and syllabus structure (cf. Munby 1978; Altman and James 1980, and references to needs analyses in Høedt 1980), there is an obvious problem in predicting what exactly the communicative needs will be for the 'general learner'. Given this 'dilemma of anticipation' in foreign language teaching, we fully agree with Knapp (1980) that instead of refining the analytical instruments of need studies, it might be more feasible to analyse how learners can make the best use of whatever specific knowledge they have of L2, in addition to their general communicative knowledge deriving from their first language, in cases where the L2 knowledge is insufficient for the attainment of a particular communicative goal. Incorporating the learner's ability to handle communication strategies as an integral part of his general communicative competence has been suggested by Canale and Swain (1980), who refer to this ability of using communication strategies as the learner's 'strategic competence'. As seen within a larger perspective, a strategic approach to L2 learning and communication is in perfect line with cognitivist ideas of the *creative* aspects of language. More specifically, in its focussing on the totality of the learner's communicative ability, the notion of a strategic competence is in accordance with recent attempts to rehabilitate the learner's knowledge and abilities from communication in the first language as a potentially valuable factor in L2 learning and communication (cf. Kellerman 1977; Breen and Candlin 1980; House forthcoming).

The articles included in this volume all fall within the area of IL speech production. This by no means reflects any deliberate attempt on our part to exclude *receptive strategies* from consideration, but we have so far been unsuccessful in finding studies which look at speech reception from the particular angle of how learners cope with problems in the reception of speech (see, however, the brief discussion of receptive communication strategies in Færch and Kasper 1980, pp. 100–101, as well as the contributions by Færch, Kasper and Tarone in Candlin and Breen forthcoming). In view of the overall importance of the receptive skills for the learner's general communicative competence, this is clearly an area in need of close investigation.

The volume is divided into the three following parts:

I: Communication strategies defined

II: Empirical studies of communication strategies

III: Problems in analysing communication strategies

A brief discussion of these areas is contained in the introductory comments which precede each of the three parts. Bibliographical references are given after each article. In addition to these, we have compiled a comprehensive bibliography which includes studies on communication strategies exclusively. Some of the entries in this bibliography overlap with the individual bibliographies following each article, but a fair number are additional and should enable the reader to pursue his studies beyond the specific topics covered by the contributors to this volume.

In addition to the specialized bibliography on communication strategies, the reader will find an index at the back of the book, which will enable him to trace a certain term or concept relating to communication strategies to those articles in which they are discussed.

Notes

1. Unless the opposite is explicitly stated, the abbreviations used all through the book will be the following:
   second language: SL
   foreign language: FL
   second or foreign language: L2
   interlanguage: IL
   native language: L1
   For the distinction between SL and FL, see Richards (1978a).
2. The term 'learning' is here used as a general term referring to the process of internalizing and automatizing language, irrespective of the nature of the context in which the process takes place (pedagogic/nonpedagogic). As there is as yet little empirical evidence for the existence of different types of underlying processes in different types of contexts, as proposed by Krashen (1981), we see no reason for observing a terminological distinction between 'learning' and 'acquisition', which would imply such a difference, and which could therefore be said to prejudge the issue (see also Færch 1978, p. 65).

References

Abbs, B., Candlin, C., Edelhoff E., Moston T. and Sexton, M. (1978). *Challenges*, London: Longman.

Albrechtsen, Dorte, Henriksen, Birgit and Færch, Claus (1980). 'Native Speaker Reactions to Learners' Spoken Interlanguage', *Language Learning*, **30**, 365–396.

Altman, Howard B. and James, C. Vaughan (eds.) (1980). *Foreign Language Teaching: Meeting Individual Needs*, Oxford: Pergamon Press.

Bausch, Karl-Richard (1976). 'Kontrastive Linguistik und Fehleranalyse', in Kühlwein, Wolfgang and Barrera-Videl, Alberto (eds.), *Kritische Bibliographie zur angewandten Linguistik*, Dortmund: Lensing.

Breen, Michael P. and Candlin, Christopher N. (1980). 'Essentials of a Communicative Curriculum', *Applied Linguistics*, **1**, 89–112.

Canale, Michael and Swain, Merrill (1980). 'Theoretical Bases of Communicative Approaches to Second Language Teaching and Testing', *Applied Linguistics*, **1**, 1–47

Candlin, Christopher N. (1981). 'Discoursal Patterning and the Equalizing of Interpretive Opportunity', in Smith, L. (ed.), *English for Cross-Cultural Communication* London: Macmillan, 166–198.

Candlin, Christopher N., Bruton, Clive J. and Leather, Jonathan H. (1974). 'Doctor–Patient Communication Skills', *Working Papers*, **1–4**, Department of Linguistics and Modern English Language, University of Lancaster.

Candlin, Christopher N. and Breen, Michael P. (eds.) (forthcoming). *Strategies in Language Learning*, Oxford University Press.

Chun, Judith (1979). 'The Importance of the Language-Learning Situation: Is "Immersion" the Same as the "Sink or Swim Method"?', *Working Papers on Bilingualism*, **18**, 131–164.

Conseil de la Coopération Culturelle du Conseil de l'Europe (eds.) (1976). *Un niveau-seuil*, Strasbourg: Council of Europe.

Corder, S. Pit (1967). 'The Significance of Learners' Errors', *IRAL*, **5**, 161–170.

Dechert, Hans W. and Raupach, Manfred (eds.) (1980a). *Temporal Variables in Speech: Studies in Honour of Frieda Goldman-Eisler*, The Hague: Mouton.

Dechert, Hans W. and Raupach, Manfred (eds.) (1980b). *Towards a Cross-Linguistic Assessment of Speech Production*, Frankfurt: Lang.

Dulay, Heidi C. and Burt, Marina K. (1975). 'A New Approach to Discovering Universal Strategies of Child Second Language Acquisition', in Dato, Daniel P. (ed.), *Developmental Psycholinguistics: Theory and Applications*, Washington, D.C.: Georgetown University Press, 209–233.

Dulay, Heidi C. and Burt, Marina K. (1980). 'On Acquisition Orders', in Felix, Sascha (ed.), *Second Language Development*, Tübingen: Narr, 265–327.

Edmondson, Willis (1981). *Spoken Discourse. A Model for Analysis*, London: Longman.

Ek, Jan A. van (1975). *The Threshold Level*, Strasbourg: Council of Europe.

Ek, Jan A. van (1976). *The Threshold Level for Modern Language Learning in Schools*, Strasbourg: Committee for General and Technical Education, Council of Europe.

Europarat (ed.) (1980). *Kontaktschwelle*, Strasbourg: Council of Europe.

Færch, Claus (1978). 'Language Learning Studies. A Survey of Some Recent Research Strategies', in Caie, Graham D., Chesnutt, Michael, Christensen, Lis and Færch, Claus (eds.), *Occasional Papers 1976–1977*, Copenhagen: Akademisk Forlag, 64–82.

Færch, Claus and Kasper, Gabriele (1980). 'Processes and Strategies in Foreign Language Learning and Communication', *Interlanguage Studies Bulletin Utrecht*, **5**, 47–118.

Hatch, Evelyn (1978a). 'Acquisition of Syntax in a Second Language', in Richards (1978b) 34–70.

Hatch, Evelyn (1978b). 'Discourse Analysis and Second Language Acquisition', in Hatch, Evelyn (ed.) (1978), *Second Language Acquisition*, Rowley, Massachusetts: Newbury House, 401–435.

Heidelberger Forschungsprojekt (1977). 'Pidgin-Deutsch. Die ungesteuerte Erlernung den Deutschen durch spanische und italienische Arbeiter', in *Osnabrücker Beiträge zur Sprachtheorie (OBST)*, Beihefte 2.

Høedt, Jørgen (1980). 'The Study of Needs Analysis', *Unesco ALSED–LSP Newsletter*, **4/1**, 14–20

House, Juliane (forthcoming). 'Zur Rolle der Muttersprache in einem kommunikativen Fremdsprachenunterricht: Überlegungen zur Theorie und Praxis', *Englisch–Amerikanische Studien*.

Johansson, Stig (1975). *Papers in Contrastive Linguistics and Language Testing*, Lund: Gleerup.

Johansson, Stig (1978). *Studies of Error Gravity*, Gothenburg: Acta Universitatis Gothoburgensis.

Johnson, Keith (1982). *Communicative Syllabus Design and Methodology*, Oxford: Pergamon Press.

Johnson, Keith and Morrow, Keith (eds.) (1978). *Functional Materials and the Classroom Teacher*, Centre for Applied Language Studies, University of Reading.

Johnson, Keith and Morrow, Keith (1979). *Communicate*, Cambridge University Press.

Kasper, Gabriele (1981). *Pragmatische Aspekte in der Interimsprache. Eine Untersuchung des Englischen fortgeschrittener deutscher Lerner*, Tübingen: Narr.

Kasper, Gabriele (1982). 'Teaching-Induced Aspects of Interlanguage Discourse', in *Studies in Second Language Acquisition*, **4/2**, 99–113.

Kellerman, Eric (1977). 'Towards a Characterization of the Strategy of Transfer in Second Language Learning', *Interlanguage Studies Bulletin Utrecht*, **2/1**, 58–145.

Kielhöfer, Bernd and Börner, Wolfgang (1979). *Lernersprache Französisch*, Tübingen: Niemeyer.

Knapp, Karlfried (1980). 'Weiterlernen', *Linguistik und Didaktik*, **43/44**, 257–271.

Knapp-Potthoff, Annelie (1977). 'Linguistische Pragmatik und Fremdsprachenunterricht — Probleme eines Verwertungszusammenhangs', *Linguistische Berichte*, **50**, 58–75.

Krashen, Stephen D. (1978) 'The Monitor Model for Second-Language Acquisition', in Gringas, Rosario C. (ed.), *Second-Language Acquisition and Foreign Language Teaching*, Arlington, Virginia: Center for Applied Linguistics, 1–26.

Krashen, Stephen D. (1981). *Second Language Acquisition and Second Language Learning*, Oxford: Pergamon Press.

Larsen-Freeman, Diane (ed.) (1980). *Discourse Analysis and Second Language Acquisition*, Rowley, Massachusetts: Newbury House.

Leech, Geoffrey N. (1980). *Explorations in Semantics and Pragmatics*, Amsterdam: John Benjamins.

Levelt, Willem J. M. and Flores d'Arcais, Giovanni B. (eds.) (1978). *Studies in the Perception of Language*, New York: John Wiley.

McLaughlin, Barry (1978). *Second-Language Acquisition in Childhood*, Hillsdale, New Jersey: Lawrence Erlbaum.
Munby, John (1978). *Communicative Syllabus Design*, Cambridge University Press.
Nemser, William J. (1971). 'Approximative Systems of Foreign Language Learners', *IRAL*, **9**, 115–123.
Palmberg, Rolf (1976). 'A Select Bibliography of Error Analysis and Related Topics', *Interlanguage Studies Bulletin Utrecht*, **1**, 2/3 340–389.
Palmberg, Rolf (1977). 'Recent Books and Articles on Error Analysis and Interlanguage Research', *Interlanguage Studies Bulletin Utrecht*, **2/3**, 91–99.
Piepho, Hans-Eberhard (1974). *Kommunikative Kompetenz als übergeordnetes Lernziel im Englischunterricht*, Dornburg-Frikkenhofen: Frankonius.
Piepho, Hans-Eberhard and Bredella, Lothar (1978). *Contacts. Integriertes Englischlehrwerk für die Klassen 5–10*, Bochum: Kamp.
Politzer, Robert L. (1978). 'Errors of English Speakers of German as Perceived and Evaluated by German Natives', *Modern Language Journal*, **63**, 253–261.
Rattunde, Eckhard and Weller, Franz-Rudolf (1977). 'Auswahlbibliographie zur Fehlerkunde (Veröffentlichungen 1967–1976)', *Die Neueren Sprachen*, **76**, 102–113.
Rehbein, Jochen (1978). 'Reparative Handlungsmuster und ihre Verwendung in Fremdsprachenunterricht', *Kommunikation in der Schule — Arbeitspapier VIII*, Seminar für Sprachlehrforschung, Ruhr-Universität Bochum.
Richards, Jack C. (1978a). 'Introduction: Understanding Second and Foreign Language Learning', in Richards (1978b), 1–14.
Richards, Jack C. (ed.) (1978b). *Understanding Second and Foreign Language Learning*, Rowley, Massachusetts: Newbury House.
Sajavaara, Kari and Lehtonen, Jaakko (eds.) (1975). *A Select Bibliography of Contrastive Analysis*, Department of English, Jyväskylä University.
Sajavaara, Kari and Lehtonen, Jaakko (eds.) (1980). *Papers in Discourse and Contrastive Discourse Analysis*, Department of English, Jyväskylä University.
Schumann, John (1978). *The Pidginization Process: a Model for Second Language Acquisition*, Rowley, Massachusetts: Newbury House.
Seliger, Herbert W. and Long, Michael (forthcoming). *Classroom Language Acquisition and Use: New Perspectives*, Rowley, Massachusetts: Newbury House.
Selinker, Larry (1972). 'Interlanguage', *IRAL*, **10**, 209–231.
Widdowson, Henry G. (1978). *Teaching Language as Communication*, Oxford University Press.
Wilkins, David A. (1976). *Notional Syllabuses*, Oxford University Press.
Wode, Henning (1981). *Learning a Second Language. Vol. I: An Integrated View of Language Acquisition*, Tübingen: Narr.
Zydatiss, Wolfgang (1976). 'Learning Problem Expanded Form — A Performance Analysis', *IRAL*, **14**, 351–372.

Part One
Communication strategies defined

Part One contains four articles which, in different ways, attempt to define the area of communication strategies and to systematize these according to various criteria.

The approach adopted by Tarone, Cohen and Dumas in their 'A closer look at some interlanguage terminology' (originally published in 1976) is firmly rooted in the tradition of error analysis: the analyst tries to account for erroneous aspects of learner language and does so by explaining these as the product of various process-level phenomena like transfer and generalization (cf. Selinker's 'five central processes' of L2 learning and communication, 1972). It is significant that communication strategies are not seen by Tarone, Cohen and Dumas as a *specific* way of communicating in an IL, as is the case with later definitions (as exemplified by the subsequent three contributions). Furthermore, communication strategies are related to the *analyst's*, not the learner's, point of view: it is irrelevant whether a specific item produced by a learner is in accordance with the learner's IL system or not, as long as it is erroneous compared to the target norm; in this case the item would be characterized as the product of a communication strategy according to Tarone, Cohen and Dumas.

Corder's survey 'Strategies of communication' represents a markedly different way of defining communication strategies. These are established in order to account for performance data *not* when these — to the analyst — are erroneous, but whenever they have been produced by learners under specific circumstances, irrespective of whether they are in accordance or not with a target language norm. Thus the point of view adopted by Corder is clearly that of the learner, and the phenomena accounted for by means of 'communication strategies' are in principle the totality of the learner's performance.

Corder observes a clear distinction between *learning strategies* and *communication strategies*, a distinction which is further discussed in our contribution and in Tarone's paper. According to Corder, learning strategies contribute to the development of IL systems, whereas communication strategies are used by a speaker when faced with some difficulty due to his communicative ends outrunning his communicative means. In such cases, the learner can either adjust his message to his communicative resources by adopting a risk-avoiding strategy, or he can expand his communicative repertoire through a risk-taking strategy. This characterization of communication strategies is further developed in our contribution, 'Plans and strategies in foreign language communication', in which communication strategies are located within a general model of speech production and defined as potentially conscious plans set up by a language user in order to solve problems in communication. We suggest that a definition of communication strategies will have to be based on the research interests of the analyst and claim that the criteria of 'problem-orientedness' and 'consciousness' are relevant criteria as seen from the perspective of FL learning and teaching.

According to this definition, communication strategies are located in the individual language user, who is the person to experience the problem and to decide on a strategic plan for its solution. A different approach is adopted in the article 'Some thoughts on the notion of communication strategy', in which Tarone defines communication strategies in interactional terms as 'a mutual attempt of two interlocutors to agree on a meaning in situations where requisite meaning structures do not seem to be shared'. Communication strategies are set apart from *production strategies*, which are defined as attempts 'to use one's linguistic system efficiently and clearly' and which are not interactional in nature.

Tarone ends her paper by discussing various research issues relating to the description of communication strategies: how learners' use of communication strategies may vary with the type of communicative situation in which they are placed by the researcher; in what ways introspective methods could be used to identify and even classify communication strategies; how the use of communication strategies relates to formal foreign language teaching and to success in language learning. Many of these issues have a direct bearing on the empirical studies contained in Part Two of this book, just as the general question of how to detect communication strategies in performance data is the topic of the two articles included in Part Three.

Although the four articles represent different approaches to the definition and general classification of communication strategies, there is considerable overlap between the specific types of strategies identified in the four studies. Unfortunately, this similarity across the articles is often obscured by terminological diversification, one and the same strategy being labelled differently by different authors. A comprehensive overview of types of communication strategies as discussed in the various studies is contained in our contribution. Also, the reader is referred to the index at the back of the volume for references to different places where the same strategy is being discussed.

1 A closer look at some interlanguage terminology: a framework for communication strategies*[1]

Elaine Tarone, Andrew D. Cohen and Guy Dumas

The field of second-language acquisition research is a relatively new one. At present, a good deal of research is being done on the interlanguages of learners in a variety of situations, and as that research is being reported in conferences, seminars and journals of various kinds, it is becoming increasingly apparent that terms such as *production strategy* need to be more fully operationalized in order to be truly useful to researchers and to teachers. This paper represents an attempt to provide a framework within which such terminology may be defined so as to represent categories of types of interlanguage phenomena which have been discussed to date. In effect, one goal of this paper is to provide some order for interlanguage data. A secondary goal is to shift the focus for language teachers and teacher trainees away from teaching methods and onto the interpretation of the learner's interlanguage. The framework which we present here is intended as a working model. We present it in order to generate discussion which will hopefully lead to a degree of consensus in the field of second-language acquisition research regarding the use of some basic terminology.

The term *production strategy* is defined in Tarone, Frauenfelder and Selinker (1976) as a 'systematic attempt by the learner to express meaning in the target language, in situations where the appropriate systematic target language rules have not been formed'. However, certain interlanguage strategies associated with production apply to comprehension of language as well. For example, the learner can systematically overgeneralize the meaning of a word he hears in one context to the same word used

* *Originally published in* Working Papers on Bilingualism, **9**, 76–90, 1976.

in another context. Likewise, he can systematically alter target language input (e.g. add, delete, substitute, or transpose forms) to make such input more consistent with his native language — hence, negative transfer in comprehension of the target language. We do not suggest that interlanguage comprehension data look like interlanguage *production* data. We aren't sure what they look like, and it is the task of another paper to deal with interlanguage comprehension. Rather, we simply wish to broaden the terminology to include this dimension of communication as well. In place of production strategy, then, we will refer to *communication strategy*, and define it as a systematic attempt by the learner to express or decode meaning in the target language, in situations where the appropriate systematic target language rules have not been formed.

We have been able to identify several distinct types of communication strategies commonly observable in interlanguages, and for the most part have found examples of those patterns as they involve the communication of phonological, morphological, syntactic and lexical elements of language (see table 'Communication strategies' on pages 6 and 7).

The first communication strategy listed in the table is that of *transfer from the native language (NL)*. Here we mean the type of negative transfer from the native language (Selinker 1969) resulting in utterances that are not just inappropriate but actually incorrect by native standards (as distinguished from inappropriate but grammatically acceptable utterances described below as examples of *overelaboration*). This phenomenon can be observed in phonology, morphology, syntax, and lexicon. In phonology, the speaker may transfer a sound from his native language to the target, e.g. /ʃip/ for /ʃɪp/. In morphology, the speaker may substitute his native language's rule for forming the possessive, e.g. *the* BOOK OF JACK for *Jack's book*. In syntax, for example, the learner transfers his native language system for indirect object pronouns to the target language, e.g. *Dió* A ELLOS instead of LES *dió* A ELLOS. In lexicon, the learner indulges in loanshift (Haugen 1950), whereby he uses a native language meaning for an already existing word in the target language, e.g. *Je* SAIS *Jean* instead of *Je* CONNAIS *Jean*.

A second communication strategy is that of *overgeneralization* — the application of a rule of the target language to inappropriate target language forms or contexts (Richards 1971). This phenomenon may also be observed in phonology, morphology,

Communication strategies

	Phonological	Morphological	Syntactic	Lexical
Transfer from NL	/ʃɪp/ for /ʃɪp/	*The* BOOK OF JACK for *Jack's book*	*Dió* A ELLOS for LES *dió* A ELLOS in Spanish-L2	*Je* SAIS *Jean* for *Je* CONNAIS *Jean* in French-L2
Overgeneralization	*El carro*/karo/ *es caro* (Flap r generalized to trill contexts — Span.-L2)	*He* GOED *Il* A *tombé* in French-L2	*I don't know* WHAT IS IT	*He is* PRETTY (Unaware of the semantic limitations)
Prefabricated pattern	—	—	*I don't know how do you do that*	—
Overelaboration	/hwʌt ar ju duɪŋ/ for /wʌtʃədun/	I WOULD NOT HAVE GONE	yo quiero ir — Span.-L2 *Buddy, that's my foot* WHICH *you're standing on*	*The people next door are rather* INDIGENT
Epenthesis	/səterei/ for / streɪ/	—	—	—
Avoidance a) Topic avoidance 1. Change topic 2. No verbal response	(To avoid using certain sounds, like /l/ and /r/ in *pollution problems*.)	(Avoiding talking about what happened yesterday.)	(Avoiding talk of a hypothetical nature and conditional clauses.)	(Avoiding talk about one's work due to lack of technical vocabulary.)

b) Semantic avoidance	It's hard to breathe for air pollution	I like to swim in response to What happened yesterday?	Q: ¿Qué quieren los pájaros que haga la mamá? R: Quieren comer. (Spanish-L2)	Il regarde et il veut boire to avoid the word for cupboard in Il ouvre l'armoire
c) Appeal to authority 1. Ask for form 2. Ask if correct 3. Look it up	Q: f...? R: fauteuil (French-L2)	Q: Je l'ai...? R: prise. (French-L2)	Q: El quiere...? R: que te vayas. (Spanish-L2)	How do you say "staple" in French?
d) Paraphrase	Les garçons et les filles for Les enfants (Thus avoiding liaison in French-L2)	Il nous faut partir for Il faut que nous partions (To avoid subjunctive in French-L2)	J'ai trois pommes for J'EN ai trois (To avoid en in French-L2)	High coverage word: tool for wrench. Low frequency word: labour for work. Word coinage: airball. Circumlocution: a thing you dry your hands on
e) Message abandonment	Les oiseaux ga... (gazouillent dans les arbres was intended in French-L2)	El quería que yo... (fuera a la tienda was intended in Spanish-L2)	What you...?	If only I had a...
f) Language switch	I want a COUTEAU²	Le livre de Paul's (French-L2)	Je ne pas GO TO SCHOOL (French-L2)	We get this HOSTIE from LE PRÊTRE (English-L2)

syntax, and lexicon. In phonology, one may find a newly-learned sound pattern used in inappropriate contexts, such as when the flap *r* in Spanish is overgeneralized to trill contexts, e.g. *El* CARRO /karo/ *es* CARO. A morphological example of overgeneralization might be the English-L2 utterance *He* GOED or the French-L2 utterance *Il* A *tombé* instead of *Il* EST *tombé*. In the latter example one notes that it is not always easy to differentiate between L2 learner overgeneralization and L1 dialect speakers' overgeneralization (Mougeon and Hébrard 1975). A look at the input language might help error analysis in such cases. A syntactic overgeneralization in English-L2 might be: *I don't know* WHAT IS IT, where the question word order with subject-verb-inversion is generalized to statements. Finally, we may find a type of overgeneralization in the use of lexical items, where an item may be used in inappropriate contexts because the learner is unaware of the semantic limitations contingent on its use, e.g. *He is* PRETTY.

At the theoretical level, overgeneralization is differentiated from transfer from NL in that in overgeneralization, it is always a rule of the *target* language which is used in place of the correct target language rule. In transfer, the learner is using a native language form (perhaps motivated by a native language rule) in place of the correct target language rule.

At the empirical level, it is a matter of controversy as to whether certain interlanguage forms should be considered a result of transfer from NL or rather overgeneralization of the target language (see, for example, Dulay and Burt 1975; Cohen 1975, Chapter 8). One way to attempt to resolve the controversy is by using the learner as informant in explaining the errors, assuming that he can provide reliable explanations (Cohen and Robbins 1976). In reality, it may not be possible to firmly establish whether a learner is utilizing the communication strategy of transfer or of overgeneralization in producing an interlanguage form. He may, in fact, be utilizing some combination of both (Selinker, Swain and Dumas 1975).

The third communication strategy we observe is the *prefabricated pattern*, defined by Hakuta (1976) as a 'regular patterned segment of speech' employed 'without knowledge of its underlying structure, but with the knowledge as to which particular situations call for what patterns'. Prefabricated patterns could in a way be considered as a subcategory of overgeneralization; to our knowledge, they have been shown to occur only in the syntactic domain. The *do-you* pattern described by Hakuta is a typical example, producing (among others): *What do you doing?* for *What are you doing?*

A fourth communication strategy which has been observed is one of *overelaboration* (after 'over-indulgence' — Levenston 1971), in which the learner, in an attempt to produce careful target language utterances, produces utterances which seem stilted and inordinately formal. While these utterances are not native-like, they might well be correct in purely grammatical terms. It is reasonable to suppose that this strategy may be closely related to the character of the learning situation. Thus, an emphasis on the written language in the learning situation would likely lead to the production in speech of forms usually restricted to writing. The identification of overelaboration calls for an awareness of context, an overelaboration being a form judged anomalous in a given context. An example of phonological overelaboration would be the production in casual speech of the utterance /hwʌt ar ju duɪŋ/, rather than the more typical /wʌt ʃəduɪn/. In morphology, a consistent use of full forms rather than contracted forms might be considered a type of overelaboration, e.g. *I* WOULD NOT HAVE *gone* for *I* WOULDN'T'VE *gone*. In syntax, similarly, one might find forms specified which are ordinarily deleted, especially in casual styles, e.g. *Buddy, that's my foot* WHICH *you're standing on.* Such overelaboration may be the result of transfer from NL. For example, in Hebrew there is no optional deletion of the relative pronoun /ʃɛ/ (that) introducing a relative clause. By the same token, English speakers learning Spanish or Hebrew, which have optional or preferred deletion of the subject pronoun in all or in certain tenses, will overuse the subject pronoun, e.g. *Yo quiero ir*, where *Quiero ir* is sufficient. An overelaboration might occur also in the use of overly-formal or esoteric lexical items in place of more frequently used target language words, e.g. *The people next door are rather* INDIGENT, where *poor* would be more appropriate.

A fifth communication strategy occurs only in the phonological domain — that of *epenthesis*, or vowel-insertion. Here the learner is unable to produce unfamiliar consonant clusters in the target language, and in attempts to produce them, he uses schwa vowels between consonants, as: /sətəreɪ/ for /streɪ/ (stray) (see Tarone 1976, for a more extensive illustration of this phenomenon).

The last six communication strategies are all classed as different types of *avoidance*, that is, these strategies are all different means of getting around target language rules or forms which are not yet an established part of the learner's competence. Upon questioning, the learner may indicate an awareness of the target language form or rule, but prefers not to attempt to use it. (Several of these patterns are described in Tarone, Frauenfelder and Selinker 1976 — some of them under different names.)

Topic avoidance is the attempt to totally evade communication about topics which require the use of target language rules or forms which the learner does not yet know very well. Topic avoidance may take the form of either a change of topic or no verbal response at all. For example, a learner may move away from a discussion about pollution problems if the pronunciation of /r/ and /l/ causes problems, or avoid a discussion of what happened the previous day because it calls for the past tense inflection. Likewise, the learner may avoid discussions of an abstract or theoretical nature due to an uncertainty as to the appropriate syntactic constructions or the appropriate technical vocabulary (see the table).

In *semantic avoidance*, the learner evades the communication of content for which the appropriate target language rules and forms are not available, by talking about *related* concepts which may presuppose the desired content. Examples of this pattern are given in the table; in one instance, where the learner wants to avoid the use of the subjunctive in Spanish, and is asked:

¿ Qué quieren los pájaros que haga la mamá?

(What do the birds want their mama to do?)

the learner responds:

Quieren comer. (They want to eat.)

Thus he avoids the subjunctive while indirectly providing the requested information.

Appeal to authority (Tarone, Frauenfelder and Selinker 1976) occurs when the learner asks someone else to supply a form or lexical item, asks if a form or item is correct, or else looks it up in a dictionary. This pattern may be used to deal with problems in all four domains depicted in the table.

Paraphrase refers to the rewording of the message in an alternate, acceptable, target language construction, in order to avoid a more difficult form or construction. So, we may find the following examples: to avoid liaison in French, learners may use *les garçons et les filles* for *les enfants* (Spilka 1976); to avoid the French partitive *en*, the learners may produce the specified form *J'ai trois pommes*, rather than *J'en ai trois*; and, to avoid the subjunctive form in *Il faut que nous partions*, the learners may say *Il nous faut partir* (Spilka 1976). In the area of lexical paraphrase, we may find several different types, as illustrated in the table. A *high coverage* word (Mackey and Savard 1967) is a superordinate term used in place of a subordinate term which carries more information in a particular context, e.g. *tool* for *wrench*. The learner may find it economical to learn abstract, superordinate words which can be used more frequently. A *low frequency* word is a relatively obscure, uncommon word used in place of the more appropriate general term, e.g. *to labour* for *to work*, where the item *to work* is being avoided. *Word coinage* (Váradi, this volume) is the creation of a non-existent lexical item in the target language, in situations where the desired lexical item is not known, e.g. *airball* for *balloon*. *Circumlocution* is a description of the desired lexical item or a definition of it in other words — as in a *thing you dry your hands on* for *towel*.

Another type of avoidance strategy is *message abandonment* whereby communication on a topic is initiated but then cut short because the learner runs into difficulty with a target language form or rule. The learner stops in mid-sentence, with no appeal to authority to help finish the utterance, e.g.

Les oiseaux ga . . . for *Les oiseaux gazouillent dans les arbres.*

El queria que yo . . . for *El queria que yo fuera a la tienda.*

The final type of avoidance strategy that we have been able to catalogue is that of linguistically motivated *language switch*. Here, the learner transports a native word or expression, untranslated, into the interlanguage utterance. Actually, the motivation for the language switch may be *either* linguistic (an attempt to avoid a difficult target language form or one that has not yet been learned) *or* social (such as a desire to fit in with one's peers). The table provides examples of avoidance-type switches. For example, an English-L2 learner might say *We get this* HOSTIE *from* LE PRÊTRE (Mougeon and Hébrard 1975), where two lexical switches occur because the learner is unfamiliar with the English words dealing with his religious experience. Gumperz and Hernández-Chávez (1970) and Lance (1969) have documented social reasons for switching, a field of investigation which is beyond the scope of this analysis.

Discussion and conclusion

This paper has redefined and operationalized in a detailed manner the notion of communication strategy, a central component of interlanguage. Perhaps a major contribution of this paper has been to explore more fully what 'non-native-like' may actually mean beyond the realm of grammatical correctness and into the murky realm of 'inappropriateness'. As we have seen in this discussion, there are really at least two such sets of strategies, over-elaboration and avoidance. In some ways, as we have used it, 'overelaboration' is dependent upon negative transfer from NL. Determining the extent to which this is the case is a research project in itself. Levenston (1971) actually attributed both what he called 'over-indulgence' and 'under-representation' to transfer from the native language. And although we have suggested that the end product of overelaboration are forms which are too formal or elegant, Levenston points out that the end result may also be excessive verbosity or informality. All of this should be explored in greater detail.

The avoidance strategies enumerated in this paper are considered to be by and large distinct from transfer and overgeneralization — perhaps the principal reason why their mention has generally been left out of much of the second-language acquisition literature. Perhaps they have been considered as behaviour at the margin. The reality is that such behaviour is in some ways central to interlanguage in that it helps reveal how the learner's interlanguage develops. But clearly there is still a lot of work to be done in this area.

It is altogether likely that this framework is nowhere near all-inclusive of communication strategies. We welcome our readers to suggest further categories or modification of existing ones. As it is, we realize that the categories described in this paper are not always mutually exclusive one from the other. As stated above, some overelaboration may be a result of transfer from NL, such as the carry-over from L1 of the relative pronoun (*that* or *which*) to an optional or preferably omitted slot in English.

Perhaps the most troublesome issue is that of multi-dimensionality. It may be too artificial an exercise to attempt to describe monolithically a series of strategies which in reality operate in multi-dimensional ways. But it seems to us that such an empirically complex state of affairs will only be substantiated by attempts on the part of our readers to use this framework to make sense out of second-language acquisition data. We welcome all criticisms and suggestions, and hope that this paper will stimulate not only greater rigor in the use of terminology in our field, but also a continuing interest in describing and explaining the data we are exposed to as teachers and researchers.

Notes

1. We wish to express our thanks to Larry Selinker, Shoshana Blum, Eddie Levenston, Marjatta Turenius and Raymond Mougeon for their comments on this paper.
2. This example of language switch attributed to a phonological motivation is documented in Celce-Murcia's study (1977). A bilingual child who had difficulty pronouncing the /f/ sound would attempt to avoid it, where she could, by using an alternate term from the other language. Hence, she would always say *couteau*, no matter what language she was using at the time, simply to avoid the /f/ in *knife*.

References

Celce-Murcia, Marianne (1977). 'Phonological Factors in Vocabulary Acquisition', *Working Papers on Bilingualism*, **13**, 27–41.

Cohen, Andrew D. (1975). *A Sociolinguistic Approach to Bilingual Education: Experiments in the American Southwest*, Rowley, Massachusetts: Newbury House.

Cohen, Andrew D. and Robbins, Margaret (1976). 'Toward Assessing Interlanguage Performance: the Relationship between Selected Errors, Learners' Characteristics, and Learners' Explanations', *Language Learning*, **26**, 45–66.

Dulay, Heidi and Burt, Marina (1975). 'You Can't Learn Without Goofing: an Analysis of Children's Second Language "Errors"', in Richards, Jack (ed.), *Error Analysis: Perspectives on Second Language Acquisition*, London: Longman, 95–123.

Gumperz, John and Hernández-Chávez, Eduardo (1970). 'Cognitive Aspects of Bilingual Communication', in Whitely, R. (ed.), *Language Use and Social Change*, Oxford University Press, 111–125.

Hakuta, Kenji (1976). 'A Case Study of a Japanese Child Learning English', *Language Learning*, **26**, 321–351.

Haugen, Einar (1950). 'The Analysis of Linguistic Borrowing', *Language*, **26**, 210–231.

Lance, D. M. (1969). 'The Mixing of English and Spanish', in Lance, D. M. et. al., *A Brief Study of Spanish–English Bilingualism*. Final Report, Research Project ORR-Liberal Arts 15504, Texas A & M University, College Station, Texas. Reprinted as 'Spanish–English Code Switching', in Hernández-Chávez, Eduardo, Cohen, Andrew D. and Beltramo, A. F. (eds.) (1975), *El lenguaje de los chicanos: Regional and Social Characteristics of Language Used by Mexican Americans*, Arlington, Virginia: Center for Applied Linguistics, 138–153.

Levenston, Edward A. (1971). 'Over-Indulgence and Under-Representation: Aspects of Mother-Tongue Interference', in Nickel, Gerhard (ed.), *Papers in Contrastive Linguistics*, Cambridge University Press, 71–121.

Mackey, William F. and Savard, J. G. (1967). 'The Indices of Coverage', *International Review of Applied Linguistics in Language Teaching*, 71–121.

Mougeon, Raymond and Hébrard, P. (1975). 'L'acquisition et la maitrise de l'anglais par les jeunes bilingues de Welland'. Publication informelle de la Section franco-ontarienne de l'IEPO (OISE), Toronto.

Richards, Jack C. (1971). 'A Non-Contrastive Approach to Error Analysis', *English Language Teaching*, **25**, 204–219.

Selinker, Larry (1969). 'Language Transfer', *General Linguistics*, **9/2**, 67–92.

Selinker, Larry, Swain, Merrill and Dumas, Guy (1975). 'The Interlanguage Hypothesis Extended to Children', *Language Learning*, **25**, 139–152.

Spilka, Irene (1976). 'Assessment of Second-Language Performance in Immersion Programs', *The Canadian Modern Language Review*, **32/5**.

Tarone, Elaine (1976). 'Some Influences on Interlanguage Phonology', *Working Papers on Bilingualism*, **8**, 87–111.

Tarone, Elaine, Frauenfelder, Uli and Selinker, Larry (1976). 'Systematicity/Variability and Stability/Instability in Interlanguage Systems', in Brown, H. Douglas (ed.), *Papers in Second Language Acquisition* (= Language Learning Special Issue No. 4), 93–134.

2   Strategies of communication*

S. Pit Corder

Strategies of communication were first invoked by Selinker (1972) in his paper entitled 'Interlanguage' to account for certain classes of errors made by learners of a second language. These errors were regarded as a by-product of the attempt of the learner to express his meaning in spontaneous speech with an inadequate grasp of the target language system. Váradi (this volume) was the first to investigate this phenomenon experimentally but little work has since been published on the topic; the most recent attempt to provide a framework for analysis of strategies of communication is Tarone, Cohen and Dumas (this volume). It is now fairly clear that all language users adopt strategies to convey their meaning, but we are only able more or less readily to perceive these when the speaker is not a native speaker.

The strategies adopted by speakers, of course, depend upon their interlocutors. What we attempt to communicate and how we set about it are determined not only by our knowledge of the language but also our current assessment of our interlocutor's linguistic competence and his knowledge of the topic of discourse. But both these are variable and actually may change and develop in the course of ongoing interaction. Furthermore, since communication is a cooperative enterprise, one must suppose that we may adopt both productive and receptive strategies of communication. So far no one has attempted within the framework of interlanguage studies to investigate the latter.

Studies of communicative strategies have therefore largely concentrated on productive strategies of language learners interacting with native speakers of the target language, where the

* Originally published in Leiwo, Matti and Räsänen, Anne (eds.) (1978). AFinLAN Vuosikirja. Publications de l'Association Finlandaise de Linguistique Appliquée, 23, 7–12.

simplifying assumption has been made that the interlocutor has 'perfect' command of the language system and also 'perfect' command of the topic of discourse.

A working definition of communicative strategies is that they are a systematic technique employed by a speaker to express his meaning when faced with some difficulty. Difficulty in this definition is taken to refer uniquely to the speaker's inadequate command of the language used in the interaction. This again is obviously a simplifying assumption, but one which permits a start to be made on investigating a difficult topic.

Much of the literature in the field seems to me to lack a general view of the problem and one of the principle confusions found is between what are called strategies of learning and strategies of communication. Some authors appear even to regard these expressions as nearly synonymous. Perhaps one of the reasons is that in both cases the data for investigating are the same, namely utterances in the interlanguage of the speaker. It is frequently difficult therefore to identify a particular feature of an utterance unequivocally as the result of one or the other strategy, i.e. the result of the learner's interlanguage system or an ad hoc result of some communicative strategy. This is particularly the case with features of an utterance which bear a resemblance to features of the speaker's mother tongue. They may be regular characteristics of his language at the time of study, in which case they could be supposed to result from the interlanguage grammar which he has created for himself, and are therefore the product of a strategy of learning which utilizes the mother tongue system as a heuristic technique. This is the feature often called 'interference' and the strategy of learning which produces it is the strategy of 'transfer'. On the other hand an interlanguage speaker may, in his attempts to communicate, simply 'borrow' for immediate purposes items or features of his mother tongue (or any other language he knows) without incorporating them into his interlanguage system. 'Successful borrowing', that is, when a 'borrowed' item is 'accepted' by the interlocutor as 'well formed' in the target language, may lead to that item being incorporated into the speaker's interlanguage repertoire. This could be regarded as 'learning'. As Hatch (1978) says: 'Language learning evolves out of learning how to carry on conversations.' 'Unsuccessful' borrowings of course will be rejected. It is because of this interaction between strategies of communication and strategies of learning that the confusion I spoke of may have arisen.

Strategies of communication have essentially to do with the relationship between ends and means. In a native speaker it is ideally assumed that these are in balance, that is, that he always has the linguistic means to express the messages he wishes to communicate. In a learner, however, these are not in balance. The learner will sometimes wish to convey messages which his linguistic resources do not permit him to express successfully. When in the course of interaction the learner finds himself faced with this situation, he has only two options open to him. He can either tailor his message to the resources he has available, that is, adjust his ends to his means. These procedures we can call *message adjustment strategies*, or risk avoidance strategies. Or he can attempt to increase his resources by one means or another in order to realize his communicative intentions. These strategies we can call *resource expansion strategies*. These are clearly 'success oriented' though risk-running strategies. If one wishes at this stage of the art to consider the pedagogical implications of studying communicative strategies, then clearly it is part of good language teaching to encourage resource expansion strategies and, as we have seen, successful strategies of communication may eventually lead to language learning.

Students of communicative strategies have identified (in a provisional way) a number of communicative strategies and they will all be found to fall into one or the other of these two macro-strategies. Thus amongst *message adjustment strategies* we have at one extreme 'topic avoidance', a refusal to enter into or continue a discourse within some field or topic because of a feeling of total linguistic inadequacy. A less extreme form of topic avoidance would be 'message abandonment': trying but giving up. A less acute form of message adjustment is 'semantic avoidance', that is, saying something slightly different from what you intended but still broadly relevant to the topic of discourse. Finally, the least acute form of message adjustment would be 'message reduction', that is, saying less, or less precisely, what you intended to say. This is often seen as rather vague general talk.

These strategies must not be regarded as admission of failure. Let us remember that in face-to-face interaction it is frequently essential from a social point of view to maintain interaction with your interlocutor. To say something is often just as important as to say what you would actually like to say!

When we turn to the *resource expansion strategies* the situation is different. Here we cannot order the techniques according to a hierarchy. We frequently find one or more strategies being employed simultaneously. All are risk-taking, in that they run the danger of failure, i.e. misunderstanding or communication breakdown. The most obvious strategy, that of 'borrowing', has been mentioned, i.e. the use of linguistic resources other than the target language, but they include guessing of a more or less informed kind, that is, an attempt to use invented or borrowed items, all more or less approximated to the rules of the target language structure as far as the learner's interlanguage allows. The extreme form of borrowing is of course simply 'switching' to another language — the most risky enterprise. Whilst a less risk-taking strategy is to use paraphrase or circumlocution, i.e. getting round your problem with the knowledge you have — inelegant perhaps but successful. One must not forget here a resort to paralinguistic devices as a resource expansion strategy — (typically, gesture) or to appeal for help from the interlocutor for a word or expression — the least risk-taking strategy of all.

How are these strategies manipulated? There is some evidence that there is a personality factor involved. Different learners will typically resort to favourite strategies — some are determined risk-takers, others value social factors of interaction above the communication of ideas, but one may assume that there is a general preference for maintaining one's intended message. Just how hard one tries will vary with personality and speech situation. One can then propose the following *encoding routine* at least as a testable hypothesis (see table p. 19).

References

Hatch, Evelyn (1978). 'Discourse Analysis and Second Language Acquisition', in Hatch, Evelyn (ed.), *Second Language Acquisition: A Book of Readings*, Rowley, Massachusetts: Newbury House, 401–435.

Selinker, Larry (1972). 'Interlanguage', *IRAL*, **10**, 209–231.

ENCODING PATHS

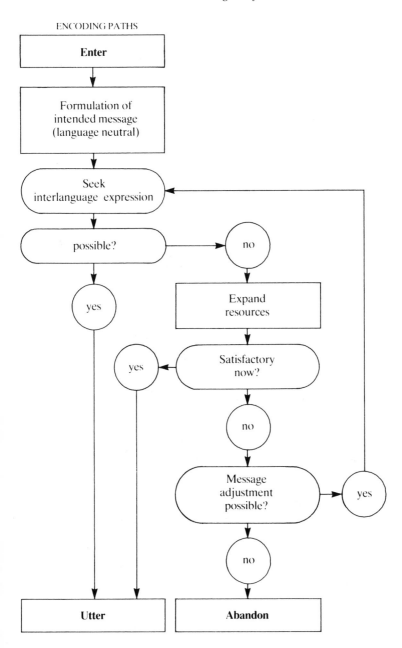

3 Plans and strategies in foreign language communication*

Claus Færch and Gabriele Kasper

L:
NS: [. . .] what do you read at home [. . .] what what do you er
L: mmmm   er historie
NS: read   what er subjects do you read about
L: and — (laugh) I read 'historie' home and sometimes
NS: mhm —
L: in my school — and — er not more —
NS: mm — do you like er
L: [. . .]
NS: history — in school — do you like learning history [. . .]
L: er yes —
NS: do you have history lessons in school —   I mean
L: kings
NS: when you learn about er I don't know   old kings —
L: oh yes I have that —   no (laugh)
NS: yes —   do you like it —   (laugh)
L: not about hist
NS: but you like reading books about history —
L: er this history   you know — er young histories — er
NS: aha —
L: not not with this old things you know kings or — all that
NS: aha
L: — but er (laugh)
NS: (laugh) in er in er for example — what — 1930 or so —
L: yes
NS: do you mean — recent — in more recent years like that
L: er [. . .] a history is — maybe on a boy — girl and — er this
NS: [. . .]
L: er young people life and   yer —
NS: oh you mean a story   maybe
L: yer   yer —
NS: — just a story   about people —   yes not not

* This is an abridged and revised version of the article 'Processes and strategies in foreign language learning and communication', which appeared in Interlanguage Studies Bulletin Utrecht, 5, 47–118, 1980.

L: no
NS: necessarily not — in the past   no — I see yes — now I
L: (laugh)
NS: understand you (laugh)
(PIF)[1]

The above conversation between a Danish learner (L, female, age 17) and a native speaker of English (NS, also female, same age) illustrates various aspects of interlanguage (IL) communication: the learner has difficulty expressing in English what she could easily have expressed in Danish (namely that she likes reading stories); her attempt to communicate leads to a misunderstanding on the part of the native speaker which then gets clarified at a later time, namely when the learner replies to a new question from the native speaker in a way which contradicts the native speaker's original interpretation of 'history'. The learner may infer from the incident that Danish *historie* does not exactly match English *history*, and there is even a possibility that she will establish a tentative hypothesis that Danish *historie*, meaning a school subject, is matched by English *history*, whereas Danish *historie*, meaning a story or a novel, is matched by English *story*.

Establishing and trying out hypotheses about L2 on the basis of active participation in communicative events is one of the central elements in contemporary, cognitively oriented models of L2 learning and acquisition, and it would be possible to describe at least some of the ways learners establish and try out hypotheses on the basis of analyses of IL data produced in various types of communicative situations (cf. Færch and Kasper 1980 for a detailed discussion of these issues). In the present article, however, we shall focus primarily on the communicative aspects of FL communication. The question of possible learning effects of various types of communication strategies will be briefly discussed in the final section of this paper.

Observing a distinction between the communication and the learning aspects of FL communication is not altogether easy when *analysing* FL performance data (see also the discussion of this by Bialystok in this volume). The distinction becomes highly problematic when applied to communicative events like classroom discourse in which 'communication' does not serve the primary function of exchanging ideas and of acting in various ways by means of language, but rather has the function of making the students learn. Nonetheless, we consider it a useful heuristic procedure to

observe the distinction between the two aspects of FL communication, and we take as our point of departure situations in
which the learners' needs to communicate clearly predominate
over any interest they might have in learning the FL.

The approach we adopt is psycholinguistic in that we locate
communication strategies within a general model of speech production. The typology of communication strategies to be suggested
below is thus dependent on this model. At the same time, the
categories included in the typology account for real phenomena,
for which empirical evidence has been provided by various
previous studies. In the following, most of the communication
strategies will be illustrated by conversational data. It is hoped
that the proposed typology can serve as a framework for analysing
communication strategies — which however does not mean that
it solves the problem of how to identify these phenomena
in textual data. This issue will be taken up in Part Three of this
volume.

General model of speech production

As a basis for our description of communication strategies, we
adopt the following simplified model of the principles behind
goal-related, intellectual behaviour (Figure 1). The notion *intellectual behaviour* is borrowed from Leont'ev (1975, p. 153), who
uses it in contradistinction to *reflectory behaviour*. 'Reflectory behaviour' refers to a fixed connection between a stimulus and a re-

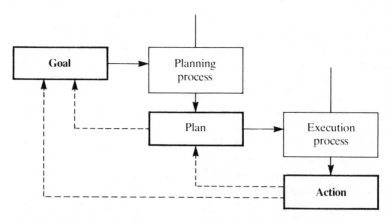

Figure 1 Planning and execution of intellectual behaviour

flectory response which is either genetically determined or learned, whereas there is no such fixed connection in the case of intellectual behaviour: rather, the individual has to choose (more or less consciously) between various alternative responses to a given stimulus in constructing 'models of the future' on the basis of 'models of the past and present'. We shall use the term 'intellectual behaviour' in a broader sense, namely, as referring to all those psychic and behavioural (observable) actions which involve cognitive processess.

The model divides into two phases: a *planning phase*, comprising 'goal', 'planning process' and 'plan', and an *execution phase*, which comprises 'plan', 'execution process' and 'action' (cf. Clark and Clark 1977, pp. 223ff for a discussion of planning and execution in speech production). In every one of these phases and their components, *feedback* or monitoring takes place, which often allows for an immediate correction of 'errors' in planning or execution (see also Sajavaara, Lehtonen and Korpimies 1980, pp. 38ff).[2]

The aim of the planning phase is to develop a plan, the execution of which will result in an action which will lead to the actional goal. In order for the plan to match the goal, the individual has to base the construction or selection of a plan on an analysis of the given situation and its resources with regard to the goal. Leont'ev characterizes the first phase in intellectual behaviour as comprising 'the orientation about the situation and the conditions of the task' which leads to the 'selection of the plan of action' (1975, p. 153). The 'assessment of the situational conditions' also constitutes the first of Rehbein's seven 'phases of the process of action' (1977, pp. 41ff).

As regards the structure of plans, Miller, Galanter and Pribram assume them to be hierarchically organized (1960, pp. 16ff). This can be exemplified from Clark and Clark (1977, pp. 223ff), in which the following hierarchically ordered levels of plans are set up: discourse plans, sentence plans, constituent plans, articulatory programme (see also Fry 1973 for a similar suggestion). This hierarchical organization of plans is of some interest in relation to strategies, a point which will be further discussed below.

In the relevant literature, one often finds that no distinction is made between the planning process and the plan itself. Thus Leont'ev says that 'the programme [= plan] is . . . nothing given, ready-made, but a process, the process of programming' (1975, p. 216), and Miller, Galanter and Pribram refer to a plan as a 'hierarchical process' (1960, p. 16). Although a distinction is arbitrary, as we are dealing with psychological constructs which have not been given any neurological support, we find that it is convenient to maintain a distinction between the planning *process*, which is sensitive to what type of goal has been selected and to the analysis of the situation, and the *plan* itself, which is what controls the execution phase. In so doing, we follow Rehbein, who explicitly distinguishes between the planning process and the plan as its result (1977, pp. 146ff).

By characterizing a plan as 'nothing given, ready-made', Leont'ev implies that plans are being constructed by the individual in generating speech. Miller, Galanter and Pribram (1960, especially pp. 177ff) and Rehbein (1977, p. 146), however, distinguish between ready-made, automatic plans which the individual can choose among, and plans which are specifically formed by the individual in a particular situation. Moreover, it is a matter of controversy to what extent the execution process, i.e. the conversion of a plan into action, can take place without the existence of plans: according to Miller, Galanter and Pribram, this is not assumed to be the case, whereas Leont'ev (1975, p. 153, pp. 194ff) and Rehbein (1977, p. 147) draw a clear distinction between 'unplanned' and 'planned' communicative behaviour. Interesting though this question is, it is of no serious consequence for our treatment of communication strategies whichever stand we take. In the following, we adopt what we consider the stronger claim as seen from a cognitivist view and consider *all* intellectual processes to be planned by either ready-made, automatic plans or by plans constructed ad hoc, as described immediately above.

The *goals* we are concerned with are *communicative* goals, i.e. goals relating to the activity of engaging in communicative events. The goals consist of actional, modal, and propositional elements. The actional element is associated with speech acts, the modal element with the role relationship holding between the interactants, and the propositional element is associated with the content of the communicative event.

A communicative event (e.g. a conversation or writing a letter) can be characterized as having both a *global goal* (or possibly a number of global goals), holding for the entire event, and a series of *local goals* which appear as part of the execution of the global goal(s). This hierarchical structure of goals is of some relevance for a discussion of communication strategies, as we shall see below.

In the *planning phase*, the language user selects rules and items which he considers most appropriate for establishing a plan, the execution of which will lead to verbal behaviour which is expected to satisfy the original goal. In L1 communication, planning processes are normally subconscious and highly automatic, a fact which may explain the occurrence of transfer from L1 in communication performed by means of an insufficiently automatized L2 (see further below). The product of the planning process is a *plan* which controls the execution phase. The *execution phase* consists of neurological and physiological processes, leading to articulation of the speech organs, writing, the use of gestures and signs, etc. This part of the communication model is of relevance for a discussion of communication strategies only in so far as the individual may anticipate or experience problems in the execution of a plan, a point we shall return to below.

We can now present the following model of speech production:

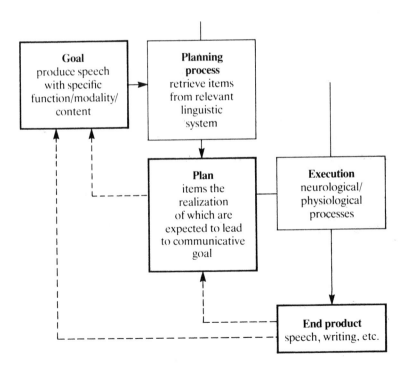

Figure 2 A model of speech production

Having established the general model of speech production, let us consider some of the individual components of the model in some detail and relate these specifically to FL communication.

Goals and plans in FL communication

In the preceding section we referred to situational assessment as part of the planning phase: the individual has to assess the situational conditions in order to select the most appropriate plan. Assessing situational conditions for communicative behaviour is not, however, a process the relevance of which is restricted to planning only: deciding on what *goal(s)* to set up clearly depends on assumptions about what can be achieved in a particular situation. Furthermore, on the basis of assumptions about what conditions hold for communication in specific situations, individuals may avoid or engage in different types of communicative situations. As the individual's need for using communication strategies and his ultimate choice of strategies are intimately related to these aspects of situational assessment, we shall go a little more into this.

As seen from a *learning* perspective it is evident that the more communicative situations the learner engages in and the greater their variety, the more possibilities he has not only for practising his IL but also for constructing hypotheses about L2 and getting them tested. However, IL users sometimes avoid situations which they expect will involve them in communication which exceeds their communicative resources, thereby preventing themselves from expanding their IL system. These may be situations which call for the use of specific types of illocutionary acts, specific topics, or situations in which special attention has to be paid to marking interpersonal relations linguistically (e.g. with respect to politeness).

If IL users avoid communicative situations which they consider problematic, — 'communication avoidance' — this blocks all subsequent stages in the communication model. Although this may be a highly significant aspect of IL users' *general* behaviour it is of very marginal interest for a discussion of IL communication which clearly presupposes that *some* communicative activity takes place. In the following, it is taken for granted that the IL user has a communicative goal, relative to the situation he engages in. As we shall see below, the goal may be 'reduced' compared to the goal which the IL user would normally have in a similar communicative situation, if this was performed in his L1.

The planning process, the objective of which is to develop a plan which can control the execution phase, is primarily sensitive to the following three variables: the communicative goal, the communicative resources available to the individual, and the assessment of the communicative situation. This is illustrated graphically in Figure 3.

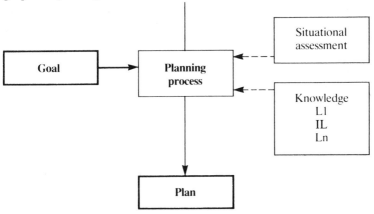

Figure 3 Variables in the planning phase

Through situational assessment the individual builds a hypothesis about which parts of his linguistic knowledge are shared by his interlocutor(s). This is an important aspect of communication in general, as it is necessary in most communicative situations to establish what one's *actual* communicative resources are relative to the specific situation, as opposed to one's *potential* resources.

In most cases the interactants choose *one* code as the basic code to be used.[3] However, within the limits imposed by the shared linguistic knowledge there is the possibility of switching codes whenever problems crop up (see further below).

The fact that the IL user builds a hypothesis about his 'actual' communicative resources in a specific situation does not imply that he will always produce utterances which are controlled by the plans based on these resources. First of all, he may have to deliberately go beyond what he considers shared knowledge in order to solve a communicative problem. Second, due to the fact that different languages are likely to be automatized to different degrees in the learner, elements originating from highly automatized languages may be realized contrarily to the situational assessment. Whether we say that such occurrences of non-intended transfer from L1 and possibly other languages is the result of subconscious, highly automatic plans which get incorporated into the general, IL specific, plan, or whether we say that these transfer features are the result of non-planned execution depends on the general stand we take on the question whether *all* intellectual goal-related behaviour is planned or not, as discussed above. However, this is of little consequence for our discussion of communication strategies, as these relate to behaviour only to the extent that this is planned.

Planning can be more or less conscious, depending on the extent to which the individual has explicit linguistic knowledge. This brings conscious planning close to 'monitoring' IL speech production: the learner controls his performance by referring to linguistic rules and items which he has a conscious knowledge about (see, e.g. Krashen 1978), either because these have been learnt explicitly or because implicitly 'acquired' elements have been 'conceptualized' (Frauenfelder and Porquier 1979; see also Bialystok 1979).

Defining communication strategies

The procedure we adopt in defining communication strategies is to localize them in the model of speech production outlined above, in which their function can be characterized through their relationship to 'processes' and 'plans'. Basic to our approach is the assumption that strategies do not constitute a class of phenomena given *a priori*, as implied by Selinker's statement that 'little is known in psychology about what constitutes a strategy and a viable definition of it does not seem possible at present' (1972, p. 219). Whereas this 'ontological assumption of a structure of the world independent of the knower' (Habermas 1971, p. 304) certainly holds true in a very general sense for specific objects in reality which can be unarbitrarily distinguished from each other (e.g. elephants from strategies), communication strategies as seen within the framework of speech production belong to an area of reality in which categorizations are neither 'arbitrary nor compelling' but rather 'appropriate or inappropriate' (Habermas 1971, p. 312). Accordingly, the class of communication strategies has to be defined on the basis of criteria which are located in the researcher's 'Erkenntnisinteresse'. We shall return to this below after a more general discussion of the relationship between processes and plans.

Strategy — process or plan?

In the literature dealing with communication strategies in ILs, one sometimes finds *strategy* being used interchangeably with *process*, which implies that both terms refer to the same class of phenomena (cf. '"simplification" is understood as the act of simplifying, the *strategy* of communication, the *process* whereby specific meanings are communicated on specific occasions', Levenston and Blum 1977, p. 52, our italics). Other researchers use the term *strategy* when referring to a specific subclass of processes, thereby implying an opposition between 'non-strategic' processes vs. 'strategic' processes (cf. Selinker's (1972) 'five central processes', two of which are 'learning strategies' and 'communication strategies'). A third way of handling the categories *process* and *strategy* has been put forward by researchers who regard them as relating to the same superordinate class of mental activities but as being distinguished into subclasses by certain defining criteria. Blum and Levenston, for instance, in a later study use the temporal dimension as a defining criterion, suggesting that *strategy* refers to 'the way the learner arrives at a certain usage at a specific point in time', *process* being used with reference to 'the systematic series of steps by which the learner arrives at the same usage over time' (1978a, p. 402). Bialystok (1978) distinguishes processes from strategies by the criteria 'obligatory/optional', processes being obligatory, strategies optional mental activities. Similar criteria are used by Frauenfelder and Porquier (1979), who classify processes as universal, strategies as optional mechanisms employed by individual L2 learners.

As the impression the reader is left with after reviewing these various implicit and explicit definitions of our two concepts is probably one of confusion rather than of clarification, we should like to venture our own attempt of defining them. In order to do so, we start off by having a closer look at the notion of *process*.

Process is frequently used in a general sense in which it is primarily opposed to (linguistic) product (cf. the general introduction to this volume). This use of the term is particularly clear in articles arguing for the relevance of 'process descriptions', rather than 'product descriptions', of language learning/acquisition (e.g. Dulay and Burt 1974). Brown defined *process* in this general sense as 'continuing development involving a number of changes' (1976a, p. 136), a definition not far from that given by Klaus and Buhr (1976), who define a process as 'a dynamic sequence of different stages of an object or system' (p. 990). It is this general sense of process which lies at the back of such otherwise disparate expressions as 'the process of L2 acquisition' (Brown 1976a, p. 136), 'the communication process', 'restructuring and recreation processes' (Corder 1978, pp. 75–76). *Process* in this general sense seems to us indeed an indispensable category in IL studies, and we shall use the term in this article as defined in the above quotes.

Given these definitions of *process*, we would, however, *not* suggest that communication strategies should be considered as a subclass thereof, but rather offer an alternative categorization which follows from the model of speech production we presented above.

If one accepts the basic distinction made in this model between the planning and the execution of speech, communication strategies can best be placed within the planning phase, more precisely, within the area of the planning process and the resulting plan. It seems possible to argue for such a categorization of strategies even without any further specification of their conceptual status, as it can be assumed that they somehow steer, monitor or control speech execution and should therefore be kept apart from the execution process itself. In analogy to our distinction between the planning process and the resulting plan, one might thus distinguish between (the process of) devising a strategy and the strategy resulting as a product of such a mental activity. Although such a distinction might be arbitrary in the case of 'prefabricated' strategies which already belong to a speaker's communicative repertoire, it becomes meaningful in cases where a speaker cannot rely on such a ready-made strategy but has to construct one 'in situ' (cf. the discussion of ready-made vs. creatively constructed plans above). Categorizing strategies as plans has also been suggested by Klaus and Buhr (1976) and Sharwood Smith (1979).

Strategies as a subclass of plans

There is no compelling reason imposed by reality why a distinction should be observed between plans and strategies — nor, for that matter, between planning processes, resulting plans and strategies. As we argued above, defining strategies as a specific category within the model of speech production is a categorization of reality, the adequacy of which can only be assessed relative to a specific Erkenntnisinteresse.

In the general introduction to this volume it is argued that communication strategies represent a highly significant aspect of IL communication, and that 'strategic competence' should be incorporated into foreign language teaching objectives as an integral part of communicative competence. The defining criteria we adopt here for identifying strategies as a subclass of plans are in line with these general considerations; the adequacy of the criteria must be assessed relative to an Erkenntnisinteresse in foreign language learning and teaching.

As a *primary* defining criterion of communication strategies we adopt *problem-orientedness*, and as a *secondary* defining criterion we adopt *consciousness*. The defining criteria relate to FL learning/teaching in the following way:

Problem-orientedness: Given communicative competence as the overall learning objective in FL teaching, one can — from a 'didactic' or syllabus construction point of view — basically adopt two procedures for reaching this goal (cf. the general introduction to this volume). First, one can aim at an exhaustive description of the communicative needs a group of learners is assumed to have when using FL, and include into the syllabus all the communicative functions and linguistic means by which these needs can be realized. After successful participation in such a course, a learner should be sufficiently well equipped to engage in FL interaction outside the classroom without experiencing any problems in communication due to a deficient FL repertoire. As has been pointed out by Knapp (1980), the assumption behind this procedure, namely that learners' future communicative needs can in fact be reliably predicted, is highly questionable, and the possibility for the learner to find himself in a communicative situation which his FL course did not sufficiently prepare him for remains very likely. Instead of basing a syllabus on the rather unrealistic assumption that it should prevent the learner from running into communicative problems, one can adopt an alternative approach which acknowledges the potential problematicity of FL communication, and incorporate ways of dealing with such problems into the syllabus. In order to be able to do so, it will be necessary to learn much more about the types of communication problems which might occur in various types of interaction, and about how learners cope with them most successfully. It follows from these considerations that problem-orientedness is a relevant defining criterion for communication strategies from both a FL learning and teaching perspective.

Consciousness: Within a cognitive framework of FL learning and teaching, it seems desirable that learners should be made aware of the communicative problems they might encounter, and of the devices they can use in order to solve them. By this we do not wish to imply that learners should always be conscious 'problem-solvers'. The point is rather that a learner who has gone through a stage of conscious analysis of a given problem in a given context in terms of an explicit situational assessment, and the conscious establishment of a plan (or alternative plans) geared at its solution, might be better capable of applying such 'strategic' knowledge to new situations in a creative and efficient way. We therefore suggest that problem-solving plans which lend themselves to such a process of consciousness-raising should be part of FL teaching, and subcategorize such plans as strategies.

We have distinguished between problem-orientedness as a *primary* and consciousness as a *secondary* defining criterion for strategies. The secondary status of consciousness is due to the fact that the criterion of consciousness is derived from the criterion of problem-orientedness, a point we shall return to presently. But first let us consider problem-orientedness as a defining criterion of communication strategies.

Problem-orientedness

The criterion of problem-orientedness presupposes a distinction between goals which the individual experiences no difficulty in reaching and goals which present themselves to the individual as 'problems': only plans that relate to the latter type of goals will be considered strategies.

The word 'problem' is sometimes used in a rather vague way as a near-synonym to 'task'. This is not in accordance with *our* usage of the word, which corresponds to the definition given by Klaus and Buhr, who define 'problem' as 'recognition by an individual . . . of the insufficiency of his . . . existing knowledge to reach a . . . goal and of the consequent need for expanding this knowledge' (1976, p. 974).

It is obvious that in the case of the FL learner, 'insufficient knowledge' refers to his IL system (but see pp. 38ff. on formal reduction for a qualification of this statement). However, the evident relevance of this notion for FL learners should not be taken to preclude its applicability to L1 users. First of all, L1 users sometimes find themselves in a situation similar to that of a learner in that they lack, for instance, a specific vocabulary needed for talking about a given topic, or situationally relevant linguistic means are not readily accessible, due to psychological constraints like fatigue or anxiety. In both cases, speakers need to expand their currently available linguistic resources. Secondly, L1 users might converse with interlocutors whose receptive competence does not match what would be a native speaker's normal language use, as happens in interaction with children, members of different social or geographical groups, or L2 learners. In those instances, the L1 user has to adjust his potential resources to those he can make use of, given his interlocutor's receptive possibilities. The problem he is faced with is then not one of insufficient *existing* knowledge, but rather one of insufficient means which can reasonably be put to use under the prevailing situational conditions.

We have characterized communication strategies as plans. This is potentially confusing unless one points out explicitly that 'strategic plans' are *not* identical with plans established in order to reach a communicative goal: the goal of a strategy (the 'strategic goal') is the *problem*, and the product of the execution phase controlled by the strategy is a *solution* to the problem. This is represented in Figure 4.

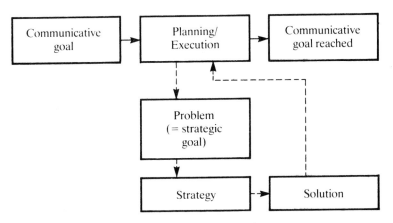

Figure 4 Communicative and strategic goals

Problem-orientedness has been used as a defining criterion by both Kellerman and Jordens in their respective descriptions of strategies: Kellerman defines a strategy as 'a well-organized approach to a problem' (1977, p. 93), and Jordens makes the point that 'strategies can only be applied when something is acknowledged as problematic' (1977, p. 14), which points to the additional criterion of consciousness: if the individual experiences a problem in reaching a goal, this implies that he is conscious about there being a difficulty.

Returning to the general model (Figure 1), we can establish two situations for the occurrence of communication strategies, depending on whether the problem is a problem in the planning phase or in the execution phase. In the first case, the individual experiences a problem in constructing a plan which he considers an adequate means for reaching his goal. In the second case, the problem crops up when the individual attempts to execute the plan.

Problems within the *planning phase* may occur either because the linguistic knowledge is felt to be insufficient by the language user, relative to a given goal, or because the language user predicts that he will have problems in executing a given plan.

The former type of problem is particularly characteristic of *IL* communication, as IL systems are typically restricted compared to L1 systems. Not surprisingly, most of the literature on communication strategies has focussed on this type of problem, and the majority of strategies to be discussed below are strategies aimed at solving problems due to insufficient linguistic knowledge.

The latter type of problem is characteristically associated with the learner being concerned with fluency or correctness. If a plan necessitates the realization of non-automatized items or rules, this may lead to non-fluent speech production which, in certain communicative situations, may be considered problematic by the IL user, who may therefore try to prevent the problem by changing his plan. Similarly, if a plan contains rules or items which are still of a hypothetical nature (cf. Færch and Kasper 1980, pp. 61ff) the execution of the plan may result in incorrect utterances which, at least in some (normally formal) contexts, may be considered undesirable. Again, the IL user may try to prevent the problem from cropping up by changing the plan.

Problems within the *execution phase* have to do with retrieving the items or rules which are contained in the plan. This is the tip-of-the-tongue phenomenon, well-known from L1 communication.

The difference between anticipating fluency or correctness problems and experiencing retrieval problems in execution is that in the former case, it is possible to *avoid* getting into a problem by developing an alternative plan, whereas in the execution phase problems *are* there and have to be solved.

Consciousness

Our secondary defining criterion, the criterion of consciousness, differs from the way consciousness has been used by some other IL researchers as a means of characterizing strategies. Thus Váradi (this volume), Kleinmann (1977) and Tarone (1977) all characterize strategies as being consciously employed by the language user which, formulated within our general model, is the same as saying that it is the *plan* which the individual is conscious about.

There are various problems in defining communication strategies as consciously employed plans. First of all, consciousness is perhaps more a matter of degree than of either-or, as is apparent from Tarone, Frauenfelder and Selinker (1976), who distinguish between 'more "conscious"'' and 'more "unconscious"'' strategies (see also Tarone, this volume, for a similar point). This, to some extent, may be related to the hierarchical organization of plans mentioned above: it is probably the exception, rather than the rule, that consciousness refers to a complete plan; in most cases, certain elements only in the plan will be consciously selected, e.g. (in connection with communicative plans) 'high-level elements' like vocabulary (Jordens 1977, p. 16) or pragmatic, semantic and syntactic, rather than articulatory, features (Leont'ev 1975, pp. 195ff).

Second, consciousness is clearly not a constant holding for specific types of plans (or parts of plans) across all individuals. As pointed out by Sharwood Smith, 'different individuals may be more or less able to become aware of their own internal mental operations' (1979), which implies a consciousness-raising process. Furthermore, the opposite situation can also be envisaged: individuals may automatize what was at one stage consciously employed plans. This points to the following classification of plans:
1. plans which are always consciously employed;
2. plans which are never consciously employed;
3. plans which to some language users and/or in some situations may be consciously used and which to other language users and/or in other situations are used unconsciously.

If such a classification could be given empirical support, this would be highly interesting from the view of FL learning/ teaching, as this covers the areas of consciousness raising and automatization, which have clear implications for the choice of teaching methods (see above, and cf. Baur and Rehbein 1979 for an attempt to establish a methodological hierarchy leading to the internalization and automatization of foreign languages on the basis of Gal'perin's theory of learning). Furthermore, the issue of consciousness is of considerable interest to IL researchers as it delimits the subgroup of plans which can be characterized by means of introspective techniques from other types of plans, the existence and nature of which can only be inferred from behavioural data or neurological investigations. We therefore want to include both plans which are *always* consciously employed and plans which are *sometimes* consciously employed (i.e. (1) and (3) above) into our category of strategic plans, and refer to these as *potentially conscious* plans. By adding together what we have said about the two defining criteria we can now define communication strategies as follows: *communication strategies are potentially conscious plans for solving what to an individual presents itself as a problem in reaching a particular communicative goal.*

We have been careful in this definition to refer to 'an individual' rather than to 'the learner', the implication being that it is meant to apply to L1 users as well. Consequently, most of the preceding and the following discussion also holds true for native speakers. However, as our *Erkenntnisinteresse* is how FL learners communicate, we shall focus on the ways this group of language users handle problems in communication.

Major types of communication strategies

A first broad categorization of communication strategies can be made on the basis of two fundamentally different ways in which learners might behave when faced with problems in communication. Learners can either solve such problems by adopting *avoidance behaviour*, trying to do away with the problem, normally by changing the communicative goal, or by relying on *achievement behaviour*, attempting to tackle the problem directly by developing an alternative plan. On the basis of these two different approaches to problem-solving, we can draw a distinction between two major types of strategies: *reduction strategies*, governed by avoidance behaviour, and *achievement strategies*,

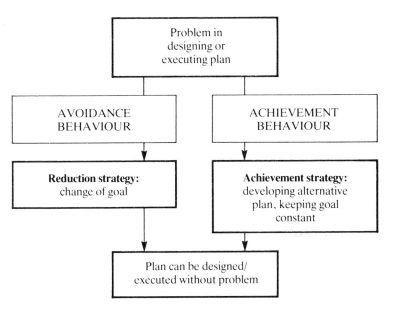

Figure 5 Types of behaviour and types of strategies

governed by achievement behaviour. The relationship between problem, type of behaviour and type of strategy is represented in Figure 5.

That reduction and achievement strategies result in very different types of solutions to problems can be seen from Figure 6, which conflates Figures 4 and 5 (see p. 38).

It is hardly surprising that the choice of strategy is not only sensitive to the underlying behaviour (avoidance/achievement) but also to the nature of the problem to be solved. In particular, problems that relate to fluency and correctness constitute a special class in that they frequently cause the language user not to use the most 'obvious' parts of his IL system because he expects that there will be problems in realizing them. 'Formal reduction' of this kind (cf. Váradi in this volume) represents a special type of communication strategies, first of all because it is neutral with respect to the underlying behaviour (see further below), second because formal reduction is frequently closely related to the subsequent use of reduction or achievement strategies: if, for example, the problem is one of fluency and the IL user 'reduces' his IL system with respect to the problematic item/rule and does not incorporate it into his plan ('formal reduction'), he may have to

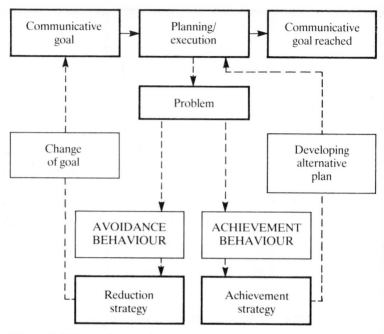

Figure 6 Effect of reduction and achievement strategies

develop an alternative plan based on his — now 'reduced' — linguistic resources in order to reach his communicative goal ('achievement strategy').

By adding together what we have said about types of problems, types of behaviour and types of strategies, we obtain Figure 7 (p. 39), which will serve as a basis for our description of individual communication strategies.

Communication strategies — a classification

1 Formal reduction strategies

In order to avoid producing non-fluent or incorrect utterances by using insufficiently automatized or hypothetical rules/items, learners may decide to communicate by means of a 'reduced' system, focussing on stable rules and items which have become reasonably well automatized. A parallel to this is found with native speakers who, in interacting with learners, may have to communi-

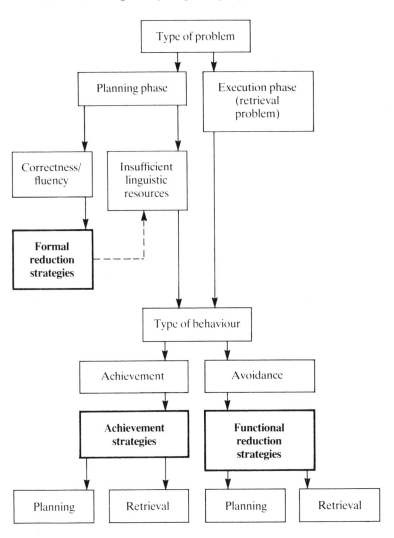

Figure 7 Overview of major types of communication strategies

cate by means of a simplified version of their L1 system, matching the learner's receptive resources (cf. the contribution by Blum-Kulka and Levenston in this volume and, further, the discussion of the interrelationship between native speakers' simplification and use of repairs in Færch and Kasper 1982). Following Váradi (this volume), we refer to this as 'formal reduction', a term which should not be taken to imply that a substantial reduction of the *system* takes place: what happens is that the language user in a specific communicative situation *avoids using* rules/items which he has at his disposal, and which in a different communicative situation would be the most appropriate way of reaching his communicative goal (cf. Kleinmann's 'linguistic avoidance', 1977, p. 102).

As mentioned, formal reduction is often closely related to functional reduction or achievement strategies. However, a distinction between formal reduction as such and the subsequent application of other strategies can often be made from an analytical point of view only, as no such clear-cut distinction between a stage of formal reduction and a following stage of functional reduction or achievement exists in actual communication.

Our discussion of formal reduction strategies will focus on the following two questions:

1. Why should the learner want to make use of his linguistic system in a reduced way?
2. Which areas of the linguistic system are susceptible to formal reduction?

Avoiding errors and facilitating speech

We have already mentioned two reasons why learners adopt formal reduction strategies: they want to avoid making errors and/or they want to increase their fluency.

Error avoidance (Jordens 1977) may to some extent be psychologically determined, some language users feeling badly about communicating in a foreign language unless they can do so without exhibiting linguistic handicaps. An additional reason may be that the language user assumes that linguistic correctness is a prerequisite for communicative success, an assumption which probably derives more from the foreign language classroom than from real-life experience (Enkvist 1973, p. 18).

That formal reduction may help increase one's fluency has been observed by Váradi (this volume), who writes that 'target language learners may notice that elimination of certain formal elements does not interfere with the transmission of meaning; it may facilitate communication by increasing fluency'. A similar view is taken by Tarone (this volume), who reserves the term 'production strategy' to strategies which are employed to increase efficiency in speech production.

The difference between formal reduction caused by error avoidance and formal reduction with a view to facilitating communication is that in the former case the result is what is considered by the learner correct language, whereas in the latter case the learner may perform utterances which he knows are not correct but which he considers appropriate from a communicative point of view. This distinction has some consequences for the subsequent choice of strategies: in the case of error avoidance the learner will employ those strategies which he assumes will result in correct L2 utterances (i.e. either functional reduction strategies or achievement strategies like paraphrase, see further below), whereas in the case of communicative facility the learner may adopt strategies that lead to performance which he knows is not correct as seen from a L2 point of view but which, in the given situation, will work. Strategies of this latter type will typically be achievement strategies such as overgeneralization and borrowing (see below).

Types of formal reduction

All areas of the IL system are susceptible to formal reduction. However, because of the different communicative status of items from different linguistic levels there are some significant differences with respect to whether the learner can reach his communicative goal by means of a reduced system, or whether he has to adopt a functional reduction or an achievement strategy.

As most items at the *phonological* level are indispensable in communication, it is not normally the case that learners can simply communicate by a reduced phonological system. Furthermore, as it is the exception, rather than the rule, that a particular phoneme is restricted to specific words (e.g. to loanwords only), a particular phoneme cannot generally be avoided through functional reduction strategies such as topic avoidance (see below) but only through achievement strategies providing a formal alternative to the IL item being avoided. To take an example, it would be impossible for learners of English to reduce on the /ð/ phoneme by completely avoiding lexemes that contain /ð/ — formal reduction with respect to /ð/ can only be achieved by adopting other ways of realizing the phoneme (e.g. by overgeneralizing the use of /d/ or by borrowing a L1 phone).

The situation at the *morphological* level is similar to that at the phonological level in that grammatical morphemes are normally obligatory in particular linguistic contexts, which in turn occur in most communicative situations. This implies that as in the case of phonological reduction, the reduction of a morphological item has often to be compensated for by the application of various achievement strategies, normally by substituting syntactic or lexical items for the avoided morphological item. This is, for instance, the case with some learners of French, described by Hamayan and Tucker, who avoided subordinate clauses containing the subjunctive, using instead an infinitival verbal complement (*il faut aller* for *il faut que j'aille*) (1979, p. 84). However, even though grammatical morphemes are normally obligatory sentence constituents, this does not imply that they also add to the meaning of the sentence — frequently they are in fact semantically redundant. For this reason learners, in order to facilitate speech production, may avoid some of these redundant features *without feeling a need to compensate*. Such morphological reduction due to 'redundancy avoidance' (cf. the discussion of 'redundancy' in Dulay and Burt 1972; Jain 1974; Taylor 1974, 1975) is exceptional among formal reduction strategies in that it does not necessitate the subsequent application of compensatory strategies.

The situation at the *syntactic* level resembles that at the morphological level insofar as there is a distinction between what learners conceive of as obligatory and optional structures. Whereas reduction of what to the learner appears to be an obligatory structure will necessarily result in either functional reduction or performance assumed to be erroneous, reduction of assumedly 'optional' rules can be achieved simply through non-application of the rules in question. An example would be the passive rule in English, which learners might avoid simply by not applying it, forming their sentences according to the rules governing active sentence structures instead. Formal reduction of this type can be difficult to detect as the result of the strategy is often a well-formed L2 sentence which is appropriate in the immediate context, and the application of the strategy only shows through 'over-indulgence' in particular structures (cf. Levenston 1971).

Formal reduction at the *lexical* level can be achieved both by means of reduction strategies (as e.g. 'topic avoidance') and by means of achievement strategies (such as 'paraphrase' and 'borrowing'). Several reasons can be given why learners should attempt to reduce their lexical system. Particular lexemes may be difficult to pronounce (Blum and Levenston 1978b, p. 10), they may belong to irregular or infrequent declensional morphological classes (ibid.), or they may impose morphological, syntactic or lexical restrictions on the context which the learner finds difficult

to observe. Reasons for lexical reduction can also be found outside the IL system, as suggested by Blum and Levenston: learners
will avoid using words for which no direct translation-equivalent
exists in their L1 (ibid.).

2 Functional reduction strategies

As can be seen from Figure 7 above, functional reduction
strategies are employed if learners experience problems in the
planning phase (due to insufficient linguistic resources) or in the
execution phase (retrieval problems), and if their behaviour in
the actual situation is one of avoidance, rather than achievement.
By adopting a functional reduction strategy the learner 'reduces'
his communicative goal in order to avoid the problem. Such reduction can attain the character of 'global reduction', affecting the
global goals, or it can be restricted to one or more local goals
('local reduction'). For obvious reasons, global reduction cannot
occur as a result of retrieval problems, which presuppose that
both goal and plan have been formed.

Functional reduction may affect any of the three types of elements of the communicative goal (actional, modal, propositional). Thus learners may experience problems in performing specific speech acts and/or in marking their utterances appropriately
for politeness/social distance ('speech act modality'). Reduction
of speech act modality has been discussed in some detail by Kasper (1979), who gives examples of how German learners of English reduce their IL performance with respect to politeness
marking (see also Nold 1978 and Kasper 1981 for a more extensive discussion of this and related types of reduction). Examples of speech act reduction can also be seen in the PIF corpus of
learner language (Færch 1979, 1982), in which learners in conversation with native speakers often do not use initiating acts.

'Global' reduction of actional features of communicative goals
is predictable communicative behaviour with learners who have
received their foreign language instruction in foreign language
classrooms in which the emphasis has been on referential speech
acts (cf. Hüllen 1973b; Piepho 1974; Wilkins 1976; Kasper 1981).
When faced with communicative tasks which demand other types
of speech acts, such as argumentative or directive functions, the
learner may experience considerable problems in performing
these and either avoid engaging in communication in situations
which are likely to necessitate the use of such functions ('com-

munication avoidance') or abstain from using them in communication no matter how relevant they appear as seen from a L1
perspective. If the learner chooses to reduce his goal globally with
respect to the actional and/or modal component, the result may
be that he conveys a distorted picture of his personality, as
observed by Harder (1980).

Functional reduction of the propositional content comprises
strategies such as 'topic avoidance', 'message abandonment' and
'meaning replacement' (or 'semantic avoidance'). *Topic avoidance* (Tarone, Frauenfelder and Selinker 1976; Tarone 1977;
Corder in this volume; Tarone, Cohen and Dumas in this
volume) refers to the strategy of avoiding formulating goals which
include topics that are perceived as problematic from a linguistic
point of view. Topic avoidance is used exclusively in connection
with problems in the planning phase, as opposed to *message
abandonment* (Tarone, Cohen and Dumas in this volume; Tarone
1977; Corder in this volume), which can also be used in connection with a retrieval problem in the execution phase. Message
abandonment is defined by Tarone, Cohen and Dumas in the following way: 'communication on a topic is initiated but then cut
short because the learner runs into difficulty with a target language form or rule. The learner stops in mid-sentence, with no
appeal to authority to help finish the utterance.'

Both topic avoidance and message abandonment result in the
learner giving up referring to a specific topic. This is not the case
with *meaning replacement* (Váradi in this volume), termed 'semantic avoidance' by Tarone, Frauenfelder and Selinker (1976);
Tarone, Cohen and Dumas; Blum-Kulka and Levenston; and
Corder (all in this volume). Here the learner, when confronted
by a planning or retrieval problem, operates within the intended
propositional content and preserves the 'topic' but refers to it
by means of a more general expression. The result of meaning
replacement is a certain amount of vagueness.

The distinction between 'topic avoidance' and 'meaning replacement' is as arbitrary as the distinction between what constitutes concepts belonging to one and the same topic and concepts
belonging to different topics. Rather than visualize the propositional reduction strategies (apart from message abandonment) as
falling neatly into one of two classes, one should see them as
forming a continuum. At the one end, the learner says 'almost'
what he wants to say about a given topic (= meaning replacement), at the other end he says nothing at all about this (= topic
avoidance).

3 Achievement strategies

By using an achievement strategy, the learner attempts to solve problems in communication by expanding his communicative resources (Corder, this volume), rather than by reducing his communicative goal (functional reduction). Most of the strategies we shall discuss relate to problems in the planning phase, some to retrieval problems in the execution phase, and one ('restructuring') to problems in both the planning and the execution phase. The problems to be solved by means of achievement strategies may occur at all linguistic levels, although most studies have concentrated on problems at the lexical level. Before we take a look at the specific types of strategies which can be used we would like to discuss one type of problem which has not so far been considered, namely problems at the level of discourse.

Problems in discourse

A number of studies have provided lists of English discourse features which are supposedly problematic for learners (Beneke 1975; Keller and Taba-Warner 1976, 1977, 1979; Edmondson and House 1981). That learners do in fact have difficulties in organizing discourse has been demonstrated by Götz (1977) and Kasper (1981), who among other things found that the following represented problems for advanced German learners of English: realizing moves in opening and closing phases; signalling change of topic and end of exchange; identifying the interlocutor's preclosing signals; using uptakers and devices for getting the floor; initiating repair work. Nold (1978) investigated how German learners of English coped with various discourse phenomena and found that they to a large extent used structures with which they were familiar from German. However, this finding should be compared to that presented in Edmondson, House, Kasper and McKeown (1979) and Kasper (1981), in which it is demonstrated that learners do not always make use of their L1 when confronted by difficulties in L2, not even in those situations where L1 and L2 are comparable in this respect. Finally, it has been shown by Stemmer (1981) that learners have problems in using appropriate cohesive devices when responding to their interlocutor's preceding act.

As has been demonstrated, even advanced learners often have discourse problems — hence from a theoretical point of view there is scope for learners to devise strategic plans to cope with such problems. However, very little research has so far been conducted within this specific area of IL communication, and suggestions relating to the use of discourse *strategies* in the literature are scarce (see for instance the discussion of how 'gambits' can be used strategically for keeping one's turn at speech in Edmondson and House 1981, pp. 66ff).

Compensatory strategies

We shall refer to achievement strategies aimed at solving problems in the planning phase due to insufficient linguistic resources as *compensatory strategies*. The compensatory strategies will be subclassified according to what resources the learner draws on in trying to solve his planning problem: a different code ('code switching' and 'interlingual transfer'), a different code and the IL code simultaneously ('inter-/intralingual transfer'), the IL code exclusively ('generalization', 'paraphrase', etc.), discourse phenomena (e.g. 'appeals'), and non-linguistic devices ('mime', etc.).

(a) Code switching

In communication in which foreign languages are involved there always exists the possibility of switching from L2 to either L1 or another foreign language. The extent to which this is done depends on the interactants' analysis of the communicative situation. Thus in the foreign language classroom, learners frequently share the L1 with their teacher, which enables them to code switch extensively between L2 and L1.

Code switching (or 'language switch', Tarone 1977; Corder 1978; and Blum-Kulka and Levenston; Corder; Tarone, Cohen and Dumas in this volume) may involve varying stretches of discourse from single words up to complete turns. When code switching affects single words only, as in example (1), the strategy is sometimes referred to as 'borrowing' (Corder 1978 and in this volume).

(1)   L: do you want to have some ah — *Zinsen* or do you want to have some more. . . .
         (BO, *Zinsen* German for 'interests')

(b) Interlingual transfer

Whereas with the code switching strategy learners ignore the IL code, strategies of interlingual transfer result in a combination of linguistic features from the IL and the L1 (or other languages different from the L2 in question). Interlingual transfer may not only involve the transfer of phonological, morphological, syntactic or lexical features of the IL (see Tarone, Cohen and Dumas in this volume), but may also occur at the pragmatic and discourse level (Kasper 1981).

If a lexical item is adjusted to IL phonology and/or morphology (cf. example (2) below), the strategy of interlingual transfer is sometimes referred to as 'foreignizing' (Ickenroth 1975), whereas adjustment at the lexical level of the IL system (e.g. translating compounds or idiomatic expressions from L1 verbatim into L2, cf. example (3) below) is described as 'literal translation' (Tarone 1977).

(2)   NS: how do you go to school [. . .]
        L: [. . .] sometimes I take my er — er what's it called — er [. . .] 'knallert' */'knælə/* —
          (PIF, *knallert* Danish for 'moped')

(3)   L: they [= my pets] eats — erm *greens* — *things*
          (PIF, 'greens things' for *grøntsager* Danish for 'vegetables')

(c) *Inter-/intralingual transfer*

Especially in situations in which the learner considers the L2 formally similar to his L1, strategies of inter-/intralingual transfer may be applied. The result of the strategy is a generalization of an IL rule (see below), but the generalization is influenced by the properties of the corresponding L1 structures (cf. Jordens 1977; Kellerman 1977, 1978). Thus Danish learners of English might generalize the regular *-ed* suffix to irregular verbs on the basis of the way verbs in Danish are distributed between the regular and the irregular declensional classes (e.g. Danish *svømme — svømmede* (past tense), English *swim — swimmed*).

(d) *IL based strategies*

The learner has various possibilities for coping with communicative problems by using his IL system: he may (i) generalize; (ii) paraphrase; (iii) coin new words. As a special type of IL based strategies we include (iv) restructuring.

(i) *Generalization* By generalization learners solve problems in the planning phase by filling the 'gaps' in their plans with IL items which they would not normally use in such contexts. As seen from a L2 perspective, the strategy resembles *over*generalization of a L2 item as it results in the extension of an item to an in-

appropriate context. However, this is not necessarily the case for the learner, who may not yet know the appropriate context for the relevant item, in which case he can hardly be said to overgeneralize. An exception to this is generalization as an achievement strategy to compensate for formal reduction: as the learner 'knows' the most appropriate item but decides to avoid using it (formal reduction), he *over*generalizes in using an alternative — and less appropriate — item.

Our usage of the term overgeneralization is more restricted than that normally found in the literature on communication strategies (see, e.g. Tarone, Frauenfelder and Selinker 1976; Tarone, Cohen and Dumas in this volume), as this usage conflates an IL with a L2 perspective and characterizes violation of restrictions which hold on rules in L2 as instances of overgeneralization.

Generalization differs from the functional reduction strategy of meaning replacement in that the learner, when generalizing, does *not* change his communicative goal: the learner assumes that his original goal can be reached by using a generalized IL item or, in other words, that the generalized item can convey the appropriate meaning in the given situation/context. Whether 'lexical substitution' (Tarone, Frauenfelder and Selinker 1976), 'approximation' (Tarone, Frauenfelder and Selinker 1976; Tarone 1977), or the use of superordinate terms (Ickenroth 1975; Blum-Kulka and Levenston in this volume), are instances of generalization strategies or of functional reduction strategies is difficult to tell from the rather vague definitions these terms have normally been given in the quoted literature, cf. the folowing: '... lexical substitution — using a word in the target language which does *not* communicate exactly the concept which the learner desires, but which shares enough semantic elements in common with the desired concept to satisfy the learner' (Tarone, Frauenfelder and Selinker 1976, p. 127). If this can be taken to mean that *the learner*, in using a lexical substitute to fill a gap in his vocabulary, believes that the substitute will convey his intended meaning, this implies that the learner's underlying behaviour is achievement, rather than reduction, and that lexical substitution is a generalization strategy. (That the *effect* of lexical substitution may be that the intended meaning does *not* get across to the interlocutor is irrelevant in the context of the present article, in which we take the learner's, and not his interlocutor's or the analyst's, point of view.)

As an instance of generalization we include the following example, in which the learner uses the superordinate term 'animals' to refer to her rabbit:

(4) NS: do you have any animals —
     L: (laugh) yes — er — er that is er — I don't know how
        I shall say that in English —
        [. . .]
     NS: I think they must be rabbits —
     L: er what
     NS: rabbits —
     L: rabbits —
     NS: yer rabbits
        [. . .]
     NS: does it — sleep on — in your room
     L: er my — *my animals* —
     NS: mm your animal
        (PIF)

(*ii*) *Paraphrase* By using a paraphrase strategy, the learner solves a problem in the planning phase by filling the 'gap' in his plan with a construction which is well-formed according to his IL system (cf. Tarone 1977, p. 198 for a related definition of paraphrase). Paraphrases can have the form of *descriptions* or *circumlocutions* (Váradi in this volume; Tarone 1977), the learner focussing on characteristic properties or functions of the intended referent. Thus in example 1 the learner describes 'interest' as 'have some more money'. In the following example, the learner tries to explain 'moped'.

(5) L: [. . .] some people have a car — and some people
        have a er bicycle — and some people have a er —
        erm — a cykel there is a m motor
     NS: oh a bicycle — with a motor
        (PIF)

As a special type of description can be mentioned the use of a converse term + negation, as discussed in Levenston and Blum 1977.

Paraphrase can also be *exemplification*, the learner using a hyponymic expression instead of the (missing) superordinate term. The learner who tried to communicate 'moped' by means of a description (example 5) earlier used exemplification, without success (example 6).

(6)   L: er (laugh) knallert – ['knælə] – er (laugh)
             [. . .] you know er *Puch*
             (PIF, *knallert* Danish for 'moped'; *Puch* a make of
             moped)

(*iii*) *Word coinage*   As the term says, a word-coinage strategy involves the learner in a creative construction of a new IL word (cf.
Váradi's 'airball' for 'balloon' in this volume). In the following
example, the learner wants to refer to the curve of a stadium.

(7)   L: we were sitting in the – *rounding* of the stadion and
             (BO)

(*iv*) *Restructuring*   A restructuring strategy is used whenever the
learner realizes that he cannot complete a local plan which he has
already begun realizing and develops an alternative local plan
which enables him to communicate his intended message without
reduction (cf. 'message abandonment', which can be considered
the reductional parallel to restructuring). In an example quoted
by Albrechtsen, Henriksen and Færch (1980), the learner gets
around the word *daughter* by restructuring his utterance: '. . . my
parents has I have er four elder sisters. . .'. In the following example the learner wants to express that he is hungry.

(8)   L: my tummy – my tummy is – I have (inaudible) I must
             eat something
             (BO)

(*e*) *Cooperative strategies*

As pointed out by Tarone (this volume), the interactional aspect
of communication is of considerable significance for a discussion
of communication strategies. She therefore proposes a definition
of communication strategy which 'make(s) it clear that the term
relates to a mutual attempt of two interlocutors to agree on a
meaning in situations where requisite meaning structures do not
seem to be shared'. That conversations between learners and native speakers often contain a fair amount of metalinguistic communication is a well-known fact, discussed, e.g., by Glahn
(1980b); Færch and Kasper (1982); and by contributors to
Larsen-Freeman (1980). However, we do not find it feasible to
restrict our definition of communication strategies in the way suggested by Tarone; although problems in interaction are necessarily 'shared' problems and *can* be solved by joint efforts, they originate in either of the interactants, and it is up to him to decide
whether to attempt a solution himself, e.g. by using a psycholing-

uistic achievement strategy, or to signal his problem to his interlocutor and attempt to get the problem solved on a cooperative basis (see also our contribution in Part Three, this volume).

If the individual decides to try to solve his problem himself and he succeeds in communicating his intended meaning to his interlocutor, the interactants clearly do not reach a state of 'mutually attempting . . . .to agree on a meaning'. If, however, the individual does not succeed in communicating his intended meaning by using a non-cooperative strategy, this may function as a 'problem indication', leading to a cooperative solution.

If the learner decides to signal to his interlocutor that he is experiencing a communicative problem and that he needs assistance, he makes use of the cooperative communication strategy of 'appealing' (cf. Tarone, Frauenfelder and Selinker 1976; Tarone 1977; Corder 1978; and Blum-Kulka and Levenston; Corder; Tarone, Cohen and Dumas in this volume). Appeals, which can be characterized as 'self-initiated other-repairs' (Schegloff, Jefferson and Sacks 1977, pp. 363ff), can be *direct* (cf. example 9), or *indirect*. In the latter case ('admission of ignorance', Palmberg 1979), the learner often supplements the (indirect) appeal by another communication strategy, as seen in example 10.

(9)   NS: what er colour is it —
        L: er skim (laugh) er — er — *what's — colour is this —*
        (points to her sweater)
        (PIF, *skimlet* Danish for 'grey' with reference to animals)

(10)   L: after my school I'll start erm (sigh) er – I learn erm shirts and er (laugh) *can't explain that* – er – sy – [sy:]
        I I can't say that
        (PIF, *sy* Danish for 'sew')

As mentioned above, an unsuccessful non-cooperative strategy may function as a 'problem indication'. In this case the strategy has the same *function* as an appeal, though this is unintended by the learner.

In communicative situations with well-defined communicative goals (e.g. problem-solving activities), and in which one of the interactants has a less elaborated linguistic system than the other(s), the interactants may change the distribution of roles in such a way that the communicative task is reduced for the linguistically 'handicapped' interactant. This can be characterized as a 'global' strategy, affecting the overall organization of discourse (see Wagner in this volume).

(f) Non-linguistic strategies

In face-to-face communication, learners frequently resort to non-linguistic strategies such as mime, gesture and sound-imitation (cf. Tarone 1977; Corder in this volume). Although non-linguistic strategies are sometimes used as the learner's one and only attempt at solving a communicative problem, they are often used to 'support' other — verbal — strategies. An important function of non-linguistic strategies is to signal an appeal to the interlocutor.

Retrieval strategies

In executing a plan, learners may have difficulties in retrieving specific IL items and may adopt achievement strategies in order to get at the problematic item. This phenomenon has been studied by Glahn, who concludes that the learners who participated in the task 'immediately realized whether they did or did not possess a term in French'. In some cases they 'knew that the term was there', and they would have to retrieve it in some way (1980a). The following six retrieval strategies were identified in the experiment: waiting for the term to appear; appealing to formal similarity; retrieval via semantic fields; searching via other languages; retrieval from learning situations; sensory procedures.

Overview of communication strategies

***Formal reduction strategies*:**
Learner communicates by means of a 'reduced' system, in order to avoid producing non-fluent or incorrect utterances by realizing insufficiently automatized or hypothetical rules/items

Subtypes:
phonological
morphological
syntactic
lexical

***Functional reduction strategies*:**
Learner reduces his communicative goal in order to avoid a problem

Subtypes:
actional reduction
modal reduction
reduction of the propositional content:
topic avoidance
message abandonment
meaning replacement

Achievement strategies:	Subtypes:

Learner attempts to solve communicative problem by expanding his communicative resources	*compensatory strategies*:
	(a) code switching
	(b) interlingual transfer
	(c) inter-/intralingual transfer
	(d) IL based strategies:
	    (*i*) *generalization*
	    (*ii*) *paraphrase*
	    (*iii*) *word coinage*
	    (*iv*) *restructuring*
	(e) cooperative strategies
	(f) non-linguistic strategies
	
	retrieval strategies

Communication strategies and L2 learning

In the introduction to this article, we briefly touched upon the relationship between learning and communication strategies. In the present section, we shall discuss how the use of communication strategies can lead to L2 learning and classify the communication strategies listed above according to their potential learning effect.

L2 learning can be conceived of as a process in which the learner gradually develops his IL system by establishing hypothetical rules (*hypothesis formation*) and by testing them out (*hypothesis testing*). Depending on the feedback obtained, hypothetical rules either get rejected or incorporated into the IL system as fixed rules. In addition to including these cognitively based processes, a comprehensive model of L2 learning has to include the process of *automatization*, in which the learner increases the availability of IL rules by using them in formal exercises or in communication (see Færch and Kasper 1980 for a more detailed description of the language learning process).

As the use of a communication strategy presupposes that the learner experiences a problem, this implies either that his IL system does not yet contain the appropriate item/rule (planning problem), or that the appropriate IL item/rule is difficult to retrieve or is considered problematic from a correctness or fluency point of view (execution problem). We can therefore conclude that communication strategies which aim at solving problems in

the planning phase can lead to L2 learning only with respect to hypothesis formation, and that communication strategies in connection with the execution phase will be associated with automatization only.

A basic condition for communication strategies to have a potential learning effect is that they are governed by achievement, rather than avoidance, behaviour: if learners avoid developing a plan and change the goal instead so that it can be reached by means of the communicative resources they already possess in their IL, no hypothesis formation takes place and their IL system remains unaffected (although the automatization of the system may hereby be increased in general due to practice). Similarly, if learners avoid using a particular IL item because of uncertainty about its correctness (formal reduction), this clearly does not lead to automatization of the relevant item (but again, possibly, to a consolidation of some other aspect of the system).

Those compensatory communication strategies by means of which the learner extends his resources without abandoning the IL system completely (as in the case of code switching and the use of non-linguistic strategies) can lead to *hypothesis formation* as the first step in the L2 learning process. These strategies are interlingual and inter-/intralingual transfer, generalization, word coinage and appeals. In addition to these *productive* strategies which were the only strategies to be considered in this article, it should be mentioned that *receptive* communication strategies can also result in hypothesis formation: the learner might use his prior L1, IL or contextual knowledge in order to understand L2 items which are not yet part of his IL system. This strategy has been discussed in the literature under the term 'inferencing' (see Carton 1971; Bialystok 1978, Færch forthcoming; Kasper forthcoming).

As regards *automatization*, retrieval strategies have a potential learning effect: if learners successfully attempt to retrieve an IL item it may be easier to use the item on future occasions. Moreover, to the extent that strategies involve the learner in using other aspects of the IL system than what is considered problematic, this can also be assumed to contribute *indirectly* to automatization of the system in general, as pointed out above.

Figure 8 contains a summary of the potential learning effect of communication strategies.

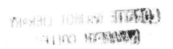

	+ potential learning	– potential learning
hypothesis formation	*automatization*	
interlingual transfer	retrieval	code switching
inter-/intralingual transfer		non-linguistic strategies
generalization		reduction strategies
word coinage	[practising IL] ←– – – – –	paraphrase
appeals		restructuring
inferencing		

Figure 8 Potential learning effect of communication strategies

Communication strategies and FL teaching

Ignoring the fact that there are many unresolved questions concerning communication strategies, we might venture to consider the *general* question whether communication strategies should be taught. If by teaching we mean passing on new information only there is probably no need to 'teach' strategies: FL learners no doubt have implicit knowledge about communication strategies and make use of this. But if by teaching we also mean making learners conscious about aspects of their (already existing) behaviour, it is obvious that we *should* teach them about strategies, in particular how to use communication strategies most appropriately. Before we can do so, however, we need more information about the potential effect of different types of strategies, as mentioned above. Furthermore, the choice of teaching methods will have to take into consideration what the relationship is between learner variables and learners' preference for strategies (cf. the two basic types of underlying behaviour: achievement and avoidance), as well as the relationship between learners' preference for strategies and teaching goals/methods. Thus one might imagine that learners would be induced to opt for reduction strategies if the FL teaching gives high priority to correctness and possibly penalizes errors against the L2 norm, even if these are a result of achievement strategies.

Would it be feasible to have learners engage in communicative situations in the classroom which require a more extensive knowledge of L2 than that which the learners can be expected to have? On the one hand, there is a risk of frustrating the learners by making too strong demands on their ability to communicate. On the other hand, there could be considerable gains in teaching learners how to compensate for insufficient linguistic resources by using the totality of their communicative resources creatively and appropriately.

With the last-mentioned question we reach a topic which has been extensively discussed in recent years: syllabus design, the pros and cons of a notional/functional syllabus as compared to a 'traditional' structural syllabus. Basic to a notional/functional approach is the attempt to establish syllabuses which are geared towards very specific communicative needs, something which is neither realistic nor desirable in connection with courses like most FL courses offered within school programmes. In connection with such courses, communication strategies can be seen as devices which enable learners to bridge the inevitable gap between classroom interaction and various communicative situations outside the classroom, hereby increasing their *communicative* competence in a way which is specific for IL communication. In other words, by learning how to use communication strategies appropriately, learners will be more able to bridge the gap between formal and informal learning situations, between pedagogic and non-pedagogic communicative situations.

Notes

1. The data originates from the PIF corpus of learner language, Department of English, University of Copenhagen. The PIF project (Færch 1979) is financed in part by a grant from the Danish Research Council for the Humanities. For a description of the corpus, see Færch (1982). In the article we also use data from the project 'Kommunikative Kompetenz als realisierbares Lernziel', Seminar für Sprachlehrforschung, Ruhr-Universität Bochum (BO). For a description of this project, see Edmondson, House, Kasper and McKeown (1979) and Edmondson, House, Kasper and Stemmer (1982). The PIF data used in this paper consist of 120 video-taped, dyadic, face-to-face conversations between Danish learners at various educational levels and native speakers of English, both having received identical instructions and conversing about everyday topics. The BO data referred to in this paper consist of 48 audio-taped, dyadic, face-to-face conversations between German first-year students and English native speakers, which were performed in role-plays involving everyday situations.
2. To date, research into these intra-individual feedback processes has concentrated on the very last execution stage, the 'myodynamic execution function', which is primarily governed by the peripheral nervous system (see, e.g. Laver 1973 and Dalton and Hardcastle 1977, pp. 15ff). As little is known about the feedback function at the earlier stages of speech production, we shall not go into this any further in the following discussion.
3. This, however, is not a necessary aspect of communication between

speakers of different L1s: as proposed by Schröder (1973), each of the interlocutors might use their respective L1s productively, provided they have a *receptive* knowledge of their interlocutor's L1.

References

Albrechtsen, Dorte, Henriksen, Birgit and Færch, Claus (1980). 'Native Speaker Reactions to Learners' Spoken Interlanguage', *Language Learning*, **30**, 365–396.
Baur, Rupprecht S. and Rehbein, Jochen (1979). 'Lerntheorie und Lernwirklichkeit — Zur Aneigung des deutschen Artikels bei türkischen Schülern: ein Versuch mit der Gal'perinschen Konzeption', *Osnabrücker Beiträge zur Sprachtheorie* (OBST), **10**, 70–104.
Beneke, Jürgen (1975). 'Verstehen und Missverstehen im Englischunterricht', *Praxis des neusprachlichen Unterrichts*, **4**, 351–362.
Bialystok, Ellen (1978). 'A Theoretical Model of Second Language Learning', *Language Learning*, **28**, 69–84.
Bialystok, Ellen (1979). 'Some Evidence for the Integrity and Interaction of Two Knowledge Sources'. Paper presented at the 13th TESOL Convention, Boston.
Blum, Shoshana and Levenston, Eddie A. (1978a). 'Universals of Lexical Simplification', *Language Learning*, **28**, 399–416.
Blum, Shoshana and Levenston, Eddie A. (1978b). 'Lexical Simplification in Second-Language Acquisition'. *Studies in Second Language Acquisition*, **2/2**, 43–64.
Brown, H. Douglas (1976a). 'Discussion of 'Systematicity/Variability and Stability/Instability in Interlanguages'', in Brown (1976b), 135–140.
Brown, H. Douglas (ed.) (1976b). *Papers in Second Language Acquisition* (= Language Learning Special Issue No. 4).
Candlin, Christopher N. and Breen, Michael P. (eds.) (forthcoming). *Strategies in Language Learning*, Oxford University Press.
Carton, Aaron S. (1971). 'Inferencing: a Process in Using and Learning Language', in Pimsleur, Paul and Quinn, Terence (eds.), *The Psychology of Second Language Learning*, Cambridge University Press, 45–58.
Clark, Herbert H. and Clark, Eve V. (1977). *Psychology and Language*, New York: Harcourt Brace Jovanovich.
Corder, S. Pit (1978). 'Language-Learner Language', in Richards, Jack C. (ed.), *Understanding Second and Foreign Language Learning*, Rowley, Massachusetts: Newbury House, 71–93.
Dalton, Peggy and Hardcastle, W. J. (1977). *Disorders of Fluency and their Effects on Communication*, London: Arnold.
Dulay, Heidi C. and Burt, Marina K. (1972). 'Goofing: an Indicator of Children's Second Language Learning Strategies', *Language Learning*, **22**, 235–252.
Dulay, Heidi C. and Burt, Marina K. (1974). 'You Can't Learn without Goofing. An Analysis of Children's Second Language "Errors"', in Richards (1974), 95–123.
Edmondson, Willis and House, Juliane (1981). *Let's Talk and Talk about It*, München: Urban und Schwarzenberg.

Edmondson, Willis, House, Juliane, Kasper, Gabriele and McKeown, John (1979). *Sprachliche Interaktion in lernzielrelevanten Situationen: Kommunikative Kompetenz als realisierbares Lernziel* (= LAUT paper No. 51, Series B, Trier).

Edmondson, Willis, House, Juliane, Kasper, Gabriele and Stemmer, Brigitte (1982). *Kommunikation lernen und lehren.* Berichte und Perspektiven aus einem Forschungsprojekt (= Manuskripte zur Sprachlehrforschung Nr. 20), Heidelberg: Groos.

Enkvist, Nils Erik (1973). 'Should We Count Errors or Measure Success?', in Svartvik, Jan (ed.), *Errata*, Lund: Gleerup, 16–33.

Færch, Claus (1979). *Research in Foreign Language Pedagogy — the PIF Project*, Department of English, University of Copenhagen.

Færch, Claus (1982). *A Corpus of Learner Language*, Department of English, University of Copenhagen.

Færch, Claus (forthcoming). 'Inferencing Procedures and Communication Strategies in Lexical Comprehension', in Candlin and Breen (forthcoming).

Færch, Claus and Kasper, Gabriele (1980). 'Processes and Strategies in Foreign Language Learning and Communication', *Interlanguage Studies Bulletin Utrecht*, **5**, 47–118.

Færch, Claus and Kasper, Gabriele (1982). 'Phatic, Metalingual and Metacommunicative Functions in Discourse: Gambits and Repairs', in Enkvist, Nils Erik (ed.), *Impromptu Speech*, Åbo: Åbo Akademi (in press).

Frauenfelder, Uli and Porquier, Remý (1979). 'Les voies d'apprentissage en langue étrangère', *Working Papers on Bilingualism*, **17**, 37–64.

Fromkin, Victoria A. (ed.) (1973). *Speech Errors as Linguistic Evidence*, The Hague: Mouton.

Fry, D. B. (1973). 'The Linguistic Evidence of Speech Errors', in Fromkin (1973), 157–163.

Glahn, Esther (1980a). 'Introspection as a Method of Elicitation in Interlanguage Studies', *Interlanguage Studies Bulletin Utrecht*, **5**, 119–128.

Glahn, Esther (1980b). '20 spørgsmål til professoren', *Skrifter om anvendt og matematisk lingvistik*, **6**, 257–280.

Götz, Dieter (1977). 'Analyse einer in der Fremdsprache (Englisch) durchgeführten Konversation', in Hunfeld, Hans (ed.), *Neue Perspektiven der Fremdsprachendidaktik*, Kronberg: Scriptor, 71–81.

Habermas, Jürgen (1971). *Knowledge and Human Interests*, Boston: Beacon Press.

Hamayan, Else V. and Tucker, G. Richard (1979). 'Strategies of Communication Used by Native and Non-Native Speakers of French', *Working Papers on Bilingualism*, **17**, 83–96.

Harder, Peter (1980). 'Discourse as Self-Expression and the Reduced Identity of the L2 Learner', *Applied Linguistics*, **1**, 262–270.

Hüllen, Werner (ed.) (1973a). *Neusser Vorträge zur Fremdsprachendidaktik*, Berlin: Cornelsen.

Hüllen, Werner (1973b), 'Pragmatik — die dritte linguistische Dimension', in Hüllen (1973a), 84–99.

Ickenroth, Jacques (1975). *On the Elusiveness of Interlanguage*, Utrecht (mimeo).

Jain, M. P. (1974). 'Error Analysis: Source, Cause and Significance', in Richards (1974), 189–215.

Jordens, Peter (1977). 'Rules, Grammatical Intuitions and Strategies in Foreign Language Learning', *Interlanguage Studies Bulletin Utrecht*, **2/2**, 5–76.

Kasper, Gabriele (1979). 'Communication Strategies: Modality Reduction', *Interlanguage Studies Bulletin Utrecht*, **4**, 266–283.

Kasper, Gabriele (1981). *Pragmatische Aspekte in der Interimsprache. Eine Untersuchung des Englischen fortgeschrittener deutscher Lerner*, Tübingen: Narr.

Kasper, Gabriele (forthcoming). 'Pragmatic Comprehension in Learner-Native Speaker Discourse', in Candlin and Breen (forthcoming).

Keller, Eric and Taba-Warner, Sylvia (1976, 1977, 1979). *Gambits 1, Openers; Gambits 2, Links; Gambits 3, Responders, Closers and Inventory. A Series of Three Modules*, Ottawa: Government of Canada.

Kellerman, Eric (1977). 'Towards a Characterization of the Strategy of Transfer in Second Language Learning', *Interlanguage Studies Bulletin Utrecht*, **2/1**, 58–145.

Kellerman, Eric (1978). 'Giving Learners a Break: Native Language Intuitions as a Source of Predictions about Transferability', *Working Papers on Bilingualism*, **15**, 59–92.

Klaus, Georg and Buhr, Manfred (eds.) (1976). *Philosophisches Wörterbuch*, Leipzig: VEB Bibliographisches Institut.

Kleinmann, Howard H. (1977). 'Avoidance Behavior in Adult Second Language Acquisition', *Language Learning*, **27**, 93–108.

Knapp, Karlfried (1980). 'Weiterlernen'. *Linguistik und Didaktik*, **43/44**, 257–271.

Krashen, Stephen (1978). 'The Monitor Model for Second-Language Acquisition', in Gringas, Rosario C. (ed.), *Second-Language Acquisition and Foreign Language Teaching*, Arlington, Virginia: Center for Applied Linguistics, 1–26.

Larsen-Freeman, Diane (ed.) (1980). *Discourse Analysis in Second Language Research*, Rowley, Massachusetts: Newbury House.

Laver, John D. M. (1973). 'The Detection and Correction of Slips of the Tongue', in Fromkin (1973), 132–143.

Leont'ev, Aleksej A. (1975). *Psycholinguistische Einheiten und die Erzeugung sprachlicher Äusserungen*, Berlin (DDR): Akademie-Verlag.

Levenston, Eddie A. (1971). 'Over-Indulgence and Under-Representation — Aspects of Mother-Tongue Interference', in Nickel, Gerhard (ed.), *Papers in Contrastive Linguistics*, Cambridge University Press, 115–121.

Levenston, Eddie A. and Blum, Shoshana (1977). 'Aspects of Lexical Simplification in the Speech and Writing of Advanced Adult Learners', in Corder, S. Pit and Roulet, Eddie (eds.), *Actes du 5ème colloque de linguistique appliquée de Neuchâtel*, Neuchâtel: Faculté des Lettres, 51–71.

Miller, George A., Galanter, Eugene and Pribram, Karl H. (1960). *Plans and the Structure of Behavior*, New York: Holt, Rinehart and Winston.

Nold, Günter (1978). 'Second Language Speech Behaviour after Nine Years of Instruction — A Contrastive Study of Discourse'. Paper presented at the 5th AILA Congress, Montreal.

Palmberg, Rolf (1979). 'Investigating Communication Strategies', in Palmberg, Rolf (ed.), *Perception and Production of English: Papers on Interlanguage*, Publications of the Department of English, Åbo Academy, 53–75.

Piepho, Hans-Eberhard (1974). *Kommunikative Kompetenz als übergeordnetes Lernziel im Englischunterricht*, Dornburg–Frikkenhofen: Frankonius.

Rehbein, Jochen (1977). *Komplexes Handeln*, Stuttgart: Metzler.

Richards, Jack C. (ed.) (1974). *Error Analysis*, London: Longman.

Sajavaara, Kari, Lehtonen, Jaakko and Korpimies, Liisa (1980). 'The Methodology and Practice of Contrastive Discourse Analysis', in Sajavaara, Kari and Lehtonen, Jaakko (eds.), *Papers in Discourse and Contrastive Discourse Analysis*, Department of English, Jyväskylä University.

Schegloff, Emanuel A., Jefferson, Gail and Sacks, Harvey (1977). 'The Preference for Self-Correction in the Organization of Repair in Conversation', *Language*, **53**, 361–382.

Schröder, Konrad (1973). 'Sprachunterricht, Sprachenpolitik und internationale Kommunikation', in Hüllen (1973a), 138–151.

Selinker, Larry (1972). 'Interlanguage', *IRAL*, **10**, 209–231.

Sharwood Smith, Michael (1979). 'Strategies, Language Transfer and the Simulation of the Second Language Learner's Mental Operations', *Interlanguage Studies Bulletin Utrecht*, **4**, 66–83.

Stemmer, Brigitte (1981). *Kohäsion im gesprochenen Diskurs deutscher Lerner des Englischen* (= Manuskripte zur Sprachlehrforschung Nr. 18), Heidelberg: Groos.

Tarone, Elaine (1977). 'Conscious Communication Strategies in Interlanguage: a Progress Report', in Brown, H. Douglas, Yorio, Carlos A. and Crymes, Ruth H. (eds.), *On TESOL '77* Washington, D.C.: TESOL, 194–203.

Tarone, Elaine, Frauenfelder, Uli and Selinker, Larry. (1976) 'Systematicity/Variability and Stability/Instability in Interlanguage Systems', in Brown (1976b), 93–134.

Taylor, Barry P. (1974). 'Toward a Theory of Language Acquisition', *Language Learning*, **24**, 23–35.

Taylor, Barry P. (1975). 'The Use of Overgeneralization and Transfer Learning Strategies by Elementary and Intermediate Students of ESL', *Language Learning*, **25**, 73–107.

Wilkins, David A. (1976). *Notional Syllabuses*, Oxford University Press.

4   Some thoughts on the notion of 'communication strategy'*[1]

Elaine Tarone

It is increasingly unclear what is meant by the term *communication strategy*, as it has appeared in the second-language acquisition literature, particularly when it begins to be used interchangeably with terms like *learning strategy, production strategy*, and *perception strategy*. Do all these terms refer to the same phenomenon? If not, what do they refer to? I would like to share some of my thoughts concerning the notion *communication strategy*, attempt to propose some means of differentiating the notion from some others, and suggest some questions raised by the perspective to be presented here. Finally, I would like to suggest some directions for future research in this area.

1 The notion of communication strategy

First of all, it is clear to me that there is a real and interesting phenomenon which occurs when second-language learners attempt to communicate with speakers of the target language. Here are some examples of this phenomenon.

A native speaker of Turkish is observed as he describes a picture of a caterpillar smoking a waterpipe; in English, his second language, he says, 'She is, uh, smoking something. I don't know what's its name. That's, uh, Persian, and we use in Turkey, a lot of.' Or again, a native speaker of Spanish is observed as he describes a picture of an applauding audience; he says, in English, his second language: 'And everybody say [claps hands].' Or again, a native speaker of English describes the principal of his school in Spanish, his second language: '... es el presidente de la

* *Originally published in* TESOL Quarterly, September 1981.

escuela' (lit.: He's the president of the school). I believe that these phenomena, documented in several recent studies (Váradi, this volume; Tarone, Frauenfelder and Selinker 1976; Tarone 1977; Galván and Campbell 1979), are *related*. They can be viewed as the speaker's attempt to communicate meaningful content, in the face of some apparent lacks in the interlanguage system. It would be useful for second-language acquisition researchers to find some way of clearly defining a term which describes this strategy and separates it out from the other types of strategies just mentioned.

As a first step in arriving at such a definition, it will be useful to examine some examples of strategies, taken from Tarone (1977). This list of strategies is not intended to be a final categorization of all existent communication strategies; it is simply provided to help us arrive at a clarification of the notion *communication strategy* and a definition of the term.

Paraphrase

Approximation — use of a single target language vocabulary item or structure, which the learner knows is not correct, but which shares enough semantic features in common with the desired item to satisfy the speaker (e.g. *pipe* for *waterpipe*)

Word coinage — the learner makes up a new word in order to communicate a desired concept (e.g. *airball* for *balloon*)

Circumlocution — the learner describes the characteristics or elements of the object or action instead of using the appropriate target language (TL) item or structure ('She is, uh, smoking something. I don't know what's its name. That's, uh, Persian, and we use in Turkey, a lot of.')

Borrowing

Literal translation — the learner translates word for word from the native language (e.g. *He invites him to drink*, for *They toast one another*.)

Language switch — the learner uses the native language (NL) term without bothering to translate (e.g. *balon* for *balloon*, *tirtil* for *caterpillar*)

Appeal for assistance — the learner asks for the correct term (e.g., 'What is this? What called?')

Mime — the learner uses non-verbal strategies in place of a lexical item or action (e.g. clapping one's hands to illustrate applause)

Avoidance

Topic avoidance — the learner simply tries not to talk about concepts for which the TL item or structure is not known

Message abandonment — the learner begins to talk about a concept but is unable to continue and stops in mid-utterance

In the light of these examples, I would like to examine several definitions of communication strategies which have been proposed in the past, and evaluate them.

Definition One: 'a systematic attempt by the learner to express or decode meaning in the target language (TL), in situations where the appropriate systematic TL rules have not been formed' (Tarone, Frauenfelder and Selinker 1976; Tarone, Cohen and Dumas in this volume). In this case, I now believe it is not clear what is meant by a 'systematic attempt', nor is it possible to distinguish, say, a production strategy from a communication strategy using this definition.

Definition Two: 'a conscious attempt to communicate the learner's thought when the interlanguage structures are inadequate to convey that thought' (Váradi in this volume; Tarone 1977; Galván and Campbell 1979). In this case, it is difficult if not impossible to say whether any of the examples above occur at a conscious or an unconscious level. In fact, if consciousness is at all a matter of degree rather than an 'on-off' matter, the definition becomes meaningless. I would, thus, prefer to avoid specifying degree of consciousness in any definition of communication strategies. Sascha Felix (personal communication) has pointed out that the real issue with communication strategies is to determine how the learner 'utilizes his limited knowledge to cope with various communication situations'; this notion of language *use* perhaps ought to be incorporated into our attempted definition of communication strategies.

These definitions do seem to capture much of what is apparently going on in the examples cited above. Communication strategies do not seem to be a part of the speaker's linguistic knowledge. Rather, they are descriptive of the learner's pattern of *use* of what he/she knows as he/she tries to communicate with speakers of the TL. To decide that communication strategies (CS) are tied up with language use is to bring into question the relationship of these strategies to communicative competence. Communicative competence has sometimes been defined as the knowledge of how to use one's linguistic system appropriately in situation. Canale and Swain (1980) have proposed a broader definition of communicative competence which would include linguistic competence, sociolinguistic competence and strategic competence; in their framework, I am attempting here to differentiate sociolinguistic competence from strategic competence. While both sociolinguistic competence and communication strategies deal with the use of linguistic knowledge, the difference lies here: communication strategies are used to *compensate for* some lack in the linguistic system, and focus on exploring alternate ways of using what one does know for the transmission of a message, without necessarily considering situational appropriateness. Sociolinguistic competence assumes the existence of a linguistic system which is shared by both interlocutors and focusses on the appropriate usage of stylistic variants of this rule system based on a shared knowledge of social norms.

Ultimately, however, our definition of the notion of communication strategy must go beyond this definition of the second-language learner's attempts to use a restricted linguistic system for communication. I think that the *interactional function* of CS has unfortunately been overlooked in my own research to date, and in much of the recent discussion in this area. It is easy to forget that language is not an *object* which is *used*, but a part of communication — a living organism created by both speaker and hearer. The interactional function of CS may be most clearly seen in an exchange which is recorded in Tarone (1977) between me and MS (see Appendix A). Whereas before this point in our interaction I had attempted to restrict my own responses to MS's utterances, in this exchange I allowed myself to respond. The conversation which then occurred can be described as a joint negotiation of an agreement on meaning — an attempt by both myself and MS to make sure that both were talking about the same thing. The purpose of the exchange does not primarily seem to be for MS to learn new English vocabulary items like *poppy*. For MS the purpose seems to be to access the Mandarin term for *waterpipe* — not to learn the English term. The *function* of the communication strategies used by both of us seems to be to exchange enough information in English to ensure that both interlocutors are talking about the same thing. In the same study, a learner used the language switch strategy in referring to a caterpillar as a *tirtil*: it is speculated in that paper that the speaker's decision to use that term may have been reached because the listener may have involuntarily, non-verbally, given some indication that she recognized the term and accepted it as a reasonable response. The function of communication strategies in both cases seems to be primarily to negotiate an agreement on meaning between two interlocutors (see Tarone 1980 for a discussion of the relationship between communication strategies, repair, and foreigner talk).

I would like to broaden the definition of communication strategies, therefore, to make it clear that the term relates to a mutual attempt of two interlocutors to agree on a meaning in situations where requisite meaning structures do not seem to be shared. (Meaning structures here would include both linguistic structures and sociolinguistic rule structures). Communication strategies, viewed from this perspective, may be seen as attempts to bridge the gap between the linguistic knowledge of the second-language learner, and the linguistic knowledge of the target language interlocutor in real communication situations. Approximation, mime and circumlocution may be used to bridge this gap. Message abandonment and avoidance may be used where the gap is perceived as unbridgeable.

To summarize, I propose that the following criteria characterize a communication strategy:

1. a speaker desires to communicate a meaning X to a listener;
2. the speaker believes the linguistic or sociolinguistic structure desired to communicate meaning X is unavailable, or is not shared with the listener;
3. the speaker chooses to:
    (a) avoid — not attempt to communicate meaning X; or,
    (b) attempt alternate means to communicate meaning X. The speaker stops trying alternatives when it seems clear to the speaker that there is shared meaning.

If we look at the examples given earlier on, they seem to fulfil these criteria, and thus may be called communication strategies. There does seem to be something odd about avoidance strategies that I will deal with shortly.

Parenthetically, in light of the criteria given above, one might ask whether communication strategies may not occur in one's native language as well as in an interlanguage. Certainly they seem to be used between dialects of the same language (Shaaban 1978). In fact, to the extent that there is always a gap between a speaker and a hearer's linguistic and semantic systems, this is undoubtedly so. No one masters the entire lexicon of one's native language, for instance; so, one may refer to an unfamiliar tool as a *thingamabob* or a *doomiflatchy*, using word coinage. One may have a memory lapse and forget a name one used to know. If George has to introduce you to Mrs X and forgets your name, he may appeal for assistance and ask you for your name. He may try to avoid introducing you until he can remember your name, or even approximate: 'This is Mmmm . . . Mary . . . no, no, Mabel!' Finally, each of us has our own semantic system, which differs from everyone else's; we use CS to negotiate shared meaning in situations where it is apparent that we may mean very different things by a term. Consider the following conversation:

A: I love you.
B: (*suspiciously*) What do you mean, love?
A: circumlocute . . . approximate . . . mime!

However, in native language interactions we may suspect that such communication strategies are used primarily with lexical items, or perhaps to clarify referents for pronouns, whereas in interlanguage they may occur with syntactic, morphological, or even phonological structures (cf. Tarone, Cohen and Dumas in this volume). Although each of us has an idiosyncratic semantic system, most of the time we go along in our native language assuming that we all mean the same thing by a particular word, and most of the time this approach gets us by. When gross discrepancies occur in our communication with others in our NL, we stop to use CS. But in communication between a second-language learner and a native speaker of the TL, such discrepancies simply occur more often, and hence the use of CS becomes more obvious.

In addition to communication strategies, there seems to be another kind of notion — the notion of *production strategy*. A production strategy, like a communication strategy, is a strategy of language *use*. I would define a production strategy as an attempt to use one's linguistic system efficiently and clearly, with a minimum of effort. Production strategies (PS) are similar to CS in that they are attempts to use one's linguistic system, but PS differ in that they lack the interactional focus on the negotiation of meaning. Thus, the use of prefabricated patterns, discourse planning and rehearsal (as in Aono and Hillis 1979) would be classified as PS because they simplify the task of speaking in a particular situation. As Aono and Hillis point out, a rehearsed segment can be impervious to unexpected interruption from the listener — and hence rehearsal seems to lack the interactional negotiation of meaning central to our proposed definition of CS. Another way of saying this is that criterion 3(b), necessary in order to have a CS, is missing.

A third kind of notion is that of *learning strategy*. I would define a learning strategy as an attempt to develop linguistic and sociolinguistic competence in the target language — to incorporate these into one's interlanguage competence. Note that criterion 1 above is not necessary for learning strategies thus defined. The basic motivating force behind learning strategies is not the desire to communicate meaning, but the desire to learn the target language. Thus, Cohen and Aphek (1981) have described strategies such as the use of mnemonics in the learning of target language vocabulary which I would classify as learning strategies, not communication strategies. Other learning strategies might include memorization or repetition of troublesome target language structures.

The relationship of learning strategies (LS) to communication strategies is somewhat problematic. Can a communication strategy also be a learning strategy? According to our definitions, one can have a CS which is not an LS and vice versa. Memorization is not a CS. Also, in the conversation with MS in Appendix A, though the terms 'poppy' and 'drug' are used in communication strategies, there is no indication that MS focussed on learning those terms; he does stop to spell the term 'opium' and repeats it several times, however. In this case, I would say that the motivations for his actions of spelling and repeating are not the communication of meaning, but rather the attempt to learn the term. Thus, I think it is theoretically possible to distinguish CS and LS on the basis of criterion 1 — the motivation underlying the use of the strategy. The problem, of course, arises (a) in that we have no way of measuring that motivation; (b) it may be that one's motivation is both to learn and to communicate; and (c) one may unconsciously acquire language even if one is using a strategy solely to communicate a meaning. If a structure works in a particular situation to communicate meaning, does it later become a part of the linguistic system? In theory, while learning strategies and communication strategies may be indistinguishable in some cases in our observation of linguistic behaviour, there does appear to be a difference between the two kinds of strategy, and there do seem to be clear observable bits of behaviour which evidence either one or the other strategy, and not both.

The differences and similarities among communication strategies, production strategies and learning strategies are outlined in Appendix B. The set of criteria which I have offered as a perspective on the use of communication strategies seems to effectively differentiate the notion of CS from the notions of production strategy and learning strategy.

The question of how to consider avoidance strategies is a difficult one. Note that there are two types of avoidance: topic avoidance and message abandonment. Message abandonment is clearly a communication strategy; there is an attempt to communicate a meaning, which is aborted midstream. In interaction, the effect of this CS is that the listener often tries to fill in and suggest an alternative means of expressing what the speaker wants to say — there is interaction and a joint effort to agree on a meaning. However, topic avoidance can theoretically occur for two reasons. In one case, the speaker may fulfil criterion 1 and desire to communicate something, but find the meaning structure necessary for that communication not shared, and avoid the topic. In another case, however, it is possible to imagine that the speaker avoids the topic because he/she does not fulfil criterion 1, and does not desire at all to communicate meaning X to the listener. In the latter case, we would have a production strategy — an attempt to simplify the speaking effort by not bringing up the topic. This is a very fine line indeed, and one which may not be determinable from observational data or introspective data. But in theory it seems reasonable that topic avoidance might be classified as either a CS or a PS depending on whether its use involves fulfilment of criterion 1 or not. The purposes underlying use of topic avoidance may be extremely complex and very difficult to get at ultimately in any given case.

One last notion deserves brief mention here. The notion of *perception strategy* seems to me to be much less likely to be confused with the three types of strategy just dealt with. The notion is dealt with in Tarone (1974) in some detail. I would define this notion as the attempt to interpret incoming utterances efficiently, with least effort. Examples of perception strategies might be principles like 'pay attention to the ends of words' or 'pay attention to stressed syllables'. Thus, due to the redundancy of speech, one does not need to decipher an entire utterance in order to understand a message in every case. Perception strategies simply take advantage of that redundancy.

2 Directions for future research

An interactional definition of the notion of communication strategy makes possible some new and innovative approaches to research, such as the introspective approach used by Aono and Hillis (1979). An advanced, linguistically sophisticated learner of English as a second language recorded his own speech in conversation with native speakers. The conversations were transcribed, and the learner then annotated the transcription, recording his retrospections as to what he had been thinking about and trying to say at various points of the discourse. A number of interesting observations are discussed in that paper. First, many of the CS described above could be identified using this approach. The researchers were able to show the existence of communication strategies like approximation, circumlocution and message abandonment in the discourse; they attempted to identify the learner's intended meaning in some cases, and they related this in concrete ways to what he said and how he said it. Given that intended meaning and intention to communicate are notions fundamental to the definition of CS, and are not easily accessible in observational data, the use of introspective data may be able to aid in the study of this phenomenon. Second, the researchers identified a production strategy which seemed to work fairly well for the learner — one which he calls 'rehearsal'. Segments of the learner's speech were 'rehearsed' if they were segments he had said before. Familiar topics which the learner had talked about often tended to draw out a great many 'rehearsed' segments. These segments seemed to be more fluent than other segments of the learner's speech, but were also less susceptible to interruption — thus there is supportive observational data to concur with Aono's introspection that these segments are in some ways different from unrehearsed segments. If the learner is interrupted in the middle of a rehearsed segment, he has great difficulty deciding how to respond, and often simply takes up his original message where it was left off without responding to the interrupter at all. Hatch (personal communication) suggests that this notion may correspond with the notion of 'narrative' in discourse analysis research. Finally, Aono and Hillis claim that the strategies used were strongly influenced by the learner's perception of the listener — how sympathetic, relaxed, or interested the listener was in what the learner was trying to say. If this is true, then this is all the more reason why communication and production strategies should be studied in the context of discourse.

Another area for future research which is suggested by an interactional definition of CS is prefigured in an ongoing study by Piranian (1979). Here, the subjects were American university students studying Russian in a formal, foreign language classroom. In a picture description task, her students used far fewer different types of CS than were found in any of the previous studies to date. Further, those foreign language learners whose experience of Russian was limited to the classroom seemed to rely to a very great extent on avoidance strategies, while those who did have extra-curricular exposure to Russian added paraphrase to their repertoire. Since this research is only just beginning, there is some question whether this pattern will prove to be a significant one. But it does raise the question whether the learning situation itself may not influence the type and variety of CS used. That is, unlike the students in all the other CS studies to date, Piranian's students were learning their other language in a formal, foreign language situation. They had had few occasions to be in situations where their main goal was communication, and where their linguistic systems were inadequate to meet this demand. If criterion 1 is not present, by definition CS are not used. Formal classrooms may encourage learning strategies, and, as Canale and Swain suggest, linguistic competence, but not encourage communication, and hence not CS. Of course, as Swain also suggests (personal communication), to encourage communication and CS in the classroom is not necessarily to encourage the development of linguistic competence.

Another direction for future research is the relation of CS and PS to success in learning. Seliger (1977) has postulated the existence of two types of second-language learners, identified in terms of their mode of interaction with others in discourse — high input generators (HIGs) and low input generators (LIGs). HIGs are defined as individuals who frequently initiate interaction with speakers of the TL; LIGs basically speak only when spoken to. Can we differentiate HIGs and LIGs in terms of the types of strategies each category uses? One might expect, for example, that LIGs would primarily use avoidance as a production/communication strategy to limit interactions with native speakers. HIGs would attempt to make use of their limited linguistic and sociolinguistic knowledge to a greater extent by use of more varied CS. It would be interesting to know, also, if some types of CS generate more input from native speakers than other types, and then to know whether HIGs use more of the CS which generate high input than LIGs. One would have to observe the use of CS in order to determine what their effect is on both learning and on native-speaker input; because of the interactional nature of CS, it is almost impossible to decide in advance what the possible effect of a particular CS is on learning.

In addition to the broad areas of research just mentioned, a very clear methodological implication develops from an interactional view of CS. Data on CS should be collected (on videotape if possible) in a discourse setting where the utterances of both interlocutors are transcribed. If possible, the task given the subjects should be one where real communication is taking place — where the hearer does not already know the information being transmitted by the speaker. The Galván and Campbell (1979) data-gathering technique is superior to the Tarone (1977) technique in this regard. However, the translation task used by Galván and Campbell is not necessarily a 'natural' one — the process of translation itself may encourage the use of some CS and discourage others. The need is for research designs which allow us to identify the second-language learner's intended meaning, in a wide variety of discourse settings, and then to see how the interlocutors attempt to use their differing linguistic systems to negotiate an agreement on that meaning — i.e. use communication strategies. The Aono and Hillis approach of using both empirical, recorded data and learner introspection is promising in that it permits the study of these CS in a wide variety of discourse situations, and provides us with two means of gaining access to the functioning of the learner's interlanguage. Its disadvantage is that it seems to require a fairly linguistically sophisticated second-language learner as subject. Of course, there are as many pitfalls inherent in the use of informants' introspections as there are in relying on observational data. Lamendella (personal communication) suggests that some of the techniques used in introspective psychology in the early part of this century may be useful in second-language acquisition research of this kind in providing the rigour which is currently needed.

More creativity is needed in the design of studies which attempt to examine the way in which restricted linguistic and sociolinguistic systems are used to deal with a variety of communication situations, and to relate research in this area to the areas of research on discourse analysis and communicative competence.

Appendix A

Conversation between MS and ET (from Tarone 1977)

ET: Do you have a single word in Mandarin that describes this?
MS: No. Uh, yes, um, we, maybe we have one, ju, just like uh do you know, um a, a poison there is, uh, no . . .
ET: A drug? *Opium*?
MS: *Yeah*, smoking . . .
ET: Opium.
MS: Op . . .
ET: Opium.
MS: How do you spell?
ET: O-P-I-U-M.
MS: O-P-I-U-M. Is a . . .
ET: It's a *drug*.
MS: *Is a* kind of, plant?
ET: Mmhm. It's a *poppy*.
MS: *Opium*.
ET: It's a poppy plant that grows and the flower is *very bright*.
MS: *Yes, yes*, oh.
ET: Opium.
MS: Oh. Yes, we, we have one called . . . Mandarin is ya pien yen. (*opium pipe*, lit.)

Appendix B

Definitions of some strategies

Strategies of language use

Communication strategy (CS) — a mutual attempt of two interlocutors to agree on a meaning in situations where requisite meaning structures do not seem to be shared. (Meaning structures include both linguistic and sociolinguistic structures.) Necessary criteria:
   1. a speaker desires to communicate meaning X to a listener;
   2. the speaker believes the linguistic or sociolinguistic structure desired to communicate meaning X is unavailable, or is not shared with the listener;

3. the speaker chooses to:
   (a) avoid — not attempt to communicate meaning X; or,
   (b) attempt alternate means to communicate meaning X. The speaker stops trying alternatives when it seems clear to the speaker that there is shared meaning.

Production strategy (PS) — an attempt to use one's linguistic system efficiently and clearly, with a minimum of effort.

Criterion 3(b) is absent. There may be no use of alternative means in the negotiation of meaning, as in cases of rehearsal, prefabricated patterns, discourse planning.

Also, in cases of avoidance, criterion 1 is absent; there may be no desire to communicate.

Language-learning strategy — an attempt to develop linguistic and sociolinguistic competence in the target language.

Criterion 1 is not necessary for LS; basic motivation is not to communicate but to learn.

Note

1. This paper was presented at the First TESOL Summer Institute in Los Angeles in 1979. Thanks to the following persons for their valuable comments and suggestions on this paper: Grant Abbott, Akira Aono, Ellen Bialystok, Evelyn Hatch, Paula Hillis, John Lamendella, Debby Piranian, Larry Selinker and Merrill Swain.

References

Aono, Akira and Hillis, Paula (1979). 'One ESL Learner's System for Communication in English: a Pilot Study'. Unpublished ms., ESL Center, University of Washington.

Canale, Michael and Swain, Merrill (1980). 'Theoretical Bases of Communicative Approaches to Second Language Teaching and Testing', *Applied Linguistics*, **1**, 1–47.

Cohen, Andrew and Aphek, Edna (1981). 'Easifying second language learning', *Studies in Second Language Acquisition*, **3**, 221–236.

Galván, José and Campbell, Russ (1979). 'An Examination of the Communication Strategies of Two Children in the Culver City Spanish Immersion Program', in Andersen, Roger (ed.), *The Acquisition and Use of Spanish and English as First and Second Languages*, Washington D.C.: TESOL.

Gorbet, Frances (1974). 'What the Teacher Can Do', in *Errors: a New Perspective*, Ottawa: Public Service Commission of Canada, Research Division, 30–78.

Piranian, Deborah (1979). 'Communication Strategies of Foreign Language Learners: a Pilot Study'. Unpublished ms., Slavic Linguistics, University of Washington.

Seliger, Herbert (1977). 'Does Practice Make Perfect? A Study of Interaction Patterns and Second Language Competence', *Language Learning*, **27**, 263–278.

Shaaban, K. (1978). 'Code-Switching in the Speech of Educated Arabs', *Journal of the Linguistic Association of the Southwest*, **III/1**, 7–19.

Tarone, Elaine (1974). 'Speech Perception in Second Language Acquisition: a Suggested Model', *Language Learning*, **24**, 223–233.

Tarone, Elaine (1977), 'Conscious Communication Strategies in Interlanguage: a Progress Report', in Brown, H. Douglas, Yorio, Carlos A. and Crymes, Ruth (eds.), *On TESOL '77: Teaching and Learning ESL*, Washington D.C.: TESOL, 194–203.

Tarone, Elaine (1980). 'Communication Strategies, Foreigner Talk and Repair in Interlanguage', *Language Learning*, **30**, 417–431.

Tarone, Elaine, Frauenfelder, Uli and Selinker, Larry (1976). 'Systematicity/Variability and Stability/Instability in Interlanguage Systems', in Brown, H. Douglas (ed.), *Papers in Second Language Acquisition* (= Language Learning Special Issue No. 4), 93–134.

Part Two
Empirical studies of communication strategies

Part Two comprises a collection of empirical investigations into the area of communication strategies. These studies vary considerably in their theoretical frameworks, methods of data collection and analysis as well as in the types of learners and the languages involved.

The part begins with Tamás Váradi's classic paper on 'Strategies of target language communication: message adjustment' (1973). Váradi establishes a model of IL production which focusses on the strategies the learner employs when he experiences a 'hiatus' in his IL repertoire. In order to adjust his message to his communicative resources, the learner either replaces the meaning or form of his intended message by using items which are part of his IL, or he reduces his intended message on either the formal or the functional level. This model was tested out in a pilot study involving adult Hungarian learners of English at the intermediate level. The experiment confirmed the hypothetical model of adjustment strategies. Although the pilot study reported on deals with learners' written performance exclusively, Váradi emphasizes that in order to assess the communicative effect of learners' utterances more precisely, they must be placed into an interactional perspective involving the native speaker's reception and responses.

In her paper on 'Some factors in the selection and implementation of communication strategies', Bialystok investigates '*who* uses *which* strategy *when* and with *what* effect?'. The focus is on strategies learners employ when faced with a gap in their vocabulary. The elicitation method is a picture reconstruction task: the subject has to describe a picture to a native speaker so that the latter can reconstruct it on a flannel board. There is virtually no verbal feedback given by the native speaker. An adult and a student group of Anglo-Canadian learners of French, all of whom received instruction in the L2, participated in the experiment. On the basis of her statistical analyses, Białystok concludes that the most efficient strategies are those which are L2 based and take account of specific features of the intended concept, and that the best strategy users combine an adequate formal L2 proficiency with the ability for flexible strategy selection.

Strategy use at the lexical level is also the topic of Blum-Kulka and Levenston's contribution on 'Universals of lexical simplification'. In contradistinction to the other articles in this section, Blum-Kulka and Levenston do not confine the scope of their analysis to IL use but make the point that simplification also operates in various other discourse types, of which foreigner talk, simplified readers and translations are included in their present investigation. The authors hypothesize that (a) lexical simplification operates according to universal principles, and that (b) their universality derives from language users' semantic competence in their L1. In their analysis of IL performance as manifested in sentence completion tests, of professional translations, teachers' FL use and simplified readers, the authors distinguish strategies and processes as two major types of simplification. Both are found to have the same semantic abilities at their basis and can be retraced in all of the four discourse types. Blum-Kulka and Levenston interpret their findings as confirming their hypotheses on lexical simplification.

In their article on 'Achievement strategies in learner/native-speaker interaction', Haastrup and Phillipson concentrate on a specific type of communication strategies. Achievement strategies (see Færch and Kasper, Part One in this volume) are employed by the learner as constructive attempts at coping with 'communication disruptions' occurring in dyadic face-to-face interactions with native speakers. The subjects are eight adolescent Danish school learners of English at intermediate level, who converse with English native-speaker peers about various topics of their everyday life. In their analysis of this data, Haastrup and Phillipson establish learner profiles in terms of the general characteristics of each conversation, the occurring communication disruptions and the types and frequency of the achievement strategies employed by the learner, which enables them to identify certain strategy styles. In evaluating to what extent various types of achievement strategies can successfully cope with communication disruptions, the authors' findings confirm those by

Bialystok: L1-based strategies seem to be least effective, whereas IL-based strategies are most likely to lead to understanding.

A qualitative approach to investigating communication strategies is also adopted in Dechert's contribution 'How a story is done in a second language'. In this case study, the oral narration of a picture story by an advanced German learner of English is analysed by means of the computation paradigm. In order to detect his subject's 'processing grammar', Dechert uses performance features like hesitation phenomena as indicators of the ongoing planning processes. In the learner's performance, fluent speech stretches alternate with non-fluent ones. The fluent stretches, which typically consist of formulaic language use, are interpreted as 'anchoring points' from which other parts of the learner's production are planned. The non-fluent stretches are explained in terms of the 'competing plans hypothesis', according to which simultaneously established or activated plans account for performance disruptions and errors. The author integrates his findings into a model of narration processing.

Dechert adopts a broad concept of communication strategy which is not specifically related to gaps in the learner's IL repertoire. A similarly broad use of the term is suggested by Wagner in his analysis 'Interlanguage communication in instructions'. His subjects are nine adult Danish learners of German attending night-school classes. Two instruction tasks are used: building a house from Lego blocks and making a clay pot. During these instructions, participants are free to provide feedback and make requests for clarification. The audio-taped data thus obtained is analysed according to the theory of action patterns ('Mustertheorie') as established by Rehbein. The pattern of an instruction is formulated, and a communication model of the discourse type 'instruction' set up. On the basis of these theoretical considerations, a qualitative analysis of the performed instructions yields an open list of communication strategies. Of these, the interactional strategy of 'handing over the verbalization to the linguistically more competent participant' is particularly interesting: it illustrates clearly the dependence of strategy selection on the learner's assessment of the communicative situation and especially of his interlocutor, and underlines the necessity for interactional data in order to obtain insight into the strategic devices of IL communication management. The following table summarizes some of the main aspects of the contributions included in Part Two.

Overview on empirical studies

	Váradi	Bialystok	Blum-Kulka/ Levenston	Haastrup/ Phillipson	Dechert	Wagner
Data						
spoken	–	+	–	+	+	+
written	+	–	+	–	–	–
interactional	–	–	–	+	–	+
type of task	picture description + translation	picture reconstruction	sentence completion	conversation	narration of picture story	instruction
Learners						
L1	Hungarian	English	various	Danish	German	Danish
L2	English	French	[Hebrew]	English	English	German
formal instruction	+	+	±	+	+	+
proficiency level	intermediate	intermediate	?	intermediate	advanced	beginner
Method of analysis						
quantitative	+	+	+	–	–	–
qualitative	+	–	+	+	+	+

5 Strategies of target language learner communication: message adjustment*[1]

Tamás Váradi

Introduction

Error analysis (EA), which was first offered as an alternative to contrastive linguistics (cf. Hamp 1968; Strevens 1971), was later assigned the function of verifying the predictions of contrastive analysis (CA) in light of empirical data collected within the more inclusive field of contrastive linguistics (Madarász 1968). In recent years various scholars have assigned a more powerful task to EA, that of investigating the 'transitional competence' (Corder 1967), 'interlanguage' (Selinker 1972), or 'approximative systems' (AS) (Nemser 1971) of foreign language learners. (The term AS is employed in this study.) This appropriate and certainly most challenging responsibility has made it necessary to revise several basic assumptions about both EA and CA and to widen their field of activity (cf. Nemser and Slama-Cazacu 1970).

As is demonstrated by Nemser (1973), current practice is characterized by certain theoretical shortcomings. To recapitulate briefly, these include: (1) a preoccupation with overt as opposed to covert errors, (2) an almost exclusive concern with learning inhibition and consequent neglect of facilitation, (3) an exclusively normative approach to errors precluding analysis in *sui generis* terms, and (4) a neglect of a simple gap — or hiatus — in the learner's knowledge of the target language as a source of errors along with structural disparities between the base language (B) and the target language (T).

In the light of these and other theoretical deficiencies discussed below,[2] the term EA loses its appropriateness — despite its brevity and currency — in reference to the research responsibility of

---

* *Originally published in* IRAL, **18**, 59–71, 1980. *Reprinted by permission of the editor.*

the field. As a merely temporary expedient, therefore, the term *approximative system analysis* (ASA) has been suggested.[3]

If interest in the acquisitional process is not restricted to the inhibitive effect of the clash of the two systems, and if the learning process is also considered, one cannot escape the fact — almost too obvious to mention — that the T does not present itself to the learner at a single stroke, as it were. Consequently, along with an analysis of inhibition and the facilitation of AS, there must be a third domain in ASA: the study of hiatus. Errors of this type result from the fact that neither the learner's B, nor his previously acquired knowledge of T — the main sources and components of his AS — is of any help, and the learner is in (perhaps temporary) ignorance of particular areas of the target language. This domain of hiatus will largely be the concern of this paper.

Besides recognizing the effect of ignorance of T elements as a legitimate concern of ASA, one should notice that CA (and EA, naturally) have in general been exclusively concerned with overt errors. From their inception, the ultimate aim of CA and EA has been to help eliminate errors in the speech of target language learners (TLs), whether by predicting or explaining them. It is one of the contentions of this paper that this exclusive concern with errors is not justified. Evidently, there is much more involved in the acquisition of near-native competence than error-free speech.

This paper proposes a theoretical framework for the examination of these neglected aspects of the speech behaviour of foreign language learners and suggests investigative procedures. Section 1 presents the framework, Section 2 describes the experimental techniques, and Section 3 offers a preliminary analysis of the results of the experiment with their implications both for the theoretical framework proposed, and for further research.

1 Description of the adjustment phenomenon

It has been largely overlooked that utterances of TLs cannot be judged entirely on their own merit, i.e. on their grammatical and semantic well-formedness. Clearly, in assessing success in foreign language acquisition, the question of how close the learner comes to communicating what he wanted to say must not be disregarded. An attempt will now be made to offer a schematic view of the communication process of TLs which takes into account the implications of this criterion. The stages of the process are

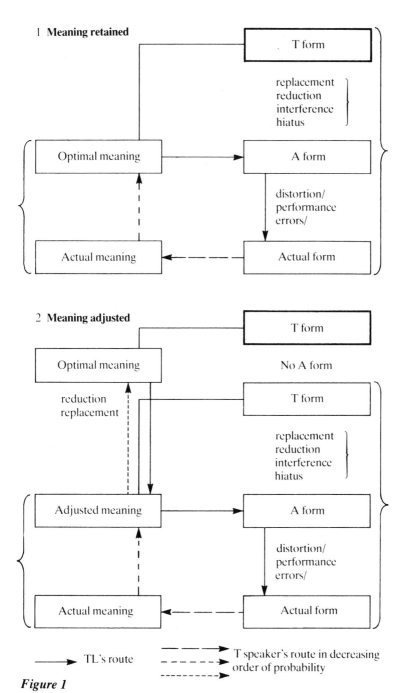

1 Meaning retained

T form

replacement
reduction
interference
hiatus

Optimal meaning → A form

distortion/
performance
errors/

Actual meaning ← Actual form

2 Meaning adjusted

T form

Optimal meaning   No A form

T form

reduction
replacement

replacement
reduction
interference
hiatus

Adjusted meaning → A form

distortion/
performance
errors/

Actual meaning ← Actual form

→ TL's route   - - - → T speaker's route in decreasing
- - - → TL's route   - - - → order of probability
- - - - →

Figure 1

Braces indicate that the distinction between the designated categories may
be lost as learner's proficiency increases.

represented in what is regarded as a logical sequence. However, it is not assumed that learners necessarily pass through all these stages in this order. Throughout the exposition the reader will be referred to Figure 1.

From the point of view of the learner, the starting point in an examination of communication in a particular T is the meaning he wishes to communicate. For our purposes 'meaning' may be regarded as those concepts, ideas, wishes, emotions, etc. that the TL desires to communicate. It is linguistically unencoded, thus neutral as between B and T and distinct from 'content', i.e. linguistically encoded meaning. However, to further simplify our exposition, we will ignore the distinction between meaning and content.[1]

The learner's problem is to find the appropriate T form to convey this meaning. This potential utterance is called here his *optimal message*, defined more precisely as the utterance the TL would use if his abilities in T matched those in B. Meaning and form of the learner's messages must be considered separately. The meaning of his optimal message is called his *optimal meaning* (OMn).

It is useful to postulate two usually different forms of the optimal message depending on whether they are considered from the point of view of the target language learner or from that of a target language speaker. In the latter case, of course, the form would be a proper *T form*; in the former case it would be a form that the learner selects in the belief that (1) it conveys his meaning and (2) that the chosen form (to be referred to as the *A form*) is a correct T form.[5] It should be noted that the posited T form is used here merely as a point of reference of which the learner, producing the kind of deviant message which concerns us here, is obviously unaware.

In terms of the concepts outlined above, the first stage of the TLs communication process may be described as a search to find a suitable A form to convey his intended meaning. The difficulties he faces are considerable. Since his AS is, by definition, impoverished (see Nemser 1971), the range of available formal means to express his meaning is much more limited in T than in B. Moreover, even the available formal alternatives are presumably less readily accessible.

1.1 *Selection of meaning*
Two possibilities may arise at this point:

(1) The learner may find a satisfactory A form through formal reduction or replacement (see 1.2 below) and having found a viable means to express his meaning, he is ready to produce an utterance which we shall call an *actual message*. The latter is defined as the utterance the learner finally produces, as literally interpreted by a target language speaker. The proviso implies that the learner may fail to achieve his aim, producing a form which is deviant or even subject to misinterpretation. The T speaker's literal interpretation of an actual message will be referred to as the *actual meaning*.[6] (2) The TL may find himself unable, by any means available to him at this stage in his acquisition of T, to formulate his optimal meaning in A, in which case it is claimed here that *he often adjusts his meaning so as to bring it within the sphere of his encoding capabilities*. This adjustment of meaning usually involves sacrifice of part of the OMn, loss of precision or it may lead to a complete shift of the optimal meaning. The meaning he finally selects for transmission in such cases will be called the *adjusted meaning*.

The process whereby under the restraining forces of his AS the TL deliberately sacrifices part of the meaning he originally wanted to communicate will be called *reduction*. As an example of this operation consider the following: a subject in the experiment to be described below (Section 3) offered 'The cat is going' as a reduced version of the OMn: 'Even the cat dashes off, who has so far watched the events from the corner.' (For a more refined view of reduction see 3.1.)

In some cases, however, instead of remaining silent — the ultimate degree of reduction — or reducing his OMn, the learner chooses to shift or *replace* it, substituting new subject matter preferably as close to his OMn as his AS allows. This manipulation of optimal meaning will be termed *replacement*. In an actual communication situation this phenomenon can probably be dismissed as of marginal importance. Yet, it has been found to have disturbing relevance for the classroom situation where learners are often called upon to produce 'nice English sentences' as ends in themselves, regardless of what they might really wish to say. The writing of test compositions in particular afford the learner with opportunities to indulge in replacement. In a survey carried out among Hungarian secondary school students of English[7] one learner, for example, did not shrink from stretching both truth and common sense to the point of claiming that when his family took a trip to Pécs for the weekend, his sister took a bus, he himself went by a ship (Pécs is over twenty miles from the Danube), his parents went by plane (there are no internal flights in Hungary), and they all arrived in Pécs at seven o'clock!

Even if the learner finds an adjusted meaning which he regards as within his communicative capabilities, there is obviously no guarantee that the learner will actually succeed in encoding it in a correct T form. In other words, discrepancies of the type posited above between an A and a T form of the OMn (1.1), resulting from hiatus, interference from B or AS, formal distortion as well as formal replacement or reduction (see 1.2 below), may equally occur in the case of adjusted messages.

1.2 *Selection of form*
The following procedures are hypothesized for the selection of an A form by the target language learner.

If the learner does not readily locate an A form appropriate to his OMn (or his adjusted meaning), he may first resort to *formal replacement*, that is, to paraphrase or circumlocution[8]. No attempt is made here to give a formal definition of these operations. For present purposes the difference between the two operations can be regarded as one of relative conciseness: while both paraphrasing and circumlocution leave the meaning unaffected, the latter is understood to involve substantial restructuring of the message, often resulting in awkward verbosity. A paraphrase, on the other hand, is a much more felicitous and concise rendition of the original form than is circumlocution, although it is still not a distributional equivalent of the form it replaces.

These attempts at finding a satisfactory formal expression are most relevant to the stage at which the learner has not yet resorted to any alteration in his meaning, i.e. the stage at which communication of the OMn remains his objective. However, circumlocution and paraphrase may occur as well in any attempt to encode an adjusted meaning. Moreover, it should be emphasized that the learner may very well find himself even unable to encode the first adjusted meaning he selects, so that further modification becomes necessary. Hence what was termed *the* adjusted meaning may very likely turn out to be only the last in a series of modified meanings, a series characterized by progressive loss of elements comprising the OMn.

Presumably, the number of such stages reflects the individual TL's attitude towards his competence in A. Between the two extremes — the TL who employs or even invents an A form without any misgivings, and the TL who would rather say things he did not really mean as long as he says them correctly — a great variety of communicational strategies can be envisaged.

In their search for an A form, learners may be reasonably supposed to resort not only to intentional reduction in meaning but also to deliberate *formal reduction*. This strategy may include (1) elimination of certain formal T elements, or more importantly, (2) reduction in the range of synonymous T forms, i.e. overuse of one form at the expense of the others. Target language learners may come to notice that recourse to (1) and/or (2) does not affect the transmission of meaning, indeed, (2) will not even result in any formal deviation from T. On the other hand, use of these strategies may facilitate communication by increasing fluency.[9] As a result, learners may either fail to make full use of their capabilities or feel little urge to improve them.[10] To differentiate formal reduction from formal impoverishment of any other source (e.g. hiatus, interference), it is essential to presume that the learner has at least a passive awareness of the correct T form, or of the range of possible formal alternatives available in T.

Research in CA and EA has been largely limited to the analysis of the discrepancy between a given A form and its T counterpart. As we know, interference from B and A or hiatus may cause TLs to inadvertently depart from the norms of T. The inadvertence of such deviations is stressed as a characteristic distinguishing them from changes in meaning and anomalies in form which are due to deliberate reduction or replacement of meaning or form.[11]

Sporadic and unsystematic formal differences between what a TL intends to say and what he actually says are considered *performance errors*.[12] When their attention is drawn to such errors of performance (slips of the tongue, memory lapses, etc.), learners are presumably able to correct them. Corder (1967) even implies that learners 'are normally immediately aware of them when they occur'.[13]

1.3 *The role of target language speakers*[14]

So far we have considered communication in T from the point of view of the TL. The listener (presumed to be a target language speaker) in perceiving the actual form communicated by the TL may succeed in attributing a literal meaning to the utterance. There may be cases, however, when the T speaker cannot impose any sensible interpretation on the perceived form. He can, of course, go beyond literal interpretation of the actual message. Frequently, he may even arrive at an approximation of the adjusted meaning. How well he succeeds in inferring the learner's meaning may depend upon the probability of occurrence of the adjusted message in the linguistic and extra-linguistic context.[15]

Furthermore, cases can be envisaged in which target language speakers succeed in inferring the optimal meaning of the learner.[16] In such cases, insofar as the transmission of meaning is concerned, communication may be regarded as successful. Curiously enough then, although learners prove unable to encode all of their meaning, they may still manage to communicate the same meaning to the listener through a felicitously reduced version of it.

This interaction of T learners and speakers — or between two T learners, for that matter — merits further investigation, partly with a view to facilitating the learner's job by helping him to make efficient temporary use of such strategies, and partly because such interaction may have been instrumental in the creation of pidgin languages, where the elimination of many mutually 'redundant' T elements has become conventionalized.

1.4 *Evaluating performance of target language learners*
The exposition given above may appear to be only an enumeration of the difficulties a learner may encounter, always focussing on the worse alternatives. But, as was noted earlier, it does not purport to be an actual case-study of a particular TL. Many of the disparities posited in the model — as, for example, that between T forms and A forms, or between adjusted and actual meanings — may disappear as successful communication is achieved in varying degrees. (This possibility is indicated in Figure 1 by braces.)

We may now return to the question of evaluating performance in T. In light of the phenomena described above, it can be readily seen that the double evaluation criterion of grammatical well-formedness and sensible meaning in context as suggested in Corder (1972) is insufficient. It will fail to disclose the aberrancy of such a sentence (found in the data of the experiment described below in 2.1) as, for example, 'The cat ran away', although this sentence surely will not pass as a T representation of the OMn: 'The cat, frightened by the unusual noise, sets off at a frantic pace miaowing furiously.' Therefore, it is suggested that a third question must be asked as well: does the utterance convey the meaning which the learner actually wanted to communicate?

In our terms, then, perfect communication may be defined as the case when the learner is not forced to adjust his meaning in any way, when his selected A form does not differ from a proper T form conveying the same meaning, and when he manages to produce the utterance without any performance distortion.[17]

It seems reasonable to suppose that learners come to develop efficient individual routines which short-cut the manipulation of their OMns. Indeed, for all TLs actually to perform all of these operations would delay the production of their utterances to an extent unacceptable in normal communication. It is tempting to speculate further that such routines for shortening the laborious route from OMns to actual messages may include the immediate and outright rejection of certain OMns by the TL as clearly beyond his capabilities for formulation in T. Moreover, inefficiencies in the encoding process itself, which is presumably much less automatic when the TL is communicating in T than in B, probably impose limitations on the range of meanings which he can even consider for communication. However, these speculations obviously call for further clarification and experimental validation.

2 Description of a pilot study

In order to investigate the adjustment phenomena discussed above, a small-scale experiment was carried out. This pilot study was not designed to meet rigorous research requirements or to obtain definitive results. Rather it sought to test the utility of one research procedure in examining such learner strategies, and, if possible, to arrive at a preliminary assessment of the validity of the theoretical formulations which have been presented.

2.1 *The design of the experiment*
Two groups of nine and ten adult learners of English at an intermediate level were selected as subjects. One group had been taught English sixteen hours a week for nine months; the other group had studied English at the same rate for only six months; but all of these students had entered the course with some knowledge of the language.

The experiment was conducted in two phases. In the first phase both groups were asked to describe a related series of drawings.[18] Group I was asked to describe the picture story in English within 45 minutes; Group II was asked to describe it in Hungarian within 30 minutes. Subjects were not allowed to use a dictionary in either phase of the experiment. The papers were collected and the two groups were asked to describe the picture again, this time in the other language. They were asked to try to avoid translating from memory, as it were, what they had written in the first version; at the same time they were asked not to invent a radically different story.

In the second phase of the experiment — for technical reasons conducted some days later — the subjects were asked to translate their Hungarian versions into English and vice versa. Before translating the Hungarian version they were given the following special instructions: make your translations as faithful to the original as possible; if, however, you have difficulty in finding a suitable word or phrase, etc., do not leave a blank space in your text but instead attempt to tell the story in your own words, keeping in mind the importance of reproducing as much of the original version as possible. Before translating the English version, the groups were urged to produce a rigorously close rendition of their composition.

2.2 *The rationale behind the experiment*
It was supposed that the native language (Hungarian) version of the picture story would very closely reflect the learner's optimal meaning. Similarly, the English versions would persumably represent the TL's adjusted messages — arrived at by reconstruction through their actual messages whenever the two did not coincide.

Our overriding concern, therefore, was to ensure that differences between the two versions could be attributable to adjustment phenomena resorted to by the learners under the compelling force of their imperfect competence in T. The task of describing a picture series was intended to furnish a fairly rigid guideline stringently controlling improvisation. At the same time, since the drawings did not constitute an overt verbal stimulus, the technique allowed for individual variation.

It had to be considered, however, that some learners may have chosen to modify their story simply because they found it boring to tell the same story twice, or that they may have noticed additional details of which they had been unaware when producing their first versions. The task of translating their Hungarian compositions back into English was assigned to filter out precisely such cases.

Furthermore, it was important to ascertain (1) whether the

learner was fully aware that the preferred form failed to convey his optimal meaning but was chosen because it provided the closest approximation his AS allowed, or (2) whether the learner felt that the chosen form did convey his OMn. For example, suppose the optimal form is *rope* and the actual form is *lace*. If the learner retranslates the actual form into Hungarian as *madzag, spárga, zsinór* ('lace') it would indicate that adjustment has occurred. If, however, he retranslates *lace as kötél* ('rope') it could indicate a lack of awareness between the differences in the Hungarian and English words.

Since there appeared to be no obvious reason for choosing one sequence rather than the other, one group of subjects was asked to write the English version first and the other the Hungarian version. It was thought that starting with Hungarian would give the learner an opportunity to consider every detail of the story so that omission on that score would be precluded. However, it was feared that the learners would probably suspect that 'something more was coming' and therefore might deliberately limit the content of their sentences with an eye to the possibly impending task of translation into English.

It must be realized that this pilot study did not aim at investigating all aspects of message adjustment. Owing to the difficulty of establishing whether omission of some formal element was done deliberately or not, the procedure would not be suitable for investigating formal reduction. For reasons discussed above, the procedure allowed the subjects only limited possibilities for meaning replacement. Unfortunately, less constraint on subject matter (e.g. in the writing of compositions, free or guided) would increase the difficulty of recovering the optimal meaning unless departure from it would happen to involve counter-factual, illogical absurdities (as in the case cited in 1.1) which learners would not be expected to produce in such situations.[19]

2.3 *Evaluation of the experimental methodology*[20]

By and large the experiment yielded the expected results. The two English versions showed essentially the same features. Cf. the following two passages:

Original English version:

Quotation 1:
   After the man left they have started to play with it. The little girl paited two ~~eis, eys, ays, eis, ays~~ ey? and a ~~mefs~~ moustache on it. The

little boy got take eff the shirt ~~off~~. After they have taken it on. It was so than a man. This 'man' hadn't any hair. It was very ugly. The two children ~~gone~~ went to the kitchen window, with a 'man'. The man is was fron of the window. The old lady was looking at the window and has seen the ugly man. She dropped away hersels to this show. The black cat excitedly run away. The two children have started to laugh at the old lady.

Translation of the Hungarian version:

Quotation 2:

The man goes away and they start to play with it. The little girl find the pen colour pens and pencils and she makes ears, eyes and so one etc. on the balloon. While she is making it the little boy take out the white shirt from the rope. The shirt and the balloon together so than the Jack. (Jack in the box) They start to play with it. The old lady was looking out of the window, when the 'man' was there. She cried a loud voice and she dropped away herself away. The cat run away. The child children laughed at a good.

[The corrections (in brackets) in the texts are those made by the learner]

In some cases, however, the translated version turned out to be considerably more elaborate and more grammatical than the one written originally in English. This difference must be ascribed in part to idiosyncratic changes in the optimal meaning which the translation was supposed to filter out. One must further consider the difference in language skills required in making a translation and in writing a composition. However, it seems clear that in certain cases subjects rejected, or failed to consider, relevant meanings which they were fully capable of encoding.

The retranslation of the English compositions into Hungarian often failed to serve the purpose of establishing the distinction between cases of adjustment and unintentional incorrect use of T elements. In many cases, learners apparently disregarded the instruction to write a literal translation of their English paper.

The subjects agreed that it was, or would have been, much easier to begin with Hungarian. Variations in the length of the two versions, and in their state of completion, appear to support this view. English versions produced *after* the Hungarian versions were, with a single exception, longer than those produced first, and in most cases even exceeded the associated Hungarian versions in length. Moreover, with the sole exception of the same English text, English versions produced second were all complete, while six of the ten produced first were unfinished.

3 A preliminary look at the data

The data examined should be regarded as merely illustrative of the kind of result yielded by the research procedure described, and as merely suggestive as regards the validity of the theoretical assumptions.

Consider the following two passages: the first is the presumed optimal message of the subject as translated from his Hungarian version by the investigator, the second is the subject's original English version.

I: presumed optimal message

Quotation 3:
   She threw up the clothes on the clothes-line with a swiftness that be-lied her age, because it occurred to her that 'Long Hot Summer' will soon start on TV. After she proceeded into the house, a young man of 50 with a Chaplin-style moustache turned up at the fence. The children playing at the back of the house noticed him. Emitting Indian war-whoops they ran up to him. The boy, since he is the one who always gets things going, put five forints into the man's palm and received the balloon due for it. The girl, because, of course, she is the one who always starts everything had the idea that they should frighten the old lady.

II: actual message

Quotation 4:
   She hangs the clothes on the washing line. The clothes dry in the soneshine. The woman goes in the house. Cam a man with ballons. The children see he. They run to he. The boy gives many and becam a ballon. They have a god idea. The girl paints on the ballon a head.

A significant reduction between the two versions is clearly evident. The second is a series of simple, isolated statements. The relationship between these statements is chronological and even this simple chronological sequence is not indicated by any overt linguistic means other than the mere concatenation of the sentences. This transitional jerkiness is particularly conspicuous in the two statements: 'The woman goes in the house. Cam a man with ballons.' (Cf. the optimal message where the connection between these two events is rendered linguistically.)

Failure to indicate explicitly another type of non-linguistic relationship — that of causality — is illustrated in the following passages written by another subject.

I: presumed optimal message:

In the street a man is selling balloons. The children are very happy because they get one from him.

II: actual message:

> Children are playing in the garden. The man is giving balloon children.
> The children very happy.

Another characteristic of the English versions by contrast with
the Hungarian versions is extreme stylistic economy and simplicity. Reference to circumstances attending the actions defined in
the picture are apparently sacrificed early in the process of meaning adjustment:

I 'Emitting Indian war-whoops, they ran up to him.'
II 'They ran to he.'

Usually, the sacrifice of humour also proved necessary:

I 'A young man of 50 with a Chaplin-style moustache'
II 'a man'[21]

Of course, certain events, things, people in the story just could
not be left unmentioned. We can briefly examine the strategies
employed by the subjects in attempting to communicate certain
concepts of key importance to the story expressed by the pictures, and formulate a somewhat more complete view of reduction.

Such a view requires a distinction between intensional and extensional reduction. *Intensional reduction* in meaning will be defined as relaxation of precision caused by the selection of forms
whose meaning, though related to it, falls short of the optimal
meaning (*salesman* > *man*). *Extensional reduction*, on the other
hand, is the elimination of part of the meaning and is manifested
in the omission of particular forms (*a young man of 50 with a
Chaplin-style moustache* > *man*). The distinction between intensional and extensional reduction seems to be blurred with regard
to form since, owing to the sequential nature of speech, all intensional reduction necessarily involves extensional reduction as
well.

Within intensional reduction it seems useful to distinguish two
different cases: (1) *generalization*, that is, the use of a superordinate term in reference to its hyponym. (2) *approximation*, which
may be roughly defined as an attempt to reconstruct the optimal
meaning by explicating (often only referring to) part of its semantic component (*balloon* > *air ring*). Sometimes approximation is

achieved through a great deal of poetic licence: it may involve recourse to ingenious associations (as in *ghost* > *Jack in the box*), word coinage (*air ring*), and undoubtedly a number of other interesting techniques (cf. *larder* > *walk-in freezer*). It should be noted that if enough of the semantic components have thus been extensionally rendered for the offered form to convey the optimal meaning inherently, it should no longer be regarded as an approximation but rather as a circumlocution. The various types of message adjustment are summarized in Table 1 (pp. 94 and 95).

The extent to which message adjustment has been carried out in relation to the intended message, as well as the distribution of the various types of adjustment relative to each other, may be taken as a rough quantitative index of the efficiency of communication in a target language. Proportions of particular interest include the ratio of unadjusted vs. adjusted messages, formal vs. semantic adjustment and intensional vs. extensional reduction. Table 2 (p. 96) shows the results of a rough statistical analysis of the above ratios in terms of the number of lexemes affected, based on an examination of fourteen translations[22] from Hungarian to English.

It must be realized that these proportions are influenced by various factors such as (obviously) the stage of development of the learner's AS, his ability to 'activate' his competence — in which his attitude towards his speech behaviour in T seems to play a prominent role — and also his assessment of the relative importance of the parts of his intended message. It has been found, for example, that the extent of extensional reduction of such key concepts as 'balloon', 'clothes-line' and 'ghost' falls far below the average percentage of omission in the entire optimal message.

The interaction of these and possible other factors should be a promising subject for further investigations.

It must be borne in mind that the analysis of the distribution of the various strategies of message adjustment discussed in the present paper can yield only a quantitative assessment of TL communication. Unfortunately, the study of the qualitative aspects of the learner's efficiency in terms of how close the adjusted message is to the optimal message is difficult to approach. The difficulty lies not only in the lack of an adequate theoretical framework in which to discuss relative closeness of meaning, but is further increased by the fact that the problem cannot be accounted for solely with reference to the performance of the *learner* but must be investigated in the light of the interaction of learners and native speakers (cf. 1.3 above).

As a further step towards gaining a comprehensive assessment of the learner's proficiency in communicating in T, the various types and the extent of message adjustment should be related to the well-formedness (acceptability and appropriateness) of the

Table 1
(Figures indicate
number of
occurrences.)

	optimal message		no adjustment	extensional
balloon	25		2	2
clothes-line	17		6	2
ghost	11			1
at a quick pace	1			
in the meantime	1			
having completed this operation	1			

actual messages. Thus it will be possible to ascertain whether error-free speech was achieved at the expense of abandoning (to a greater or lesser extent) the learner's optimal meaning on the one hand, or whether, on the other hand, errors are largely due to the learner's refusal to compromise his optimal meaning despite the inordinate gap that exists between his optimal meaning and his encoding capabilities in T.[23]

message adjustment				
reduction		replacement		
intensional		formal		
generalization	approximation	circumlocution	paraphrase	semantic

ball   3
something   2
some present   1
some toy   1
⎯
7
	gas ball 1
	air ball 5
	air ring 1
	luft ball 3
	lufi, lifi 2
	⎯
	12
		special toys for
		   children . . .
		they are filled
		   by gas 1
		bowls . . . they
		   are light and
		   they are flying
		   1
		⎯
		2		

rope 2	string 3
	strong string 1
	lace 1
	lace for wet
	   clothes 1
	⎯
	6
		line for drying
		   wet clothes 1		

				Ankel Georg 1
	old man 2 an awful 1 ugly man 1 ugly sir 1 awful man 1 awful body 1 Jack in the box 1 man with a big head 1 ⎯ 9			

			quickly 1
			while she was
			   doing it 1
			after she hanged
			   up the dresses 1	

Table 2

Student's number	unadjusted/adjusted message		formal/semantic adjustment		intensional/extensional reduction	
1	55.22	44.78	10.67	89.33	25.41	74.59
2	72.82	27.18	24.53	75.47	0.59	99.41
3	87.82	12.18	15.79	84.21	50.00	50.00
4	83.33	16.67	24.00	76.00	77.78	22.22
5	90.94	9.06	00.00	100.00	72.00	28.00
6	53.45	46.55	18.52	81.48	3.16	96.84
7	54.08	45.92	25.93	74.07	1.64	98.36
8	41.52	58.48	6.51	93.49	3.25	96.75
9	69.59	30.41	49.15	50.85	68.18	31.82
10	20.98	79.02	4.42	95.58	0.15	99.85
11	75.73	24.27	8.00	92.00	3.08	96.92
12	68.93	31.07	20.69	79.31	18.64	81.36
13	76.04	23.96	30.77	69.23	00.00	100.00
14	69.82	30.18	10.10	89.90	12.56	87.44
Total	63.70	36.30	17.79	82.21	24.10	75.90

3.1 *Conclusion*

The results of this preliminary investigation suggest the general validity of the theoretical presuppositions presented, in particular the concept of *message adjustment*. They also suggest the utility of similar experimental techniques for investigations of this type. It is hoped that these results will also help to stimulate further research yielding more definitive information on an apparently significant characteristic of the speech behaviour of foreign language learners.

Notes

1. The author wishes to record his indebtedness to Dr William J. Nemser for the invaluable assistance he so generously gave him at all stages of his work.
2. Some of the points raised in this section have also been noted elsewhere, e.g. by Corder (1973), Hammarberg (1974), and Jain (1974).
3. By William J. Nemser in personal communication.
4. Despite its importance, we will not concern ourselves with questions regarding the extent to which the TL first encodes this meaning in B before attempting to communicate it in T.
5. However, there are also cases of guessing, when this belief amounts to wishful thinking. Moreover, the learner sometimes even deliberately distorts the optimal message. (See the discussion of 'formal reduction' 1.2.)
6. Note that not every discrepancy between a T and an A form brings about a semantic change between the optimal and the actual mean-

ing. Therefore, one can speak of an actual message being formally incorrect even though the optimal meaning is communicated.

7. The survey was carried out by the International Association for the Evaluation of Educational Development (IEA) in 1971.

8. The question may be raised here: What is actually being paraphrased or circumlocuted? Two different cases suggest themselves:

   (1) While the question is not considered in this study, we may suppose that the TL often first encodes his meaning in B. If he then fails to find an A equivalent for the B form, he presumably resorts to a paraphrase or circumlocution of the B form.

   (2) It is also possible to imagine instances where the A form is similarly manipulated: as when, for example, the learner is uncertain about its correctness, or its propriety in the given context, or when it offers serious difficulties in pronunciation, and therefore he avoids its use.

9. One finds numerous examples of such formal reduction in certain types of communication among native speakers as well, e.g. in the jargon of Hungarian waiters, as in *Két sültcsirke rendel* lit. 'two fried chicken order', where both nominal and verbal inflections have been omitted.

   Interestingly enough, T speakers also often resort to formal reduction in an attempt to meet learners of their language on their own terms.

10. Selinker (1972), speaking of an unpublished study by Coulter (1968), states that the latter 'presents convincing data to demonstrate not only language transfer but also a strategy of communication common to many second language learners. This strategy of communication dictates to them, internally as it were, that they know enough of the TL [target language] in order to communicate. And they stop learning.' Cf. further.Richards (1971, p. 19): 'The learner may simplify the syntax of the language in an effort to make the language into an instrument of his own intentions.'

11. From the point of view of the target language speaker the difference is, of course, irrelevant.

12. Cf. Corder (1967, pp. 166–167), where they are called 'mistakes'. In Corder (1973, p. 261) they are redesignated as 'lapses'.

13. Corder's statement that foreign language learners and native speakers are subject to similar external and internal conditions (i.e. memory lapses, tiredness, emotional overcharge, etc.) seems reasonable. However, rejection of such performance errors as being of no relevance to the (transitional) competence of the learner seems questionable. It is argued that under these conditions, speakers will still produce a significantly greater number of 'lapses' in their target language than in their mother tongue. Furthermore, informal observation suggests that under the same conditions, the errors of a TL of a higher proficiency level will differ both quantitatively — as less numerous — and qualitatively — as less serious — from those of a TL at a lower level, i.e. one utilizing a more elemental approximative system. This fact strongly suggests that performance errors do reflect — even if in such an indirect way — the competence of the learner.

14. The term 'target language speaker' is used here in a relative sense to refer to anyone communicating with the TL whose T competence is significantly superior to that of the learner himself.

15. Among the factors reflected in this probability of occurrence — along with redundancies normally present in a speech situation — are the target language speaker's knowledge of B, his experience in communicating with non-native speakers and the closeness of his acquaintanceship with the TL.

16. Of course, reconstruction of an optimal meaning is extremely difficult in case of replacement, when the T speaker may not suspect that what he is being told is not at all what the learner would, in fact, like to say.

17. While attainment of such proficiency is obviously a long-range objective in language acquisition, it can be argued that it is counter-productive for teachers to insist upon reaching it throughout the learning process. Indeed, recourse to approximating the optimal meaning by reduction or, especially, to expressing it through paraphrase or circumlocution might even be encouraged in the short run, particularly at the earliest stages of foreign language acquisition when there is a conspicuous discrepancy between what a learner may want to say and his formal means for saying it.

18. Picture story 6 from L.A. Hill, *Picture Composition Book*, Longman, 1960, pp. 14–15.

19. Notice, however, that since the learner's actual message is analysed *only in relation to his optimal message,* the present framework makes it possible to distinguish semantic anomalies that originate in the encoding process from those inherent in the optimal message. In other words, it is possible to avoid the assumption — imposed by necessity on current practice in evaluating performance of especially adult learners — that the learner's optimal message is always coherent, true, consistent, logical, etc., i.e. semantically well formed.

20. Although it is felt that the procedure provides insight into the nature of the learner's transitional competence, it is probably too elaborate for direct use in language teaching. However, a simplified version of the experiment, with the students translating a suitable text from B into T without using a dictionary and with proper motivation for communicating the meaning, could furnish the teacher with information of considerable practical utility.

21. Pragmatically, failure to convey the humour is doubtless less serious than the failure to explain how the children got the balloon in the first place.

22. Unfortunately, only fourteen subjects were available for the second phase of the experiment.

23. To find the most efficient alternatives for the learner to choose along the continuum indicated by the two extreme points would seem to be of great pedagogical importance.

References

Corder, S. Pit (1967). 'The Significance of Learners' Errors', *IRAL*, **5**, 161–170

Corder, S. Pit (1972). 'Idiosyncratic Dialects and Error Analysis', *IRAL*, **9**, 147–159.

Corder, S. Pit (1973). *Introducing Applied Linguistics*, Harmondsworth: Penguin.

Coulter, Kenneth (1968). 'Linguistic Error Analysis of the Spoken-English of Two Native Russians'. Unpublished M.A. thesis, University of Washington.

Hammarberg, Bjørn (1974). 'The Insufficiency of Error Analysis', *IRAL*, **12**, 185–192.

Hamp, Eric P. (1968). 'What a Contrastive Grammar Is Not, if It Is', in Alatis, James E. (ed.), *Report of the Nineteenth Annual Round Table Meeting on Linguistics and Language Studies*, Washington, D.C.: Georgetown University Press, 137–147.

Jain, Mahavir P. (1968). 'Error Analysis: Source, Cause and Significance', in Richards, Jack C. (ed.) (1974), *Error Analysis*, London: Longman, 189–215.

Madarász, Paul Huba (1968). 'Contrastive Linguistic Analysis and Error Analysis', Unpublished Ph.D. dissertation, Berkeley, University of California.

Nemser, William J. (1971). 'Approximative Systems of Foreign Language Learners', *IRAL*, **9**, 115–123.

Nemser, William J. (1973). 'Neglected Aspects of Data Analysis', Paper presented at the VI Meeting of the Rumanian–English Linguistic Project, Timisoara, May 1973.

Nemser, William J. and Slama-Cazacu, Tatiana (1970). 'A Contribution to Contrastive Linguistics', *Revue roumaine de linguistique*, **15**, 101–128.

Richards, Jack C. (1971). 'Error Analysis and Second Language Strategies', *Language Sciences*, October 1971, 12–22.

Selinker, Larry (1972). 'Interlanguage', *IRAL*, **10**, 209–231.

Strevens, Peter (1971) 'Two Ways of Looking at Error Analysis', *Zielsprache Deutsch*, **2**, 1–6.

6 Some factors in the selection and implementation of communication strategies[1]

Ellen Bialystok

While aptitude and motivational differences among learners provide an important estimate of the success achieved in mastering a foreign language (see for example, Naiman, Fröhlich, Stern and Todesco 1978), they cannot account for the modifications which can be made to the learners' competence through specific language learning activities. As Carroll (1977, p. 2) points out: 'it is through the adoption of appropriate learning sets and strategies that learners can often be successful even when the talents they bring to the task are moderate, or indeed only minimal'.

There is little consensus in the literature concerning either the definition or the identification of language learning strategies. Moreover, there is little agreement as to which behaviours are not strategies but more properly belong to the domain of language learning 'processes'. Selinker (1972), for example, posits five central *processes* for language learning:

1. language transfer
2. transfer-of-training
3. strategies of second-language learning
4. strategies of second-language communication
5. overgeneralization of TL linguistic material

But strategies and processes are not disentangled: he offers 'simplification' of the target language as an example of 'strategies of second-language learning' but it is unclear why such a strategy does not assume equal status with the processes of 'language transfer' or 'overgeneralization of TL material'.

Not only is there confusion in the literature between strategies and processes but also between types of strategies — learning, communication, interlanguage, and the like. *Consciousness* does not discriminate among these varieties of behaviour — most mental processes are relatively automatic, but it is difficult to accept *automatic* as equivalent to *unconscious*. Further, the presence or absence of the introspective function does not convincingly distinguish conscious from unconscious mental activity; introspection provides a notoriously poor description of mental events. Hence even if the distinction between conscious and unconscious is accepted theoretically, its practical measurement is virtually impossible and its usefulness thereby decreased.

A more palatable version of this distinction would be in terms of the learner's degree of control over the exercise of the strategy. The learner, for example, may be more or less systematic in the application of a particular strategy to different material. However, while this distinction may help to classify behaviour, it does not help to classify strategies: the same strategy used for different purposes may be associated with different degrees of control. Simplification of linguistic material, for example, may be used deliberately and systematically for some communication tasks but almost accidentally for others.

The distinction between *learning strategies* and *communication strategies* has been particularly controversial. One expedient for highlighting their difference is to consider the extent to which the strategy is based on a feature of the learner or a feature of the language. The former result in *learning strategies*, the latter in *communication strategies*. Both may be accompanied by varying degrees of learner control.

The learning strategies refer to activities in which the learner may engage for the purpose of improving target language competence and hence, are revealed by the learner. Even here, however, the range of activities cited by investigators under the rubric *learning strategies* indicates little consensus regarding the precise domain of this concept. Included in these lists are activities as diverse as the following: being a good guesser, being willing to appear foolish (Rubin 1975); having a tolerance of the language and empathy with the speakers (Stern 1975); and always attempting to convert passive knowledge into active productive knowledge (Carroll 1977). These three respectively refer to an ability, an attitude, and an activity, yet all have been assigned importance as learning strategies.

Communication strategies are revealed through linguistic analyses of the learner's interlanguage. These strategies indicate the extent to which the learner's utterances in the target language are affected by the native language (Taylor 1975), the procedures used to express concepts for which target language words are unknown (Tarone 1977), the extent to which and the manner in which the lexicon of the target language is simplified (Blum-Kulka and Levenston in this volume).

More theoretically motivated descriptions of the difference between types of strategies, particularly learning and communication strategies, have recently been proposed. Tarone (1980) argues for differences between communication and production strategies as two types of what had previously been called communication strategies. The former category she reserves only for those cases in which communication is disrupted because of an impasse in the minds of both speaker *and* listener. Learning strategies, in her scheme, have no role in communication. Færch and Kasper (this volume) place the strategies in an elaborate analytical conception of language use. In both cases, the motivation for deploying strategies is clearly related to a communicative situation, but the nature of the strategy used and the effect of using that strategy is less well documented.

There is no doubt of the need for theoretical attempts to disentangle strategy from process, and learning strategy from communication strategy, but the *a priori* classification of strategies according to these criteria may obscure a simple pragmatic consideration, namely, given a situation, what will learners do to communicate? Specifically, what strategy will learners select and how successful will it be in achieving the desired goal? The designation of certain strategies as, for example, *communication strategies*, precludes their role as *learning strategies* in the same situation if these two types of strategies are proposed as categorical alternatives. There is some value, therefore, in relaxing these criteria for the sake of observing the behaviour of various strategies in particular situations, irrespective of their theoretical designation, in order to observe their communicative effect. Thus we may say that any strategy may potentially operate as either a learning or a communication strategy: ideally the implementation of a strategy leaves a positive mark on both learning and communication.

Based on these considerations, the definition of communication strategies followed in the present study includes all attempts to manipulate a limited linguistic system in order to promote communication. Should learning result from the exercise, the strategy has also functioned as a learning strategy, but there is no inherent feature of the strategy itself which can determine which of these roles it will serve. This *post hoc* approach has, in fact, been proposed by Kurt Kohn (1979, personal communication) who suggests that strategies can be classified as learning or communication *only* after their effects are known.

Much productive research in the field of communication strategies has led to the identification (Hamayan and Tucker 1979; Dittmar and Rieck 1979; Blum-Kulka and Levenston in this volume) and classification (Tarone 1977) of communication strategies. The result of these studies is that they have provided a rich and systematic framework describing the ways in which learners can operate within their own interlanguage in order to communicate difficult concepts. What has not been explored, however, is the extent to which the implementation of this framework is also systematic, that is, a description of the conditions which serve to make learners more likely to adopt certain of the strategies. In addition, the strategies themselves have not been compared for their relative effectiveness in conveying certain concepts.

In broad terms, the present study attempted to examine the issue of implementation of strategies by dealing with the question: *Who* uses *which* strategy, *when*, and with *what* effect? The purpose was to locate regularities attributable to any of these factors with respect to the approach by various second-language learners to specific communication problems. As a starting point, then, a communication task and a taxonomy of strategies needed to be developed.

Picture reconstruction task

In order to elicit the use of communication strategies when appropriate target language vocabulary is lacking, a task had to be designed which would meet three criteria — first, it had to simulate real communicative exchange in which one of the interlocutors was a monolingual speaker of the target language; second, the task had to provide an incentive for the learner to attempt to convey difficult information; and third, it was necessary to have control over the items for which the communication strategies were to be examined.

In the task developed for these purposes, the subject is asked to describe a picture so that a native speaker of French can accurately reconstruct it. The subject is given a 25 cm × 35 cm colour illustration depicting a young girl standing on a stool to hang a Christmas stocking on the fireplace mantle. Three items, a mantle clock and two lighted candles, sit on the mantle, and three fireplace tools stand beside the fireplace — a bellows, a shovel and a pair of tongs. The eight items which needed to be conveyed and hence were designated as target items were: (1) *tabouret* (stool), (2) *deux chandelles* (two candles), (3) *horloge* (clock), (4) *chaussette/bas* (stocking), (5) *ruban* (ribbon), (6) *soufflet* (bellows), (7) *pelle* (shovel), (8) *pinces* (tongs).

The picture is to be reconstructed on a large flannelboard using cardboard cut-out objects with adhesive backing. To provide a shared context, the fireplace is drawn on the flannelboard. As well as the correct items, the experimenter also has available a series of incorrect items, or distractors, from which to choose when reconstructing the picture. These distractor items were based on one of the following:

1. items with semantic similarities to the target item, e.g. a wristwatch for the mantle clock;
2. items with phonetic similarities in the second language, e.g. *chaussure* (shoe) for *chaussette* (stocking), or cross-lingual similarities, e.g. *cloche* (church bell) for *clock*; and
3. items which fit into the context of the picture, e.g. a poker and a basket with firewood.

Two researchers administered this task to each student individually. The first experimenter explained in English the requirements of the task to the subject. The subject was instructed to look carefully at the picture and then to describe it in detail, in French, so that the second experimenter, introduced as a native speaker of French and a non-English speaker, could reconstruct the same picture on the flannelboard without looking at the subject's illustration. Two French lexical items were provided — *la cheminée* (fireplace) and *le feu* (fire). Before the subject started, the reconstructor repeated the instructions in French. During the course of the task, the reconstructor selected either the appropriate item, an incorrect item, or made no selection at all, according to the instructions given by the subject. Subjects generally continued until all the correct items were placed on the board.

During the task the first experimenter noted any non-verbal or paralinguistic device used by the informant to elaborate the oral description given or possibly even to replace it.

Although there was no time limit imposed, subjects generally completed the task in about 15–30 minutes. Occasionally, some encouragement was given or simple questions, such as 'Qu'est-ce qui est à droite?', were asked, but the reconstructor refrained from speaking as much as possible. Feedback was provided by the items put on the flannelboard.

Each session was tape-recorded and later transcribed.

Taxonomy of communication strategies

The taxonomy of strategies developed for the present study was based on existing typologies, most notably that of Tarone (1977), but was conceptually reorganized. The basis of our taxonomy is a consideration of the source of the information on which the strategy is based. To this end, a trichotomy was proposed: the information incorporated into the strategic effort may be derived from (a) the learner's source language, or any language other than the target language, (b) the target language itself, or (c) non-linguistic or contextual information given with the situation. These distinctions should be critical not only in determining the success of the strategic effort, in that intralingual strategies should be more effective for native speaker listeners than those based on some other language, but also in their potential for discriminating speakers according to their proficiency in the target language. Learners with greater formal ability in the target language or more experience in employing communication strategies may be more likely to use those strategies based on the target language than on some other language. In the taxonomy, these distinctions are referred to as L1-based strategies and L2-based strategies. No systematic examination of non-linguistic strategies was conducted.

1 L1-based strategies

(*a*) *Language switch* refers to the insertion of a word or phrase in a language other than the target language, usually the learner's native language; for example:

> Il y a deux *candles* sur la cheminée.

(*b*) *Foreignizing* native language (L1) items is the creation of non-existent or contextually inappropriate target language (L2) words by applying L2 morphology and/or phonology to L1 lexical items, for example:

(1)   Il y a deux /kãdɛl/ sur la cheminée.

(2)   Il y a une *cloche* sur la cheminée.

In the second example, *cloche* is formed by applying a French pronunciation to the English word 'clock'. The result is a word which exists in French (church bell) but is inappropriate in the context. It is possible that the informant knew that such a word *cloche* exists in French, was uncertain of its meaning and since it seemed to be derived through a phonetic manipulation of the English, tried it out in the context.

(*c*) *Transliteration* reflects the use of L2 lexicon and structure to create a (usually non-existent) literal translation of an L1 item or phrase, such as *place de feu* for English 'fireplace' or *pièce de temps* for 'timepiece'.

Although the strategies foreignizing and transliteration incorporate elements of the target language they originate in native language knowledge.

2 L2-based strategies

(*a*) *Semantic contiguity* is defined as the use of a single lexical item which shares certain semantic features with the target item. In our task, for example, *tabouret* (stool) was frequently replaced by *chaise* (chair) or *table* (table), and *horloge* (clock) by *montre* (watch). In these cases the learner was selecting a word which provided an approximate translation of the unknown concept by referring to a similar but known item.

(*b*) *Description*, the second strategy, has three subclassifications which indicate the information which has been incorporated into the description. These three are general physical properties, specific features, and interactional/functional characteristics.

The general physical properties refer to universal features of objects, that is, colour, size, material and spatial dimension, the latter including the concept of shape, such as *it is round*, as well as location within space, e.g. *it is something that hangs on the wall*. Specific distinguishing features are usually marked by the surface structure *has*, e.g. *it has four legs*. The interactional descriptions indicate the functions of an object and the actions that can be performed with it.

These different types of descriptions are usually used in some combination and often accompany semantic contiguity. Thus *tabouret*, for example, could be described as *une petite chaise de bois, pour reposer les jambes quand on est fatigué, elle n'a pas de dos*. This description combines semantic contiguity (*une chaise*), size (*petite*), material (*de bois*), function (*pour reposer les jambes* ...), and a specific feature (*elle n'a pas de dos*).

Both the above strategies are included in other taxonomies but in a more general form. Their use in the present taxonomy is intended to be more specific than has previously been the case.

(*c*) *Word coinage*, the third strategy, is the creation of a L2 lexical item by selecting a conceptual feature of the target item and incorporating it into the L2 morphological system. For example, 'clock' was referred to as *heurot*, the noun suffix *-ot* was attached to 'heure' meaning 'time'. This strategy usually produces items which do not exist in the target language or, if they do, have a contextually inappropriate meaning. Thus the noun *souffleuse*, which was given to denote 'bellows', can be categorized as an attempt on the learner's part to create a noun from 'to blow'. This coined word, however, does exist in French but means 'prompter in a theatre'. Such coincidences may even impede communication.

The L2-based strategy description frequently contained items or expressions which reflected the use of L1. For example, to convey the meaning of *soufflet* (bellows) one subject said '*avec les mains je apply le /prɛfýr/ de l'objet et adder de l'air*'. The speaker has attempted to give a functional description of the desired object, but the description contains one English insertion and two foreignizations — /prɛfýr/ from English 'pressure' and 'adder' from 'to add'. Both the English insertion and the foreignizations relate only indirectly to the target item. These L1-based strategies which occur within the framework of a L2-based description have been called 'embedded' and are treated separately in the analyses.

Who uses which strategy?

The subjects in the study were a group of sixteen grade 12 students learning French in high school and a group of fourteen adults learning French in a Civil Service French Language Training Programme. For some analyses, the grade 12 students were divided into two groups — ten from the regular French programme and six from an advanced class. The adults were generally more advanced in their studies than were the students. In addition, all subjects completed a cloze test to provide an individual assessment of proficiency, and a more difficult test was required for the adult learners than for the students.

For every student, a figure was calculated to represent the average number of distinct strategies that were recruited for each unknown target item, irrespective of the nature of those strategies in terms of our typology. Embedded L1-based strategies were not included in this count. By considering the grade 12 advanced and regular students separately, there were no differences among the three groups in their quantitative use of the strategies.

A significant difference in selection emerges, however, by considering the L1-based and L2-based strategies separately. The grade 12 advanced students used significantly fewer L1-based strategies that did the other two groups ($F(2.27) = 4.73$, $p < .025$). Nonetheless, since they used the same mean number of strategies per item as the other two groups, they compensated by a relative increase in L2-based strategies. The selection of strategies by all groups is reported in Table 1.

In addition to these group differences, individual differences on these measures can be obtained through the correlation between proficiency as indicated by the cloze test and the individual's strategy use measured in these ways. Again, the average number of strategies used bore no relation to proficiency, but the blend of those strategies, in terms of their base in the L1 or L2, did. For the adults, there was a significant negative relationship between cloze test performance and the proportion of L1-based strategies used ($r_{14} = -.65$, $p < .001$). For the students, the relationship was negative but not significant ($r_{16} = -.22$, n.s.), although when separated into the two groups, it is found that the advanced class, who used these L1-based strategies most profusely, displayed a positive non-significant relationship between cloze scores and proportion of L1-based strategies ($r_6 = .66$, n.s.). That is, in that group only, it was the *best* students who used the L1-based strategies, although the tendency for those students was to avoid L1-based strategies. Hence the anomaly in the advanced 12 group makes the overall relationship found for grade 12 students difficult to interpret.

Aside from these general categories of L1-based and L2-based strategies, a series of chi-square analyses comparing the selection of each strategy by adults and students showed no significant dif-

Table 1 Group differences in strategy selection

	L1-based strategies						L2-based strategies				
	Language switch		Foreignizing		Transliteration		Semantic contiguity	Description			Coinage
								General properties	Features	Interaction	
Subjects	$\bar{x}_1$	$\bar{x}_2$	$\bar{x}_1$	$\bar{x}_2$	$\bar{x}_1$	$\bar{x}_2$	$\bar{x}_1$	$\bar{x}_1$	$\bar{x}_1$	$\bar{x}_1$	$\bar{x}_1$
Adults N = 14	.15	.18	.06	.09	.01	.04	.15	.22	.08	.32	.01
Grade 12 Advanced N = 6	.02	.12	0	.08	0	.01	.14	.37	.1	.37	0
Grade 12 Regular N = 10	.14	.26	.04	.05	.01	.05	.12	.25	.09	.36	0

x_1 = excluding embedded strategies
x_2 = including embedded strategies

ference in selection. Hence target language proficiency biases the learner to select differentially between L1- and L2-based strategies, but does not predict the selection of specific strategies.

Which strategy when?

Although the proficiency of the student determines to some extent whether the strategy will be L1-based or L2-based, it does not determine the exact strategy that will be selected. Therefore does the specific intention to be conveyed have an effect in selecting a particular strategy from those broad categories? To examine this possibility, the distribution of strategies in terms of the eight target items was calculated. These data are reported in Table 2.

There were few differences among the items in the extent to which they elicited any of the L1-based strategies. The item *horloge* produced a higher incidence of foreignizing than did the other items because many learners attempted to use *cloche* for 'clock'.

For the L2-based strategies there was some accommodation in selection by both the adults and the students to the particular target item involved. The descriptions especially took account of the critical features of the intended concept: size was relevant for *tabouret*, spatial dimension for *chaussette*, and material for *ruban*. The functional/interaction strategy was predominantly used for the fireplace instruments, although it was a popular strategy for all the items.

Although the adult and the student selections were largely consistent with each other, the adults varied their strategy more freely in terms of the item and thus displayed more flexibility than did the students. Flexibility is indicated by the frequency footnotes in Table 2.

With what effect?

The problem of communicative effectiveness is difficult to handle quantitatively. In a real linguistic interaction, a myriad of social, contextual, and cognitive factors will impinge on the successful interpretation of every utterance. When one of the interlocutors is additionally a learner rather than a proficient speaker of the language, the problem is confounded accordingly.

In the stylized communication situation created for this study, objective criteria were established by the experimenter for deter-

Table 2 Distribution of strategy type per target item

Target items	L1-based strategies				L2-based strategies						
	L1 insertion	Foreignizing	Transliteration	Semantic contiguity	Description						Coinage
					General properties			Material	Features	Interaction/ function	
					Colour	Size	Spatial dimension				
Horloge	0.04	0.12[1]	0.01	0.16	0.03	0.22[1]	0.14	0	0.04	0.23[2]	0
Tabouret	0.08	0.02	0	0.29[1]	0.02	0.31½	0.01	0.02	0.16	0.09	0
Ruban	0.18	0	0	0.08	0.11	0.10	0.05	0.10	0.02	0.37½[2]	0
Chandelle	0.19	0.04	0	0.20[1]	0.04	0.03	0.03	0.06	0.10	0.28[2]	0.03
Soufflet	0.10	0.02	0	0	0.06	0.02	0.04	0	0.02	0.72½	0.02
Pelle	0.17	0.01	0	0.03	0.01	0.11	0.08	0.03	0.05	0.51½	0
Pinces	0.06	0.02	0	0.07	0.05	0.03	0.10	0.01	0.14	0.52½	0
Chaussette	0.15	0	0	0.12	0.06	0.03	0.21	0.03	0	0.41½	0

[1] most frequently used strategy by adults
[2] most frequently used strategy by students

mining whether or not a particular utterance would be considered successful and result in the correct item being placed on the board. Whether or not those criteria accurately reflected most real communication situations (certainly no criteria could ever represent *all* situations), there was at least the empirical advantage of having a consistent standard by which to judge all responses for all subjects in the study. For this reason, comparisons across subjects (the first question) and across items (the second question) have statistical credibility. The problem of effectiveness, however, is more complex, and cannot be handled without losing some objectivity and certainly not without recruiting native speakers to provide their own perspective to at least supplement our objective decisions.

Table 3   Communicative effectiveness of strategies for each item

| Item | Adults strategies | | |
	Most effective	Score	Least effective
soufflet	description-function	7	coinage
pinces	description-function	7	switch (2×) foreignizing
pelle	description-function (2×)	8	switch (3×) ──────── description-function
chandelle	description-function	6	switch
horloge	foreignizing semantic contiguity size (2×) spatial dimension	6	foreignizing
chaussette	colour spatial dimension function	8	semantic contiguity function switch
ruban	description-function material	7	semantic contiguity colour spatial dimension
tabouret	semantic contiguity size feature	7	semantic contiguity size

MEAN   7.0

A total of seventeen native speakers of French participated in this phase of the study — ten of them dealt with the adult responses and seven of them with the students. Two questions were examined: first, were all the strategies equally effective in conveying meaning; and second, did the different learners (groups and individuals) use them with equal effectiveness?

To answer the first question, all the judges for each group were given eight sets of cards grouped by target item. Each card contained the transcript for a learner's attempt to convey that item. The judges were required to rank order all the cards in the set from most effective to least effective thereby generating an ordered list for each target item. Definitions for 'effective' and criteria for determining effectiveness were deliberately left vague.

Students strategies

Most effective	Score	Least effective
description-function	8	switch
description-function	9	size function (2×)
description-function (2×) semantic contiguity size	5	foreignizing
semantic contiguity switch description-function	7	switch
semantic contiguity size spatial dimension features, function	7	function
colour size (2×) spatial dimension (2×) function (2×)	2	switch
colour material function	6	switch (2×)
semantic contiguity (2×) size (2×) features (2×) function	9	semantic contiguity size

6.6

Nonetheless, the interjudge reliability for the adults' judges was .90 and for the students' was .78, both figures respectably high.

From the rank order lists produced in this manner, the strategies or set of strategies designated the most effective and the least effective were extracted for further examination. These strategies are reported in Table 3.

The specific strategies designated as 'most effective' appear to interact both with the target item being conveyed and the proficiency of the learner indicated by the two categories of adults and students. Moreover, although L1-based strategies never appear in the 'most effective' column, they frequently occur in the 'least effective' listing.

There is a large overlap between the strategy deemed most effective by the judges and the strategy most frequently selected by the subjects for a particular item. This convergence reflects, in part, the sensitivity of the subjects to the most appropriate means of expression for particular items. Furthermore, the greater variation of strategies used by the adults for different items suggests that they are more flexible than the students in their ability to adapt their strategic attempts to meet the needs of specific concepts.

It is sometimes the case that the same strategy appears both as the most effective and least effective for a particular item. The use of semantic contiguity for *tabouret* is an example of this. Hence while the general category descriptions of the strategies provide an important means of differentiating among them, the selection of a specific strategy still requires the clear statement of appropriate information for that strategy to be effective.

To determine the relationship between strategy effectiveness and group, a means of comparing the rankings of effectiveness for the adults and students was required. Accordingly, the native-speaker judges were asked to assign a score out of 10 to the strategy or set of strategies ranked best for each item. While the adult scores are quite stable across items, the student scores vary considerably. Thus, for the students, strategies which may have been ranked first for different items were not necessarily equally effective in conveying the meaning of the item. Nonetheless, the difference between these scores when collapsed across items and compared for the two groups is not significant: the best attempts by both groups were relatively equivalent in their effectiveness.

A more detailed view of the role of proficiency was obtained by computing a mean rank per subject based on the rank order assigned by the judges to each of their target item responses. The lowest ranks, that is, first, second, etc., indicate the highest placing in the overall rank order. A correlation analysis between these rank order mean scores and performance on the cloze test showed significant negative correlations for both the adults ($r = -.50$, $p < .05$) and the students ($r = -.40$, $p < .05$). That is, the better the learner performed on the cloze test, the better ranked were his/her strategic attempts by the native speaker judges. Thus formal proficiency in the target language as demonstrated by the learner's ability to operate in a rather formal written test intervenes between the appropriate selection of a communication strategy and the effective implementation of that strategy to convey meaning. The role of proficiency is seen as an intervening variable rather than a determining variable because there were relatively few differences between adults and students and between the individuals in each of those groups in terms of the selection of strategy types. The differences emerged primarily in the realization of those strategies as effective forms of communication. Nonetheless, the differences in selection which do emerge may be attributable to proficiency through a threshold paradigm: a minimal level of proficiency is initially required for appropriate selection of strategies. Clearly, without some minimal formal competence, learners do not even have at their disposal an adequate range of possible strategies from which to select.

The role of strategies in communication

By examining the attempts of language learners to convey meaning in highly controlled communicative situations, it is possible to gain insight into the role of communication strategies. This role will be discussed in terms of the initial questions, namely, *who* uses them, which strategies for *which* concepts, and with *what* effect.

In spite of the difference among the learners in this study in terms of their level of formal proficiency in the language and their own experience in using this and other languages, all their strategic attempts to function in this communication task could be adequately described by a rather simple taxonomy of strategies. The basis of the taxonomy was its distinction between L1-based and L2-based strategies, and this dichotomy was reflected in the selection of strategies by learners of different proficiency levels, specifically, the L2-based strategies being preferred by more advanced learners.

In addition, the more advanced learners were more sensitive to other constraints in the selection of specific strategies, namely, in this case, the particular target concept to be conveyed. Although all learners showed some modification in their strategy selection as a function of the target concept, the adult learners did so with greater flexibility.

The result of these selection and proficiency variables was that the same strategies were more effective when used by learners who had greater formal control over the target language. Thus, in the final analysis, the variables, who, which, and what, interact to determine the success of implementing particular communication strategies.

What, then, distinguishes the best strategies and the best strategy users? The best strategies, it seems, are those which are based in the target language and take account of the specific features of the intended concept. The best strategy users, on the other hand, are those who have adequate formal proficiency in the target language and are able to modify their strategy selection to account for the nature of the specific concept to be conveyed.

An additional distinguishing characteristic of the best strategy users is revealed by examining the background of the adult subjects in this study. Of the fourteen adults tested, five of them spoke at least three languages and had travelled extensively. It was precisely these five learners who contributed *all* the responses ranked as best by the native-speaker judges. Thus there is an experiential factor which may be critical in assuring effective use of strategies.

The informal evidence of the role of experience in using language provided by the adult group in this study may be used to support the notion of an ability called 'strategic competence' (Canale and Swain 1980) which is distinct from formal mastery of a language. This would involve the ability to use language effectively in spite of formal limitations and would presumably be developed through experience in using language in those ways. But in spite of this experience, the effective use of communication strategies is unambiguously related to formal proficiency, and in spite of efforts to disentangle formal from communicative uses of language, the evidence from this study places formal mastery firmly within the construct of communicative competence.

Although the results of this study do not bear much on questions concerning the relationship among strategy types, that is learning versus communication strategies, they do contribute to an understanding of the relationship between strategy use and communicative competence. If we disregard the possible differences among strategies in terms of their potential to increase learning or their motivation for being selected with respect to learning considerations, then we can examine more directly their role in communication. For example, the L2-based strategies may be less effective as a learning device than a L1-based strategy such as 'appeal for assistance' (not included in our analysis because all such appeals were denied), but they are more effective than such strategies in conveying meaning. Thus the analysis of these strategies in terms of their role in communication makes no assumptions about their potential to act as learning strategies.

Clearly, the effective use of appropriate strategies is an important aspect of communicating in an imperfectly learned language. The evidence indicates, however, that this ability is not entirely separate from the level of formal mastery achieved in that language, and the informal communicative use of language is constrained in this way by formal control over the system.

Notes

1. This study was funded by a grant from the Department of the Secretary of State, Canada. I am indebted to Maria Fröhlich and Joan Howard who were the two experimenters and did much of the work in constructing the task materials and the taxonomy of strategies used in the analysis.

References

Canale, Michael and Swain, Merrill (1980). 'Theoretical Bases of Communicative Approaches to Second Language Teaching and Testing', *Applied Linguistics*, **1**, 1–47.

Carroll, John B. (1977. 'Characteristics of Successful Second Language Learners', in Burt, Marina, Dulay, Heidi and Finocchiaro, Mary (ed.), *Viewpoints on English as a Second Language*, New York: Regents, 1–7.

Dittmar, Norbert and Rieck, Bert-Olaf (1979). 'An Exploratory Study of the Verbal Organization of L2 Tense Marking in an Elicited Translation Task by Spanish Immigrants in Germany', Berlin: Freie Universität (manuscript).

Hamayan, Else V. and Tucker, G. Richard (1979). 'Strategies of Communication Used by Native and Non-Native Speakers of French', *Working Papers on Bilingualism*, **17**, 83–96.

Naiman, Neil, Fröhlich, Maria, Stern, H. H. and Todesco, Angela (1978). *The Good Language Learner*, Toronto: Ontario Institute for Studies in Education.

Rubin, Joan (1975). 'What the "Good Language Learner" Can Teach Us', *TESOL Quarterly*, **9**, 41–51.

Selinker, Larry (1972). 'Interlanguage', *IRAL*, **10**, 209–231.

Stern, H. H. (1975). 'What Can We Learn from the Good Language Learner?' *Canadian Modern Language Review*, **31**, 304–318.

Tarone, Elaine (1977). 'Conscious Communication Strategies in Interlanguage: a Progress Report', in Brown, H. Douglas, Yorio, Carlos A. and Crymes, Ruth H. (eds.), *On TESOL '77: Teaching and Learning English as a Second Language*, Washington D.C.: TESOL, 194–203.

Tarone, Elaine (1980). 'Communication Strategies, Foreigner Talk and Repair in Interlanguage', *Language Learning*, **30**, 417–431.

Taylor, Barry P. (1975). 'The Use of Overgeneralization and Transfer Learning Strategies by Elementary and Intermediate Students of ESL', *Language Learning*, **25**, 73–107.

7 Universals of lexical simplification*

Shoshana Blum-Kulka and Eddie A. Levenston

Introduction

The simplest way of looking at lexical simplification is numerical: it is the process and/or result of making do with *less* words. And both the process and the result can be observed and studied in a number of different linguistic contexts:

1. in the speech and writing of second-language learners — at all stages their total vocabulary is less than the vocabulary available to native speakers;
2. in the speech (and, later, writing) of children acquiring their first language, before they possess the full range of vocabulary available to adult speakers;
3. in the speech of adult native speakers when addressing children, foreigners (Ferguson 1971), learners of their language (Henzl 1973) or other native speakers they feel it necessary to 'talk down' to because they possess a poorer vocabulary;
4. in simplified reading texts prepared by native speakers for the use of second-language learners (Blum 1972); the reduced range of vocabulary in which such texts are produced is often clearly specified by the publisher;
5. in pidgins (Samarin 1971, p. 119: 'the total lexical inventories of pidgins are known to be impoverished by comparison with those of natural languages');
6   in translation, when the lack of precise equivalents in the target language may lead to various devices similar to the kinds of lexical simplification found in the above situations (Dagut 1971).

Since lexical simplification is a feature of so many diverse linguistic activities, it seems reasonable to assume that it operates

* Originally published in Language Learning, **28**, 399–415, 1978. *Revised for inclusion in this volume.*

according to universal principles. And these universals of lexical simplification derive from certain aspects of *semantic competence*, particularly:

a)   the awareness of hyponymy, antonymy, converseness and possibly other systemic relationships between lexical items, by means of which we can explain why in specific contexts one lexical item can substitute for another (see also Richards 1976 and Slobin 1974)

b)   the ability to avoid the use of specific lexical items by means of circumlocution and paraphrase

c)   the ability to recognize degrees of paraphrastic equivalence.

These aspects of semantic competence are at the basis of the communicative strategies that we use, when the need arises, to express complex meanings by indirect means with minimal vocabulary. For the language learner it is the difficulty, or impossibility, of both internalizing the exact nature of the interrelationships mentioned above and acquiring the native speaker's awareness of degrees of polysemy and figurative extension and his sensitivity to formal, collocational and idiomatic restrictions on lexical choice that lead to the continual use of simplification as a communicative strategy.

The learner's need to simplify is thus explained by the complexity of the task of acquiring command of all aspects of the native speaker's semantic competence; his ability to do so derives from his own semantic competence in his first language. As a native speaker he will at times experience a need for paraphrase and circumlocution, for hyponymy and synonymy, in some of the situations listed in the introductory paragraph above (especially (3)). As a language learner he is compelled to reorganize semantic fields in the early stages, when he lacks vocabulary, and to do so according to the principles that govern his semantic competence as a native speaker.

The aim of the present paper is to examine the validity of this suggestion — that lexical simplification operates according to universal principles, and that these derive from the individual's semantic competence in his mother tongue — by means of a comparative study of lexical simplification in four of the contexts listed above: (1) the speech and writing of second-language learners; (3) the speech of teachers or other native speakers when addressing non-native speakers; (4) simplified reading texts prepared for second-language learners; and (6) translation. Evidence will be cited both from our own research with learners of Hebrew, and from a variety of publications in different fields. Before proceeding to survey the evidence, however, it is necessary to clarify further the meaning of 'simplification'. In particular, we must examine the significance of the basic ambiguity of the term as demonstrated in the form of the definition: 'the process and/or result'.

Lexical simplification as end-product

An over-simple view of lexical simplification would concentrate on the *result* of making do with less words, and view the task of research as lexicographic. For every word in the target language one would just have to list all the alternatives, single words or paraphrases, found in the learner's utterances. The end-product would be an 'interlanguage dictionary'. It would lack information, however, about the *processes*, or *strategies*, of derivation whereby the alternatives were formed, or the structural relations between items in the list.

A subtler view of lexical simplification, though still concerned with an end-product, would attempt semantic 'mapping', acknowledging that vocabulary cannot be adequately studied merely in terms of one-for-one equivalences. Instead of narrowing the focus of the study to lexical items, it would compare broader areas of lexical territory or — to change the metaphor and the number of dimensions — greater volumes of semantic space. For any given area — or volume — of vocabulary, it would be necessary to chart the way it was divided up (a) in the learner's native language, (b) in the learner's interlanguage and (c) in the target language (cf. Selinker, Swain and Dumas 1975: 'the psychologically relevant data on second-language learning are utterances in TL [target language] by native speakers, and in NL [native language] and IL [interlanguage] by second-language learners').

The main focus of attention would be the comparison of (b) and (c); comparison with the mother tongue should be explanatory, not predictive. Such a study would be qualitative as well as quantitative. It would not merely demonstrate how lexical simplification meant managing with less words; it would also show how the range of uses of each word was affected by its place in the total structure of vocabulary.

And not only the structural relations between words would have to be studied. Words also differ in connotations, in collocability, in degree of formality, in other register restrictions, and in their ability to combine into idioms. And all these aspects of word usage are reflected in the learner's language. A word may be given not only a greater range of referential meaning; it may be used with inappropriate connotations, deviant collocations, too (in)formally, in the wrong register, unidiomatically.

Clearly an adequate description of lexical simplification must take account of all these dimensions of meaning. The mapping should take place in multi-dimensional space. And to the extent that information along any dimension is lacking for the first and second language — dictionaries are notoriously inadequate, for example, in their treatment of collocability — it will be necessary to include in the research programme a study of native speakers' usage, observed or elicited in both languages.

Even the data required for referential distinctions in the mapping is hard to come by. Much of it may be lying there in the dictionaries and thesauruses, but in completely unorganized fashion. And the lack of organization is a major obstacle to research.

Lexical simplification as process

Any study of lexical simplification, however understood, must of course necessarily take as raw data examples of learners' performance, published translations, simplified texts, teachers' utterances as heard in the classroom. We have no direct access to the mind of the learner or native speaker when he produces lexically simplified forms. Nevertheless, our main concern is with the processes of simplification that underlie such usages and can be inferred from them.

As the major aim of research we hence propose the investigation of the general processes of lexical simplification. One of the first steps in such an investigation is to clarify conceptually the nature of the phenomena we are studying and to set up a terminological framework for describing it. In the ensuing discussion we shall try to clarify what we mean by three of the terms that have been used in reference to interlanguage phenomena: 'avoidance', 'process', and 'strategy'.

Avoidance

Common to all cases of lexical simplification is the attempt to express meaning while 'avoiding' certain lexical items. But the term *avoidance* obviously applies with different degrees of appropriateness to the different contexts discussed. It is most appropriate for the teacher, who knows what he is avoiding, and least appropriate for the translator, where 'avoidance' is created by lexical voids in the target language. As for learners, some are in the position of teachers and some in the position of translators, depending on the extent of their knowledge of the target language vocabulary.

Two basic types of avoidance can therefore be distinguished:
1. apparent avoidance, caused by lack of vocabulary, whether in language learning or in translation;
2. true avoidance, practised by advanced language learners, teachers and editors of simplified texts.

The learner who does not have the vocabulary to express his meaning and the translator faced with a lexical void in the target language use various strategies to fill the semantic gap. One practised by learners is complete abandonment of the subject; 'topic avoidance' (Tarone, Frauenfelder and Selinker 1976) or 'message abandonment' (Váradi in this volume) refer to this behaviour. Change of topic or complete silence are clearly strategies of communication, or non-communication, common to contexts of interaction whether between language learners or between native speakers. When used by language learners, these strategies are probably often motivated by the need to avoid unknown lexical items.

True avoidance presupposes choice. Words which the teacher or the editor of simplified texts assume will be unknown to the student are omitted, replaced or paraphrased. For language learners at the advanced stage, avoidance occurs when the learner has a passive knowledge of lexical alternatives, but fails to exploit the distinctions in his own speech and writing.

There are several possible motivations for avoidance at this stage:
1. *Phonological avoidance.* Given the choice of two words or phrases sufficiently synonymous to be equally acceptable in many contexts, the learner will prefer the one he finds easier to pronounce. The Hebrew word *zi'za'* shock; appal) will be replaced by *hifḥid* (frighten); *hikhḥiš* (deny) will be replaced by *amar šelo* . . . (say that . . . not . . .).
2. *Graphological avoidance.* The learner when writing will prefer the word he has no difficulty in spelling: *get* rather than *receive*.

3. *Morphological avoidance*. The learner will prefer regular to irregular verbs whose forms he is not sure of. Of the two verbs which can translate 'express' — *bite*' and *hibi'a* — the second is easier to conjugate in the past, perhaps because of its similarity to the common verb *higi'a*, and thus preferred. (Similarly, one of us suspects that in his French, he prefers *penser* in the past, though quite happy to use *croire* in the present.)
4. *Syntactic avoidance*. The learner will prefer the word that requires a regular, known syntactic structure rather than one whose syntactic environment is unclear or difficult. Learners of English might avoid *provide* (*someone with something*) and prefer *give* (*something to someone*) (Levenston 1980).
5. *Void avoidance*. Learners tend to avoid words for which no precise equivalents occur in their mother tongues, especially when the semantic components of such words require them to make distinctions they are not used to making at the level of single words. An example is the verb *šibec* (to insert in a suitable place). This is replaced by *hixnis* (insert) or *sim* (put) or by paraphrase.

More detail on these kinds of avoidance is given in Levenston and Blum (1977), and in Kleinmann's (1977) study, which focusses on avoidance of grammatical 'categories' of the kind we would call *void avoidance*.

The term *avoidance*, therefore, apparent or true, can be used to answer two questions: *what* occurs in the different linguistic contexts and *why*. Comparison of interlanguage usage, for instance, with expected native-speaker usage in the same context — or of target language with source language in the case of translation — will show *what* is avoided. Explanations of the kind listed, from morphological to void avoidance whether postulated by the investigator or given by the learner, will suggest *why* avoidance takes place. But to answer the question *how* meaning is conveyed in spite of avoidance, we need to study the various strategies of communication used. The sub-classification of strategies derives from the different kinds of answer to the question 'how'.

Strategies and processes

The terms *strategy* and *process* have often been used in second-language acquisition literature in a way that might imply that they are interchangeable (Tarone, Frauenfelder and Selinker 1976; Levenston and Blum 1977. For further discussion of this point, see the contribution by Færch and Kasper in Part One of this volume). In the original version of this paper we defined *strategy* as 'the way the learner arrives at a certain usage at a specific point in time' and *process* as 'the systematic series of steps by which the learner arrives at the same usage over time' (p. 402).

The temporal criterion suggested has important methodological consequences: a single usage can indicate a certain strategy. Thus if a learner's specific usage is traceable to his mother tongue we say that the strategy used has been transfer. But to speak about transfer as a process we have to know to what extent and in which ways the learner's mother tongue has influenced his interlanguage. If we find the same specific usage repeated by the learner in the same contexts over time, we might say that a certain aspect of the learner's interlanguage has been formulated as a result of a process of transfer. In this view, the distinction between processes and strategies is not necessarily one of ± consciousness (see the discussion of this in the contribution by Færch and Kasper in Part One of this volume). Rather, the difference is one of levels of analysis: processes are the underlying cognitive principles we are searching for in analysing strategies.

Processes are inferable from strategies, just as strategies are inferable from spoken and written interlanguage performance. A single form used as a strategy of communication can either disappear from the learner's speech or become fossilized and part of a stable interlanguage. The distinction becomes clear when we compare lexical simplification by language learners with its occurrence in other linguistic contexts. The use of a hyperonym (e.g. *flower* in place of *rose*) by a teacher in the classroom is a *strategy* of communication, used to overcome the learner's lack of vocabulary. The same technique used by the learner at a stage when the needed word is not at his disposal also serves as a *strategy* of communication. However, when this technique appears at a later stage, when the learner knows both words, it indicates that a *process* of overgeneralization has taken place, possibly followed by one of *fossilization*. With teachers, techniques of simplification are always strategies, even when used to excess; with learners, the same strategies may indicate processes of interlanguage formation.

Following this distinction, we propose to divide all strategies of lexical simplification into groups: A, strategies that can initiate processes; B, strategies that are situation bound. Usages produced by strategies of group A are potentially fossilizable. In the realization of strategies from group A the speaker utilizes the linguistic resources at his disposal. Hence, the limits on the number of strategies that might be included in group A are set by the nature of semantic systems. In the realization of strategies from group B, any feature of the communicative event can come into play, including the non-linguistic ones. Hence, there is no real limit to the number of strategies that might be included in group B — the only limit being the resourcefulness of speakers and the ingenuity of researchers in describing their actions.

Communication strategies of lexical simplification

Group A: Potentially process initiating	Group B: Situation bound

1 Overgeneralization realized by:
  a) the use of superordinate terms
  b) approximation
  c) the use of synonymy
  d) word coinage
  e) the use of converse terms
2 Transfer
	1 Circumlocution and
	   paraphrase
	2 Language switch
	3 Appeal to authority
	4 Change of topic
	5 Semantic avoidance

As the subdivision in group A indicates, there are two main processes that create lexical simplification: overgeneralization and transfer. Both are cognitive processes that are not specific to language learning.

The strategies listed as a–e are specific to lexical simplification; we consider these as indicating overgeneralization because they all entail disregard for restrictions on meaning and usage.

All but one of the strategies in the above list have been reported in the literature of second-language acquisition, though the grouping and to some extent the labelling differ from previous taxonomies (see Ickenroth 1975; Tarone, Frauenfelder and Selinker 1976, and the contributions by Tarone, Cohen and Dumas, and by Váradi in this volume. The only strategy not reported in one or other of these papers is the use of converse terms, for which see Levenston and Blum 1977).

We have chosen five of these strategies for comparative study: the use of superordinate terms, approximation, the use of synonyms, transfer, and circumlocution and paraphrase. In each case, we shall try to supply data not only from learners' interlanguage performance data — using both our own research and other published studies of learners' usage — but also from translation, teachers' usage and simplified reading texts.

Superordinate terms

Semantic competence for a native speaker includes the ability to recognize when relations of hyponymy exist between items in the lexical system, and when a number of items have a common 'superordinate' which can replace them.

Hence the translator, confronted with semantic voids, can exploit such relations between items in the lexical system of the target language, and try to convey the source language meaning by using the superordinate term in the target language. By adding a 'qualifier' — the technical term used by Wonderly (1968) for explanatory additions to a word in translation — the full meaning can sometimes be conveyed. 'Unqualified', the use of the superordinate term alone always results in the depletion of meaning. Dagut (1971, p. 85) cites the sentence 'It now became apparent that the man in civilian dress...' where the original Hebrew word *almoni*, here translated *man*, has no equivalent in English. Its semantic components are 'human' and 'name unknown'. By using the superordinate term *man* the translation obviously depletes the explicit meaning, though in the total context the missing component can perhaps be inferred.

Effective use of superordinate terms is probably at its highest in the simplification of reading texts. From the versions of *Oliver Twist* quoted in Davies and Widdowson (1974) one may cite the replacement of *gazed* by *looked*, of *rushed* by *ran*. And an example of superordinate term plus qualifier is the replacement of *ladle* by *serving-spoon*.

Henzl's (1973) study of lexical simplification by native speakers of Czech when addressing learners of Czech, gives two examples of the use of superordinate terms: the verbs *plakat* (to weep) and *videt* (to see), both replaced, when addressing a Czech audience, by synonyms of various extended meanings.

In an earlier article (Levenston and Blum 1977), we claimed that advanced learners, who have at their disposal some or all of the co-hyponyms at the disposal of the native speaker, tend to use a word set up as superordinate in their interlanguage in contexts where the majority of the native speakers use a co-hyponym: *sameaḥ* (happy) for *sameaḥ/meušar/meruce* (happy/content/ satisfied). Looking at the data[1] again, and this time at the answers of those learners who did not know the required word in each sentence, we found that the use of appropriate or non-appropriate superordinates was a major strategy for overcoming lack of vocabulary. This applies to all the test sentences, not only those set up to test the hyponymy hypothesis:

(1)   hu haya muxan leqabel et ha 'ahrayut se samti 'alav.
       He was ready to accept the responsibility that had been put upon him.

(2)   ani mictaer šehu lo qibel et drišat hašalom mimxa, pašut šaxaḥti *lehagid*.
       I'm sorry he didn't receive your kind regards, I simply forgot to say.

The results vary in acceptability. *samti* (put) in sentence 1, though superordinate to *hitalti* ('imposed' — the required word) is in no way acceptable, and was not used by any of the Israelis. In sentence 2, however, though the required word — *limsor* (convey) — was supplied by 77.5 per cent of the Israelis, among the 22.5 per cent who did not use it, one used *lehagid* (say) and another *l'omar* (say), both superordinate to *limsor* in this context. This provides further evidence for the claim that strategies of simplification are basically universal in nature and are often used by native speakers, even when addressing other natives, and in contexts where the need for simplification is by no means obvious.

An example of the danger to communication created by learners who overgeneralize one of a group of synonyms is given by Abberton (1968). Serbo-Croat *pametan* is used where English uses either *sensible* or *clever*. Serbo-Croat speakers tend to use *clever*, even when the context demands *sensible*. They will thus often give a connotation of 'cunning' quite unwittingly when they use *clever* in the wrong context.

Approximation

The term is used here as in translation theory: 'the selection of words whose area bounds upon the blank space and which by insertion into the context of the word they are made to translate will suggest to the reader the association of that word' (Rabin 1958). In both the following examples the need for approximation derives from the use in the source of the Hebrew word *hupa* (bridal canopy) in contexts where the reference is clearly to the act of marriage:

(3)   nixnasnu laḥupa — we were married [Lit. we came under the bridal canopy.]

Here the translation has nothing of the specifically Jewish religio-cultural meaning, but the effect of this depletion is barely felt by the reader in the target language.

(4)   lo zaxu lehagi'a laḥupa — (...how many girls) never reached the canopy...

Here the translation is probably quite obscure to most readers, especially those with no knowledge of Jewish marriage customs.

We find a similar range of effect when the technique is used in text-simplification — the examples again are from Davies and Widdowson (1974):

(5)   He gazed...on the small rebel → He looked...at the small boy.
        (The associations of 'rebel' are lost completely.)
(6)   The master aimed a blow with the ladle → hit Oliver with his spoon.
        (The original does not actually specify whether he hit him or not.)

One danger of using approximation in the classroom is that it may lead to misunderstanding. When a teacher, observed by Sela and Arad (1977), asks:

(7)   at roça latet et haḥeder?
        Would you like to give your room?

meaning 'rent it', the student may in fact both misunderstand her and learn a deviant collocation.

Examples of approximation are hard to find in published accounts of interlanguage performance data, which tend to concentrate on unacceptable usage; approximation may well succeed as a strategy of communication and also be acceptable. But one clear example is cited by Lo Coco (1975): the use of *años simpaticos* (friendly years) instead of *años agradables* (pleasant years).

In our own data the effects of approximation on communication range from comprehensible though deviant collocations to complete obscurity:

(8)   ani ḥošev šenatnu lo maspiq hizdamnuyot. ḥacara hi šehu lo yodea ex lefateaḥ otan.
        I think he's been given enough opportunities. The trouble is that he doesn't know how to develop them.

lefateaḥ hizdamnuyot (develop opportunities) is as unusual collocationally in Hebrew as in English, but the word does have a semantic component [+ use] in common with the appropriate item (*lenacel*, 'exploit'), so the meaning the learner is trying to convey by approximation is clear and appropriate.

But this technique is not always so successful:

(9)   hem natnu lo avoda tova. hu ḥasax/asaf harbe kesef.
        They gave him a good job. He saved/gathered a lot of
        money.

The word needed in the context and supplied by 68 per cent of the Israelis was *hirviaḥ* (earned). In using *ḥasax* (saved) and *asaf* (gathered), the learners avoid the proper term — which they do not know — by presupposing it, since in this context 'saving' money implies receiving a good salary. But whereas the sentence with *ḥasax* is acceptable in Hebrew — *ḥasax* (save) collocates with *kesef* (money) — the sentence with *asaf* (gathered) is not, neither in English nor in Hebrew.

Rabin's definition of approximation in translation emphasizes the importance of the *context* in suggesting to the reader (or hearer) the desired meaning. Rewritten to cover its use in all the linguistic contexts under discussion, the definition might read: 'using a word in the target language (or simplified text) which does not convey the concept required in the context — a concept for which a single term may exist that is commonly used by native speakers — but which shows enough semantic elements with the derived concept to more or less convey its meaning in the given context'.

Synonymy

The use of 'common-level' or 'familiar' synonyms is considered by Wonderly (1968) the easiest solution to the lexical problems that arise in preparing Bible translations for popular use. In the common language versions he quotes, *remained* is replaced by *stayed*, *chanced* by *happened*, and *fetters* by *chains*. Simplified reading texts for language learners use the same technique when they replace register-marked but infrequent words by their unmarked, more frequent synonym; in Hebrew the literary form *natal* is regularly replaced by the common *laqaḥ* — they both mean 'take', and differ only in stylistic level.

In both these linguistic contexts the use of synonyms is aimed at improving readability by increasing the number of familiar words. To ensure successful preservation of the original meaning of the text, replacements must be limited to words that differ in frequency and/or register but not in semantic content. Even then, especially when the original text has literary value, the simplified version is bound to change the connotative meaning. In one of the versions of *Oliver Twist*, 'nobody controverted the prophetic gentleman's opinion' becomes 'nobody disagreed with his opinion'. Whereas one may disagree in silence, controversion implies an explicit statement of an opposite opinion; despite the synonymy, the difference is significant.

Henzl (1973) also found that Czechs preferred 'common-level' synonyms when addressing non-native speakers; she quotes the substitution of the standard *straznik* (policeman) for the register-restricted *policast* (cop; fuzz). The common-level words are often taught first because of their high frequency. Hence it is not surprising that their relative frequency in the learner's interlanguage exceeds their relative frequency in commonly acceptable native usage even in advanced stages, when the learner knows more than one alternative.

Three of the sentences in the sentence completion test in our previous study (Levenston and Blum 1977) were devised to test this hypothesis. All three were phrased in a way that marked them for register. We expected the native speakers of Hebrew to prefer in each case the word appropriate to the style, and the non-natives to disregard this constraint. Both groups conformed — in one case, for example, given by the context a possible choice between *natal* (formal and marked for 'wash') and *raḥac* (unmarked for 'wash') 85 per cent of the Israelis used *natal*, versus only 38 per cent of those learners who knew — that is, they could translate at sight — both words.

Interestingly, though the majority of Israelis chose the expected, marked, term there were always some (in the case of *natal* — 12.5 per cent) who chose the unmarked. Awareness of synonymy is a component of semantic competence. It is used by learners as a strategy for a simple task of sentence completion. And it is this same strategy of simplification that is used deliberately by the native speaker when he wishes to simplify for others.

Altogether there seem to exist three distinct kinds of situation that may develop with respect to the use of synonyms in a learner's interlanguage:

1. Of a pair of synonyms that differ in register only (e.g. *natal/ raḥac*) the more frequent is learned first and as a result, its

relative frequency in the learner's interlanguage is greater, at all stages, than in normal usage by native speakers. But this does not lead to inappropriate usage.

2.   A pair of synonyms share the same components of meaning but differ in register and take different collocations. The learner, aware of only one of the pair, uses it regardless of collocational and stylistic restrictions. The result is often inappropriate usage, e.g. *a beautiful man* used by a learner who does not know the word *handsome*.

3.   Two words that share most of their semantic components but are not true synonyms become such in the learner's interlanguage semantic system and are used interchangeably. In the written exercises of one student in one week we found such interchangeability in the use of *diber* (speak) and *amar* (say).

Transfer

All second-language learners probably begin by assuming that for every word in their mother tongue there is a single translation-equivalent in the second language. More precisely, perhaps, the assumption of word-for-word translation-equivalence as a working hypothesis — 'thinking in the mother tongue' — is the only way a learner can even begin to communicate in a second language. Mastery of the second language involves the gradual abandonment of the equivalence hypothesis, the internalization of the semantic relationships in the second language independently of their first-language equivalent, the ability to 'think in the *second* language'.

If, then, by lexical transfer we mean attributing to a lexical item of the second language all the functions — referential and conceptual meaning, connotation, collocability, register-restriction — of its assumed first-language translation-equivalent, then it is not a strategy of avoidance but a strategy of communication, in fact the means whereby communication becomes possible. 'Positive' transfer is also probably the main way we increase our control of the second-language vocabulary. Take the word *way* itself. One English-speaking student of Hebrew was observed to use the word *derex* in the context *lo zu haderex la'asot et ha'avodah* (that's not the way to do the work), though the word had only been encountered for the first time a few days earlier in class in its literal topographical sense — *haderex mikan lehefa* (the way from here to Haifa). One may, however, place too great a reliance on transfer and fail to realize its limitations. Even the professional translator may remain too tied to his source language and produce the kind of transfer effect known as translatorese. The Hebrew idiom, for instance, rendered 'thou shall not uncover the nakedness of . . .' in the Authorized Version is less obscurely translated by the New English Bible 'you shall not have intercourse with . . .' (Leviticus 18: 6–15).

Such infelicities in published translations are, or should be, rare. In learners' utterances, by contrast, they are or should be common; without such creations and their subsequent correction, no progress can be made. To give just one example, after transferring the Hebrew *na'alei 'avoda* to English as *workshoes* the learner discovers the need in English, not found in Hebrew, to distinguish between *shoes* and *boots. Workshoes* is an unacceptable loan-translation. Legitimate loan-translations are those lexical transfers that have acquired respectability. Whereas English borrowed *kindergarten* from German, Hebrew transferred the word as *gan yeladim* (garden of children), preserving even the plural of *Kinder* (Rabin 1958).

Some kinds of borrowing may also be classified as transfer, though for learners a careful distinction must be made here between *transfer* and *language switch*. If a learner, attempting to communicate in the second language, uses a term from his mother tongue and makes no attempt to adjust the morphology or the phonology, he is employing the strategy we have labelled 'language switch'. This too is a strategy common to learners and translators, who when faced with a lexical void in the target language, resort to italicized citation of the source-language term, with or without footnotes and a glossary. If, however, the learner creates appropriate second-language morphology and phonology, he may be said to have resorted to *transfer*. At best he may hit on a form already borrowed, already accepted in the target language. At worst, he will produce a pseudo-borrowing, a form possessing all the features of a genuine borrowing except acceptability. Our own elicitation procedures did net one example of this type: *ekstati*. A third possibility is the creation of false cognates. This, of course, is always likely to happen when the word in question originated in the second language, was borrowed into the learner's first language with a changed meaning, and is then translated back by the unsuspecting Israeli student of English, e.g. *I took a tramp from Jerusalem to Tel Aviv* (English *tramp* is used in Hebrew in the sense of 'lift, free ride'). The same effect may be produced through processes akin to loan-translation, e.g. when a Hebrew speaker translates *lašon hara* word by word as 'bad language', not knowing that the correct English term for *lašon hara* is 'slander'.

Between pairs of languages more closely related than English and Hebrew, the existence of cognates, real and apparent, is a well-known source for errors of transfer; Lo Coco (1975) quotes the use of *una familia larga* (for *grande*) by English-speaking learners of Spanish. (For a detailed attempt at sub-categorizing these phenomena, see Nash 1974.)

Finally, a word about the use of transfer by teachers in the class-room. One would not normally expect such a phenomenon to occur. Unlike translators, teachers can avoid the problems of lexical voids, or difficulties forced upon them by unknown texts. Unlike learners they tend to be at home in both languages. Nevertheless, we have seen teachers indulging in transfer. Faced with the need to describe grammatical phenomena, and realizing that the Hebrew term would be unfamiliar to the learner, a Hebrew teacher talked about the [subjekt] of a sentence, pronouncing the word as it would be if a normal borrowing. But it is a pseudo-borrowing; Hebrew speakers do not normally use the word in a grammatical sense. Such transfers are most likely to occur with 'international' words, especially in heterogeneous classes with more than one mother tongue.

Circumlocution and paraphrase

The translation of a high-level word by a descriptive phrase is rec-ommended by Wonderly (1968) as a useful solution in Bible translations for popular use, especially in cases where theological, cultural and other technical terms are involved. Among his exam-ples are:

repent → turn away from your sins, blasfema (blasphemes) → ofende a Dios con sus palabros (offends God with his words), fidel (faithful) → siempre cumple sus promesos (always keeps his promises) (Wonderly 1968).

From a semantic point of view the technique involved is the separate specification of component features.

When used in dictionary definitions, and thus context-free, cir-cumlocutions are expected to specify all the semantic features of the defined word: '*island* — a tract of land surrounded by water'.

In translations, text-simplifications and learners' speech, circumlocutions are never context-free, and hence tend to vary in their
degree of accuracy, if considered as definitions of the words they
replace. In translation proper, circumlocution may be replaced by
paraphrase, which does not necessarily specify even all those
semantic components required by the context; such periphrastic
renderings are a last resort, employed mainly in cases of 'cultural
voids':

(10)   tihye micvah levaqer eclo bevet ḥolim.
        It would be a good deed to visit him in hospital.

A *micvah* in Hebrew is a religious commandment, either positive ('Honour thy father and thy mother . . .') or negative ('Thou
shalt not covet . . .'). Whereas the fulfilment of many positive
micvot — including the commandment to visit the sick — would
qualify as a 'good deed', this paraphrase contains neither the
semantic component 'duty', nor the essential connotation (+
religious).

An example of paraphrase in a simplified reading text is the replacement of 'God will clear me' (from George Eliot, *Silas Marner*) by 'God will prove me innocent' (*Silas Marner* simplified and
brought within the vocabulary of New Method Reader 6 — Longman 1936).

Such periphrastic renderings can at best supply the referential
meaning of the original. When the connotative meaning is an important feature of the original, the text-simplifier and the translator are in trouble. In the following example the informality and
direct criticism found in the source are replaced by a rather formal, not to say pedantic, use of irony in a periphrastic translation
that completely changes the tone of the original:

(11)   . . . said it didn't seem very 'spunky' of Mr Irving . . .
        hixriz al hamore šelo hir'a simanei gvura yetera (de-
        clared that the teacher did not show signs of being over-
        heroic). (From Upton Sinclair, *Oil*, and the translation
        by M. Avishai 1929, quoted in Toury 1977.)

Teachers also use paraphrase, both to avoid unknown lexical
items and to introduce new ones. Used skilfully this is obviously a
useful tool of lexical simplification in language teaching. On the
other hand, the price paid for misuse of this strategy in teaching
is higher than in translation. An unsuccessful paraphrase in translation will affect the accuracy and acceptability of one specific

text. An unsuccessful paraphrase offered as explanation in class may lead the student to misapprehend the meaning of a word and thus later to misuse it. One teacher explained *sexuna* (neighbourhood) as *maqom šeyeš bo harbe binyanim* (where there are lots of houses), leading students to think it meant 'a built-up area'.

The other danger, common to all strategies of simplification, is that the distinction between acceptable and non-acceptable usage is blurred. A *kennel/meluna* may be a *dog's house/bayit šel kelev*, but only the single word is normal usage in either language. When the teacher systematically avoids lexical items by paraphrase, he often uses collocations unacceptable under normal circumstances. The learner, lacking any independent criteria for judging degrees of acceptability in the target language, accepts the teacher's usage as the norm, not realizing that he is thereby widening the gap between his interlanguage and the target language. This danger is not specific to the use of paraphrase. All strategies of lexical simplification may have this unwished-for effect. We mention it here because it is often the misuse of circumlocution by learners that produces the oddest interlanguage uses, and it is important to remember that the use of this strategy by learners is clearly encouraged by its use as a teaching device.

The nature of the elicitation procedures used in our own study (Levenston and Blum 1977) did not much allow for the use of circumlocution: the test given required the completion of sentences, with single blanks for single missing words. Nevertheless, learners did use a special kind of circumlocution, one that entailed the use of two words instead of one: instead of the required word *nixšal* (failed), students wrote *lo hicliah* (did not succeed). This technique is also well known to translators. By exploiting the various semantic relationships of 'oppositeness' of meaning (to use Lyons' 1968 terminology), translators can solve the problem of lexical voids in the target language. Just as 'she is not married' is an intralanguage translation of 'she is single', so the same device can be used for translating 'single' into a language that lacks such a term.

In conclusion

The probably universal nature of lexical simplification is supported by two arguments:
1. the *need* is constant, deriving from limits placed on the size of the vocabulary at the disposal of the speaker. These limits

may stem from the speaker's own lack of knowledge, the addressee's linguistic immaturity, or — in the case of pidgins — features of the language itself;

2. the *strategies employed* by a speaker to achieve his communicative goals despite such restraints are based on certain aspects of semantic competence shared by all speakers.

In the specific case of second-language acquisition, it is necessary to distinguish between those aspects of semantic structure — hyperonymy, antonymy, converseness, synonymy, etc. — which make lexical simplification possible, and those complexities of language use — register-variety, metaphorical extension, collocational restriction, etc. — which make it *necessary*. However, though hyperonymy, antonymy, converseness and synonymy are universals of semantic structure, their realization will differ from one language to another, and thus the *end-product* of lexical simplification in a learner's speech will not always be acceptable to a native speaker.

In fact, a quite separate study needs to be made of possible/ universal communicative *effects* of simplification by learners upon native speakers. In addition to the clear recognition by the listener of referential errors and inappropriate collocations or registers, there will also be cases of misunderstanding, obscurity and ambiguity. For a preliminary attempt to categorize some of these effects, see again Levenston and Blum 1977.

It is indeed the preliminary state of all research on lexical simplification that is still most noticeable. We have tried in this paper to survey some of the empirical evidence for the hypothesis that lexical simplification is based on universal principles of semantic competence. The preliminary nature of our inquiry is only too obvious:

1. The categories of the taxonomy proposed could be subclassified with even greater delicacy. In particular the different kinds of oppositeness (Lyons 1968) and hyponymy (Cruise 1975) need to be taken more fully into account.

2. We have not examined all the contexts of linguistic simplification. In particular, the evidence from pidginization and creolization should be compared for similar phenomena (Schuman 1974).

3. We have not compared *all* the strategies and processes postulated, even within the contexts chosen. There is clearly room for more systematic investigation of all the phenomena noted, both in the same and other linguistic contexts and in other pairs of languages.

138   *Shoshana Blum-Kulka and Eddie A. Levenston*

Notes

1. In this research both learners and native speakers were required to fill
   in the lexical gaps in the test sentences. In addition, learners were
   subsequently required to translate into their mother tongue a list of
   words which included all those used by native speakers to complete
   the same set of test sentences.

References

Abberton, Evelyn (1968). 'Some Persistent English Vocabulary Problems for Speakers of Serbo-Croatian', *English Language Teaching*, **22**, 167–172.

Blum, Shoshana (1972). 'Easy Hebrew as a Means for Teaching Hebrew to Adults'. Unpublished Ph.D. thesis, the Hebrew University of Jerusalem.

Cruise, D. A. (1975). 'Hyponymy and Lexical Hierarchies', in Cambell, I. M. and Mitchel, T. F. (eds.), *Archivum Linguisticum*, Vol. VI.

Dagut, Menachem B. (1971). 'A Linguistic Analysis of Some Semantic Problems of Hebrew–English Translation'. Unpublished doctoral thesis, Jerusalem.

Davies, Alan and Widdowson, Henry G. (1974). 'Simplified Readers', in Allen, J. P. B. and Corder, S. Pit (eds.), *Techniques in Applied Linguistics*, The Edinburgh Course in Applied Linguistics, Vol. 3, Oxford University Press, 176–177.

Ferguson, Charles A. (1971). 'Absence of Copula and the Notion of Simplicity: a Study of Normal Speech, Baby Talk, Foreigner Talk and Pidgins', in Hymes (1971), 140–150.

Henzl, Vera M. (1973). 'Linguistic Register of Foreign Language Instruction', *Language Learning*, **23**, 206–223.

Hymes, Dell (ed.) (1971). *Pidginization and Creolization of Languages*, Cambridge University Press.

Ickenroth, Jacques (1975). *On the Elusiveness of Interlanguage*, Progress Report, Utrecht.

Kleinmann, Howard H. (1977). 'Avoidance Behavior in Adult Second Language Acquisition', *Language Learning*, **27**, 93–108.

Levenston, Eddie (1980). 'Second Language Acquisition: Issues and Problems', *Interlanguage Studies Bulletin Utrecht*, **4**, 147–160.

Levenston, Eddie and Blum, Shoshana (1977). 'Aspects of Lexical Simplification in the Speech and Writing of Advanced Adult Learners', in Corder, S. Pit and Roulet, Eddie (eds.), *The Notions of Simplification, Interlanguages and Pidgins and their Relation to Second Language Pedagogy* (= Actes du 5ème colloque de linguistique appliquée de Neuchâtel 20–22 Mai 1976), Genève: Droz and Neuchâtel: Faculté des Lettres, 51–71.

Lo Coco, Veronica Gonzales Mena (1975). 'An Analysis of Spanish and German Learners' Errors', *Working Papers on Bilingualism*, **7**, 29–37.

Lyons, John (1968). *Introduction to Theoretical Linguistics*, Cambridge University Press.

Nash, Rose (1974). 'Phantom Cognates and Other Curiosities in Puerto

Rican Englanol'. Paper presented at the TESOL Convention, Denver, Colorado.

Rabin, Chaim (1958). 'The Linguistics of Translation', in Smith, H. (ed.), *Aspects of Translation: Studies in Communication*, London.

Richards, Jack C. (1976). 'The Role of Vocabulary Teaching', *TESOL Quarterly*, **10/1.**

Samarin, William J. (1971). 'Salient and Substantive Pidginization', in Hymes (1971), 117–140.

Schuman, John H. (1974). 'The Implications of Interlanguage, Pidginization and Creolization for the Study of Adult Language Acquisition', *TESOL Quarterly*, **8**, 145–152.

Sela, Pasia and Arad, Ariela (1977). 'Simplification and Over-Simplification in the Language of Teachers'. Unpublished seminar paper, Hebrew University, Jerusalem.

Selinker, Larry, Swain, Merrill and Dumas, Guy (1975). 'The Interlanguage Hypothesis Extended to Children', *Language Learning*, **25**, 139–152.

Slobin, Dan I. (1974). *Psycholinguistics*, London: Scott and Foreman.

Tarone, Elaine, Frauenfelder, Uli and Selinker, Larry (1976). 'Systematicity/Variability and Stability/Instability in Interlanguage Systems', in Brown, H. Douglas (ed.), *Papers in Second Language Acquisition* (= Language Learning Special Issue No. 4), 93–134.

Toury, Gideon (1977). 'Norms of Literary Translation into Hebrew, 1930–1945'. Unpublished doctoral thesis, Tel Aviv University.

Wonderly, William L. (1968). *Bible Translation for Popular Use*, United Bible Societies.

8 Achievement strategies in learner/native speaker interaction

Kirsten Haastrup and Robert Phillipson

1 Introduction

1.1 *Aims*

This is a study of how learners cope in real communication situations. Our aim is to analyse when communication breaks down or is disrupted in the interactional context of a Danish learner of English talking to a native speaker of English, and to study what resources the learners draw on to solve their problems. In many cases they resort to achievement strategies. These have been described by Færch and Kasper as attempts by the learner 'to solve problems in communication by expanding his communicative resources . . ., rather than by reducing his communicative goal' (Part One, this volume). Within the theoretical framework established by these authors we assess how Danish learners vary in their use of the achievement strategies open to them. The reason for concentrating on achievement strategies and excluding reduction strategies (see Færch and Kasper, Part One) from our analysis is that a major interest is the question of how learners solve problems in reaching their communicative goals, rather than how they avoid problems by reducing communicative objectives. We are interested in whether there is any link between strategy use and learners attending different types of school and pursuing different academic goals. We also wish to test the hypothesis that some achievement strategies are inherently of greater communicative potential than others. The article contains two detailed portraits of individual learners, and makes a comparative study of eight. We relate our empirical study of how achievement strategies are actually used to the theory of communicative competence presented in Canale and Swain (1980). We go on to state in what way the descriptions of learner performance will be of immediate relevance to teachers of English and can be of importance in the assessment of oral proficiency.

2 Corpus and method

2.1 *Research context*
This study is part of PIF (Project in Foreign Language Pedagogy), Department of English, University of Copenhagen. PIF is concerned with describing various aspects of the spoken and written English of 120 Danish learners, drawn from all levels of the Danish education system. For a full description of the project's aims see Færch (1979). There are three samples of the spoken language of each subject, but only one is relevant here, namely the videotaped, 20-minute conversation with a native speaker of English. The PIF conversations were designed to test whether school English could be applied in the more genuine communication situation of chatting to a native speaker about school, holidays, interests and the like. The samples of learner language were recorded in conditions which were as close to real communication as studio recording conditions would permit. Often the atmosphere is very relaxed, and the rapport between the two very good, although they are meeting for the first time, in unfamiliar surroundings. For a full description of the data collection phase of the PIF project, see Færch (1982).

2.2 *Native speakers*
The British people who interacted with the Danish learners had recently arrived in Denmark, knew virtually no Danish, and were unfamiliar with things Danish. This put the learners in the position of providing the native speakers with a good deal of very basic information about their own lives and experiences.

2.3 *Learners*
Eight learners were selected for this study. They have all had five years of English as part of their compulsory schooling, and at the time of the interviews they are in their sixth year of English and in three different types of school. Three learners are in their final year of compulsory schooling, and probably about to leave formal education; three learners are in their first year of a three-year course of an academic kind which qualifies for higher education; two learners are in a parallel two-year course which is more flexible and intended for people with some experience out of school. All are 16–17 years old, with the exception of one person who

has been out and about for a few years before returning to school. One reason for choosing learners from different types of school is that we assume that the learners vary in their motivation and aspirations, and we are interested in the relationship between learner types and strategy use. It is highly likely that Danish teachers would regard our subjects as being typical of learners in the three institutions.

2.4 *The conversations*
The native speaker had more briefing and more experience of the situation than the learners. The native speakers had a dry run in the pilot phase of the project, were told about the general aims of the project, and some of them engaged in a fair number of conversations. In our limited corpus, five native speakers were represented, one of whom conducted four of the conversations. The learners knew that they would be expected to speak English to an English person, and had been reassured that they were not being 'tested' in any way. Both parties were given a list of topics that they could refer to if needed. The list is in fact adhered to in almost all the conversations, and there is thus a fair consistency as regards topics discussed. There is much less uniformity about how the conversations proceed, and how much initiative the learners show, as personality is obviously of critical importance. The discourse structure frequently follows the rough pattern of the native speaker putting questions, which induce a response from the learner, which one of them then follows up (cf. Holmen forthcoming, for a detailed analysis of this). Neither of the labels 'interview' and 'conversation' is ideal, because the confrontations of our subjects did not have the specific purpose of pursuing facts or attitudes, in the way the term 'interview' suggests, nor were they as desultory and thematically unstructured as much informal 'conversation' is. Broadly speaking, as our examples will demonstrate, the two people give the impression of making polite talk to a stranger, of genuinely wanting to discuss matters of mutual interest, with the native speaker making most of the running. For want of a better term we will use the term 'conversations'.

2.5 *Types of data*
Interactional data is exciting but messy. What is captured on video is a complex interpersonal exchange, and this the investigators observe and interpret. Our data is thus very different from language elicited in a test situation and then vetted by a panel of judges. Elsewhere communication disruptions have been investi-

gated in terms of the ability of native speakers to correct imperfect sentences produced by learners (Phillipson 1979; Tomiyana 1980). Native-speaker tolerance has been indirectly investigated through ingenious tests of the perception of and attitudes to learner language, e.g. when ranking sentences on a scale of acceptability (Johansson 1975). Like Bialystok and Fröhlich (1980) we were interested in the relationship of learners' strategy use to proficiency level, but whereas they used elicited data, which facilitates tighter control of a number of variables, we used spontaneous, interactional data, which is closer to natural communication.

2.6 *Procedure*
Two investigators (the authors, one Danish and one English) watched each tape and identified when communication was disrupted. The relevant extracts of the videotape were transcribed, any significant contextual information noted down, and all achievement strategies in each extract identified. For each disruption, an assessment was made of whether the parties reached mutual comprehension or not. The typology and terms used are exemplified below (see 3, Definitions). On the basis of the transcriptions and our impressions from the videotapes we proceeded to draw up profiles of each learner (see below, 4 and 5), involving a general characterization of the interview, the pattern of communication disruptions, the kinds of achievement strategy used, and reception problems.

3 Definitions

3.1 *Communication disruptions*
One can rigidly distinguish between problems seen from the learner's point of view, the native speaker's, or from the detached investigator's, but in practice these aspects are interwoven. Communication disruptions are often explicitly signalled by one of the speakers, and followed by repair, clarification, or similar shared efforts to negotiate towards mutual comprehension. We define a communication disruption as occurring when mutual comprehension is impaired by one of the speakers misunderstanding the other or when the learner is manifestly in trouble in putting across what he/she wants to say. In the first case either the learner or the native speaker will explicitly indicate presence of a linguistic code problem. In the second case the learner will mark a pro-

duction difficulty by hesitation or non-verbal signals, and will generally have recourse to a communication strategy.

Occasionally the two speakers are unaware of a misunderstanding, but the investigators, from their detailed knowledge of Danish and English, can infer presence of a communication disruption in the context.

3.2 *Strategy types*

The strategies investigated are those that Færch and Kasper call 'compensatory strategies'. In order to be able to present a checklist here, very short examples of each strategy are listed, without the context being given. Longer examples are provided in the learner portraits which follow.

Achievement strategies	*Example from our corpus*
L1-based strategies	
borrowing[1]	'fagforening' (= trade union)
anglicizing[2]	in the marine (= navy)
literal translation	meanings (= opinions)
IL-based strategies	
generalization	people from all country
	(= all parts of the world)
paraphrase	we have — when we talk
	(= oral exam)
word coinage	a funny (= fancy) dress ball
restructuring	if something is er doesn't work
Cooperative strategies	
appeals	what do you call it?
Non-verbal strategies (NV)[3]	gesture
Strategies aimed at solving retrieval problems	er now I have to think

4 Profile of learner 2[4]

4.1 *General characterization of the conversation*

The conversation is 'sticky', as the learner has serious problems both in saying what he wants and in understanding the native speaker. The tempo is generally rather slow, and utterances short, but not because of any reluctance to talk on the part of the learner. Both speakers are eager to please each other, but the learner is anxious not to reveal his weaknesses. His pronunciation is good. The native speaker talks very naturally, but she is occasionally nervous, which results in her not marking a change of topic and not always being entirely clear. It is a boy (learner) meets girl (native speaker) situation, both of them belonging to the same age group. A considerable amount of non-verbal communication facilitates the solution of the linguistic problems.

4.2 *Communication disruptions*
There are 21 communication disruptions in the conversation. So far as causes are concerned, there is no evidence of either pronunciation or grammar causing communication disruptions: the origin of these lies almost entirely in the learner's lexical limitations, both in reception and production.

4.3 *Learner production*
The learner has great difficulty in formulating what he wants to say. Pauses are frequent and long. He seldom appeals to the native speaker for help but prefers other achievement strategies. The majority of these are L1-based rather then IL-based: there is a good deal of 'borrowing', literal translation into English, and 'anglicizing'.

Extract 1 (p. 146) demonstrates the learner needing to use a series of strategies to reach a particular communicative goal. The learner is about to describe his part-time job.

The learner's first utterance causes the communication disruption, and the second, a paraphrase which is in effect a circumlocution, does not succeed in clarifying the issue. The first utterance is a good example of the use of two L1-based strategies not leading to success. The Danish word *bringe* means deliver, and the Danish word *petroleum* has been anglicized as *petrol*. The first paraphrase provides background information, but the native speaker's guess about cars confirms that she has not understood. The second paraphrase, providing a justification for what the learner is trying to explain, sets the native speaker off in the right direction, and the learner's use of the Danish word for a jerrycan, supported by a gesture shaping this object, enables the native speaker, after pause for thought, to find an appropriate word. The final utterance in this extract shows the learner repeating his transfer error, literally translating into English; the crucial lexical item *deliver*, absence of which triggered off this compli-

Extract 1

(L = learner; NS = native speaker)

Transcript	Comment	Strategies
L: I bring petrol	= I deliver paraffin	literal translation/ anglicizing
NS: mm	simulates comprehension	
L: here in the winter there are a lot to do	an explanation of the need for such work	paraphrase
[...]		
NS: do you fill people's cars?		
L: no er		
NS: no is it?		
L: to heat up a room you need petrol	gesture	paraphrase + NV
and it's in 'dunke' you know	= jerry can; gesture	borrowing + NV
NS: yeah it er I mean in containers		
L: yeah in containers		
NS: yeah		
L: and ten litres in each		
NS: oh and you take it to people's houses and pour it in		
L: yeah bring it		lit. translation

cated sequence of learner/native-speaker communication, has not actually been used, though comprehension has been reached.

In the conversation as a whole there is a pattern of L1-based strategies not working very effectively to achieve understanding, and needing an IL strategy in support. However, little use is made of generalization, word coinage and restructuring in the conversation, and even paraphrase is used only five times. The positive advantages of paraphrase are clear in the second extract,

Extract 2

Transcript	Comment	Strategies
NS: why do you think they do that?		
L: mm they want a 'parcelhuset'	= a detached house	borrowing
NS: uhuh what's that?		
L: erm it's a house erm it it's not an apartment	gesture indicates a plot of land	paraphrase + NV
NS: mm		
L: but it's a big house where just THEY live	gesture models a house	paraphrase + NV
NS: oh I see a a sort of totally detached house	gesture, in shape of a house	
L: yeah		

when the two are discussing people moving out of Copenhagen to the surrounding region.

In Extract 2 the learner's borrowing causes a communication disruption: the native speaker is baffled by the Danish word and asks for clarification. The two paraphrases enable the native speaker to understand what the learner is referring to, upon which she provides the appropriate lexical item, and the discussion continues.

Otherwise there is in the conversation no distinct pattern in the use of communicative strategies: they sometimes occur singly, sometimes in pairs or clusters, in which case there is a tendency for the L1-based strategies to be used first and to trigger off a communication disruption. In general, mutual comprehension is reached, with the exception of a lengthy stretch towards the middle of the conversation where the speakers talk at cross-purposes for nearly a minute.

4.4 *Learner reception*
Of the 21 communication disruptions, no fewer than 7 are caused by the learner failing to understand a question, and with a

single lexical item being the stumbling-block. Examples of these are:

- you don't mind *committing yourself* for three years?
- have you been *abroad* for holidays?
- do you have to say *in advance* that you're coming?
- do you think there are any ways of *solving* the unemployment problem in Denmark?

In such circumstances the learner resorts to a cooperative strategy, an *appeal*, which is either non-verbal, a facial movement, or verbal, in which case he repeats the troublesome lexical item. In all, 13 appeals are used by the learner during the conversation with extensive use of supportive non-verbal communication.

4.5 *Summary — learner 2 strategy style*
The learner runs into a considerable number of difficulties. His reception problems are immediately solved by appealing to the native speaker for clarification of the linguistic problem. His production problems are caused by him not having the necessary lexis to discuss his part-time job, future employment plans, or hobby (sailing), or topical political issues (social democrat education policy and housing problems linked to this). His lexical limitations make for a halting, non-fluent advance. He uses a wide range of achievement strategies, but often the L1-based ones do not enable him to reach his communicative goal. The IL-based strategies are more effective, particularly paraphrase.

5 Profile of learner 5[5]

5.1 *General characterization of the conversation*
The learner is an adult whose school English has clearly been extended through informal use in many contexts. English flows from him very freely and fast, and he appears to be confident that he can communicate all that he wants: he makes extensive and vivid use of non-linguistic communication and he is verbally fluent despite encountering frequent linguistic problems. The native speaker (female) treats him as a linguistic equal, making few concessions to his non-nativeness, and his comprehension is generally unerring and swift.

5.2 *Communication disruptions*
The total number of communication disruptions is 42, the highest

figure in our corpus. A couple of them are caused by the native speaker asking a question in an unclear, rushed manner, but the vast majority are caused by the learner having production difficulties: typically he sets off on one track, fails to complete the sentence, and restructures, thereby indicating that he is in linguistic trouble.

5.3 *Learner production*
The learner makes extensive use of achievement strategies, at least 60 of them in the 20-minute conversation. The full range are represented, L1-based, IL-based, cooperative, non-linguistic and retrieval strategies. The first extract demonstrates use of his favourite L1-based strategy, literal translation.

The learner is aware that he does not know how to express degrees above and below zero in English. He holds the floor while trying to solve the problem, hesitating momentarily before retrieving. There is no appeal to the native speaker until the 'you know'. In fact the native speaker can understand this first literal translation, and the two succeeding ones in the extract, as there is little risk of confusion in the context.

Of the IL-based strategies there is a clear preference for restructuring, of which there are no fewer than 28. The learner often

Extract 3

Transcript	Comment	Strategies
L: I came down from twenty degrees — er I don't know how you say twe it was twenty degrees hot you know.	floorholding = plus twenty (rising intonation)	retrieval restructuring lit. translation appeal
NS: mm		
L: and I came up er in Scotland to twenty degrees freezing so I got very sick (L and NS laugh) just before Christmas	= minus twenty	lit. translation
NS: this Christmas?		
L: er last Christmas — and I didn't want to stay sick in a hotel ov — the Christmas over	= over Christmas	lit. translation

has to use a succession of two or more strategies to get his message across, as in extract 4, where he is describing his job in a laundry.

Extract 4

Transcript	Comment	Strategies
L: I have to look after a machine if something is er doesn't work I have to well it's not difficult because there's only three buttons you know (laughs) all automatical you know	NV throughout — gesture	restructuring restructuring NV paraphrase
NS: mm		

This shows the learner making a succession of statements, and producing a torrent of language before the native speaker can break in again. Twice a restructuring strategy is used, with so little hesitation that if one only watched the videotape once, one might not notice the shift in sentence structure. The learner likes to keep talking. We can take it that the native speaker has grasped what was intended in this extract.

However, having worked with the videotape of this particular learner for some time we became very suspicious. On the face of it he seems to reach his communicative goals. What happens though is that he talks so fast and so much that the native speaker often does not get a chance to query anything. Extract 5 is a typical example of a disruption where the learner's efforts result in partial comprehension or perhaps even miscomprehension.

The learner is discussing what it means to exchange a life of working abroad for one of studying.

The learner's first utterance shows his familiar restructuring strategy. His second is garbled, but seems to include a paraphrase which enables the native speaker to understand that the learner is complaining of his day being worked out for him. His third utterance contains a good deal of information, but is so unclear that the native speaker interprets it as referring to filling out forms, whereas it is highly likely that he is attempting to describe a life

Extract 5

Transcript	Comment	Strategies
L: so suddenly you have to plan your — all your whole day you know		restructuring
NS: mm		
L: and it's all sets up you know you are not very free in a way	shows boxes with his hands	NV ? paraphrase
NS: have you got into the habit now or is it still hard?		
L: well I've got into it now but er then there's problems with the tax people and (blows) you know there's too much	'the' is held	
things — it's all set down in very little (unfinished)	same gesture of parcelling things out	generalization NV (message abandonment)
NS: forms to fill in		

regulated by a whole range of obligations and pressures. Our conclusion is therefore that they only reach partial understanding of one another.

5.4 *Learner reception*

The learner has little difficulty in understanding anything the native speaker says to him. As we have already indicated, he talks a lot, which means that he has a good deal of influence on the way the conversation progresses. It results in him not being exposed to so much detailed questioning.

5.5 *Summary — learner 5 strategy style*

Learner 5 uses a wide range of achievement strategies, of which the most common are restructurings and literal translations. It is normally the case that two or more strategies are used in succession. His language often results in partial comprehension, with literal translations submerged in a mass of language, bolstered by 'you know'. His fluency is genuine enough but his ability to communicate precisely in English is spurious.

6 Learner strategy styles

6.1 *From profiles to comparison*
In order to compare the strategy use of the eight learners in our corpus, we compiled mini-profiles of each of them covering the same ground as the full-length profiles just presented. These mini-profiles have not been included here, because we feel their brevity makes them incomprehensible unless there is access to the videotapes or transcripts. What we have done is to transfer the information from the mini-profiles to Table 1, which records the number of communication disruptions per conversation, and the strategy use of each subject. The eight subjects have been grouped according to the type of school they attend.[6]

The table is a crude attempt to portray the range of strategy use visually. No strict statistical principles have been followed: we abandoned an attempt to distinguish between frequent use, infrequent use and no use, and have merely recorded, inevitably in a somewhat subjective fashion, regularity. The bracketed cross (X) notes use spread over a number of strategy types within the major categories of IL- or L1-based strategies. Under cooperative strategies we have recorded appeals of two types: one occurs when the learner has a production problem and asks for help in finding a lexical item (marked P); the other involves the learner acknowledging that he/she has a reception problem and appealing to the native speaker for clarification (marked R).

In what follows we summarize what can be read from Table 1.

6.2 *Frequency of communication disruptions*
A word of warning is needed about how to interpret the figures for the number of communication disruptions per conversation. It would be wrong to assume that a low figure indicates a high degree of communicative success. In addition to the way learners vary in their use of strategies, there is the native speaker to reckon with. In virtually all the conversations the native speakers provoke communication disruptions by occasionally asking an incoherent question. Furthermore they vary in the degree to which they follow up learner contributions, particularly when these are opaque. The native speakers may prefer to keep the conversation going by changing topic rather than probing. The conversation with

Table 1

Learner number	communication disruptions	L1-based strategies			IL-based strategies				cooperative strategies	non-verbal strategies	retrieval strategies
		borrowing	anglicizing	literal translation	generalization	paraphrase	word coinage	restructuring			
1	11	X	X						P	X	
2	21	X	X	X	X				PR		
3	15		X		(X)						
4	16				X				P	X	
5	42			X				X		X	
6	26			X	(X)				P		
7	30		(X)					X	PR		
8	30	X		X				X	P	X	X

X   = regular use of the strategy
(X) = occasional use of each of the strategies in the set, i.e. L1-based or IL-based
P   = presence of a production problem
R   = presence of a reception problem

learner 1 has a very low figure for disruptions, but the chat is disjointed: the native speaker senses that the topic has been exhausted after rather feeble contributions from the learner, bolstered by non-linguistic strategies (used as a substitute for language rather than as support for it). By contrast the figure for disruptions is higher in the conversation with learner 6, who is a fluent, willing participant. Here the disruptions are caused by native-speaker incoherence four times, and otherwise by gaps in the learner's vocabulary, productive and receptive, and one occasion by a mispronunciation. A further factor is the degree to which the learner monitors output by correcting him- or herself, and here practice varies. Self-corrections mostly take the form of a paraphrase or a restructuring. They generally demonstrate the learner correcting a grammatical item, removing an error so that output conforms with target language norms. There is thus a communication disruption, within our definition, but there was never any risk of a misunderstanding and the correction does not improve on comprehensibility. Some learners correct themselves, others do not. The important point being made here, where we have stressed diversity among both native speakers and learners, is that the statistics for the frequency of communication disruptions in the conversations need qualitative analysis before any conclusions can be drawn.

6.3 *Learners' use of L1-based strategies*

It is to be expected that learners at this level, and even more advanced ones, will have gaps in their lexical repertoire, the central question then being how they solve their communicative problems. However, we were quite surprised that most of our learners make frequent use of L1-based strategies, as one might expect that learners, after five years of English teaching, would rely more heavily on IL-based strategies. The tendency in our corpus is definitely for an L1-based strategy to be used first, after which the native speaker may elicit a clarification, for instance a paraphrase. But native speakers do not always follow up in this way. This is illustrated by learner 7, who makes extensive use of L1-based strategies. In fact in nearly one third of the 30 communication disruptions in this conversation full comprehension is not reached, because the learner is not pressed hard, and the native speaker does not let on that there is still less than complete mutual understanding. By contrast learner 4 solves linguistic code problems swiftly by paraphrase and appeal, and occasionally by anglicizing.

6.4 *How many strategy styles?*

Our point of departure for this study was an interest in finding out which strategies a sample of Danish learners actually use, and what triggers them off. One reason for choosing learners from three distinct types of school was that we wanted to investigate whether a particular educational tradition, and the attitudes, norms and expectations of teachers and learners associated with it, could dictate use of particular strategies. A glance at Table 1 is enough to disprove this. The distribution of communication strategies varies considerably; appeals are widely used; non-linguistic strategies are common (possibly thus exploding the myth that Danes are undemonstrative!); and learners in the less academic school context, numbers 1 to 3, are over-dependent on their mother tongue. Rather than concluding that there are three strategy styles, it is more reasonable to claim that there are eight.

6.5 *Strategies for communicative success*

A further hypothesis was that some strategies, namely IL-based strategies, were inherently of greater communicative potential than others. We wished to investigate whether there is a continuum of the following nature, in some way running parallel to increasing mastery of the target language:

Least effective   Most effective

$$\longrightarrow$$

L1-based strategies   IL-based strategies

Our findings support the existence of such a continuum. L1-based strategies nearly always lead to partial or non-comprehension and IL-based strategies often lead to full comprehension. As might be expected. To this we can add that overuse of non-linguistic strategies (not as a supplement but as a substitute for linguistic strategies) as well as appeals in Danish seldom lead to success. We cannot say very much about the relative effectiveness of IL-based strategies since they are not extensively used by our eight learners. Generalization, word coinage, and restructuring are used by few of them, whereas paraphrase is more common. Table 1 shows that half of the learners use paraphrase regularly; virtually all the learners make some use of it. One could hypothesize that paraphrase is the strategy that has the highest potential for communicative success. Our findings, however, are inconclusive on this point. Some learners use paraphrase with great effect, others attempt paraphrase but are so vague that the result is partial comprehension. The general pattern though is undoubtedly that IL-based strategies have great potential for leading to communicative success.

7 Further perspectives

7.1 *Achievement strategies and evaluation*

If one accepts the existence of a continuum going from relatively less to relatively more effective strategies, the next question is: should the 'strategic' aspect of spoken language use also be covered when oral proficiency is assessed? Our study supports the assumption that strategic competence exists alongside grammatical and sociolinguistic competence, and that Canale and Swain's model (1980) including these three components is a helpful way of looking at communicative competence. They describe strategic competence as follows. 'This component will be made up of verbal and non-verbal communication strategies that may be called into action to compensate for breakdowns in communication due to performance variables or to insufficient competence' (1980, p. 30). Their 'breakdowns' we see as a parallel to our 'communication disruptions'. On the basis of our eight conversations one could tentatively classify two of our learners (1 and 2) as having limited strategic competence, two (4 and 6) as having effective strategic competence, and four would be very difficult to place. This is perhaps a timely warning against premature attempts to measure this particular aspect of communicative competence. Clearly teachers or evaluators would need extensive experience and briefing before being able to administer any assessment scheme relating to strategic competence. A Danish research project has been started to see whether teachers can actually administer evaluation sheets for oral proficiency where strategy use is one component.[7] We are definitely in favour of promoting work in this area, because, as we explain in our concluding paragraph (**7.2**), we believe that learners can be guided to greater communicative success through strategies.

7.2 *Achievement strategies and foreign language teaching*
We regard this study as one small step towards clarifying the relationship between learners' preference for certain communicative strategies and the goals and methods of the English teaching they have received (see Færch and Kasper in this volume). Our findings indicate that there are as many styles as there are individuals, rather than specific carry-over from a particular educational tradition. Before any causal link between teaching and strategy use in non-classroom interaction can be substantiated, a number of issues need further exploration, for instance:
– the question of personaiity and strategy use, where the picture we see is one of diversity;
– the question of whether language courses which, roughly speaking, focus on correctness rather than comprehensibility, or vice versa, necessarily foster particular types of strategy use;
– whether classroom practices such as learners being asked to provide definitions of word meanings or paraphrases, or treating the teacher as a 'dictionary' that converts L1 forms to the target language, encourage particular types of strategy use.
A quite different issue is the matter of making learners aware of the elements of strategic competence and of the strategy style of themselves and their fellow learners. We believe that many of

our learners would benefit from greater consciousness of the positive advantages that paraphrase offers, and that a learner like the one in the second profile, learner 5, could learn from a study of his own strategic competence. His strategy use, consisting mainly of literal translations and restructurings, which he uses with blithe confidence, seems to have fossilized in the sense that effective communication is out of reach: his strategic competence seems to have got stuck near the least communicative end of the continuum. We agree with Færch and Kasper (Part One, this volume): 'If by teaching we mean passing on new information only there is probably no need to 'teach' strategies. . . . But if by teaching we also mean making learners conscious about aspects of their (already existing) behaviour it is obvious that we *should* teach them about strategies. . .'.

It is our personal experience from courses and seminars that teachers of English agree with this. Many who have seen our videotapes would like to be able to use them in their teaching. We do not see strategy teaching as a substitute for vocabulary learning, but as a useful supplement, involving attention to a different aspect of the learner's communicative competence.

Notes

Research reported in this article has been financed in part by a grant from the Danish Research Council for the Humanities.

1. 'Borrowing' covers all code-switching, whether a single word or more.
2. 'Anglicizing' is foreignizing into English.
3. Non-verbal strategies have only been recorded when they are central in the context, whether as an alternative or as a supplement to linguistic strategies.
4. Learner 2 is PIF subject 89. Extract 1 is three minutes into the conversation; extract 2 is right at the end of it. He is number 2 in our list of the 8 subjects, see Table 1.
5. Learner 5 is PIF subject 59. Extract 3 is five minutes into the conversation; extract 4 comes after a further two minutes; and extract 5 occurs just before extract 4. He is number 5 in our list of the 8 subjects, see Table 1.
6. Learners 1 to 8 on Table 1 are PIF research subject numbers 86, 89, 98, 58, 59, 25, 27, and 57. 1, 2 and 3 are in their final year of 'Folkeskole'; 6, 7 and 8 are in their first year of 'Gymnasieskole'; 4 and 5 are in a parallel two-year course. See text, paragraph **2.3**.
7. This is the Brøndby project, supported by 'Folkeskolens Forsøgsråd'. Information, in Danish only, is available from the Danish Ministry of Education.

References

Bialystok, Ellen and Fröhlich, Maria (1980). 'Oral Communication Strategies for Lexical Difficulties', *Interlanguage Studies Bulletin Utrecht*, **5,** 3–30.

Canale, Michael and Swain, Merrill (1980). 'Theoretical Bases of Communicative Approaches to Second Language Teaching and Testing', *Applied Linguistics*, **1**, 1–47.

Færch, Claus (1979). *Research in Foreign Language Pedagogy — the PIF Project*, Department of English, University of Copenhagen.

Færch, Claus (1982). *A Corpus of Learner Language*, Department of English, University of Copenhagen.

Holmen, Anne (forthcoming). 'Learner — Native Speaker Interaction', *Indian Journal of Applied Linguistics*.

Johansson, Stig (1975). *Papers in Contrastive Linguistics and Language Testing*, Lund: Gleerup.

Phillipson, Robert (1979) 'Tolerance Tests — Measuring the Linguistic and Communicative Content of Samples of Learner Language', in von Faber, Helm, Eichheim, Hubert and Howell, Thelma (eds.), *Evaluation mündlicher Sprachleistungen*, München: Goethe Institut, 117–129.

Tomiyana, Machiko (1980). 'Grammatical Errors and Communication Breakdown', *TESOL Quarterly*, **14**, 71–79.

9 Dann du tagen eineeee — weisse Platte — an analysis of interlanguage communication in instructions*

Johannes Wagner

In recent years, an increasing number of studies in interlanguage (IL) research have focussed on the improvising techniques used by language learners, referred to as communication strategies. A definition of communication strategies which can be taken as being representative for the literature on this topic is given by Tarone, Cohen and Dumas (Part One, this volume), who define them as 'a systematic attempt by the learner to express or decode meaning in the target language, in situations where the appropriate systematic target language rules have not been formed'.

A learner thus makes use of communication strategies in cases of emergency only, namely, if he cannot produce an utterance which is in accordance with target language norms on the basis of his IL. This definition is potentially misleading as it implies that learners only have recourse to strategies in very special types of situations. We shall attempt to develop a broader concept of communication strategies in this article.

In the literature, one comes across different lists of communication strategies, which particularly aim at the lexical level (see e.g. Tarone, Cohen and Dumas in this volume; Váradi in this volume; Tarone 1977; Palmberg 1979; Glahn 1980).

This procedure can be criticized under various aspects:
1. One has so far analysed the product, the utterance, but not the process by which it is brought about. The statements on communication strategies are, however, hypotheses about

* The original version of this article appeared (in German) in Hyltenstam, Kenneth and Linnarud, Moira (eds.), Interlanguage Workshop at the Fifth Scandinavian Conference of Linguistics, Frostavallen, April 27–29, 1979, Stockholm: Almquist and Wiksell, 55–76, 1979. Translated by the editors.

the underlying process. It is this disparity which makes the identification and delimitation of different strategies so difficult (see the literature referred to above). In this respect, IL research regresses to the position of error analysis which investigates product level phenomena and speculates about the causal processes.

2.   Communication strategies are coding strategies. Coding is a process whereby a set A is projected onto a set B. However, what is the status of set A in our case? To put the question differently: what form has the information taken on *before* communication strategies operate?

3.   The investigations to date have analysed marginal, if not deficient, cases of communication. Description exercises and translations which are not addressed to a specific recipient constitute text types which are fundamentally different from oral communication. The transferability of the results seems questionable. One of the first demands to be made on research into communication strategies must be to investigate genuine verbal interaction. Methodologically, this entails a transition to discourse and communication analyses. In this context, it should be noted that the investigations available are not based on any explicit theory of communication. This implies that the results obtained in those studies are difficult to interpret.

In the following, communication between IL speakers will be analysed. This type of communication will therefore also differ from everyday communication. The participants are two learners who share the same L1 and a foreign language which neither of them speaks well enough to make himself understood without running into problems. Furthermore, the intention and the plan behind the verbal communication are predetermined and can only be modified by the speakers as they execute it. On the other hand, it is exactly this predetermination which allows for basing the analysis on reliable assumptions about speakers' intentions. From a methodological point of view, it is therefore reasonable to maintain a certain artificiality in the analysis. Genuine communication between a language learner and a native speaker is often distorted as the native speaker tends to take over large parts of the verbalization (up to the point of taking over all of the verbalization through questions and by providing alternatives) so that the IL speaker only has to produce positive and negative feedback (cf. Wunderlich 1976, pp. 363ff). The risk one runs in recording such interactions is that one obtains a lot of material on the native speaker's foreigner talk but very little on the language learner's IL and communication strategies.

Elicitation of communication

In the experiment dyads of adult Danish learners of German cooperate in performing a precisely defined communicative task. First, one subject is instructed by the experimenter in a non-verbal action which the subject has to perform himself. Thus one can assess whether the instruction has been understood. In a second step, the subject instructs another learner who also performs the instruction. Both subjects are allowed to ask as many requests for clarification as they wish. Two instructions are used so that every subject is instructed by the experimenter in an action which is unknown to him. The subjects are asked to produce a clay pot and a house from Lego blocks. The wordings of the instructions used by the experimenter are included in Appendix 1, page 171.

Nine adults took part in the experiment. They were all participants in a German course run by a Danish institution which offers adults the possibility of taking the school-leaving examination after the 10th form.

The experiment is to be regarded as a pilot study as it was only audio-taped. Accordingly, there were a few instances which called for a considerable amount of interpretation. For a precise analysis of communicative behaviour, video-recordings are necessary.

The complete wording of two learner texts are included in Appendix 2, page 172. Both of them contain directions how to build a house from Lego blocks. Text VI can be considered as an optimally realized instruction which includes requests for clarification and even comments by the instructor. Text VIII, on the other hand, is one of the most drastically reduced versions from the experiment in that the participants restrict themselves to realizing the minimal task-specific requirements, as will be shown in the analysis below.

Some preliminary considerations for analysing the discourse

The verbal interaction is structured by the goal and contextual conditions of the entire communication. One of the participants has information which the other one needs in order to perform the non-verbal action. The instructor has to give the necessary directions and — after these have been executed by the instructee — evaluate whether they have been followed correctly. These basic characteristics of the interaction result in the following idealized discourse structure:

1	s:	do X	direction
2	H:	(non-verbal)	execution
3	s:	yes okay	evaluation

4	s:	now do Y	direction
5	H:	(non-verbal)	execution
6	s:	good	evaluation[1]

The three-phase discourse structure reflects the instruction pattern. Patterns are conventionalized action-functional units (see Rehbein 1977). The evaluation phase is optional within the instruction pattern: it can be left out but is then contained implicitly in the subsequent direction. In this way, a discourse structure with only two phases evolves which can alternate with a three-phase structure.

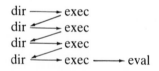

Questions and requests for clarification can be fitted into this basic structure of direction – non-verbal execution – evaluation. The question consists of a two-phase pattern 'question – answer', which can combine with the instruction pattern into a complex pattern in specific ways. If the instructor cannot verbalize an instruction, he can ask the instructee. By supplying the answer, the instructee then completes the instruction himself.

1	s:	es/es ist/ eller — das soll eine	(direction)
2		was heisst das hier (laughs)	request for clarification
3	H:	ein kleines loch	answer
4		ahja — das verstehe ich	metacomment
5		(non-verbal)	execution

(Text VI, 6/8 Appendix 2)

Similarly, the instructee can ask for clarification. If the addressee of this request does not make sure that his interlocutor understands the information he gives, the communication is in danger of breaking down, as in the following example. Instead of giving a direct answer or a further explanation, the instructor partially repeats the instruction. This procedure, which at a first glance seems incomprehensible, will be easier to understand after our discussion of a model of the communication process.

1	S:	Dann machst du ein Loch mit deinem Daumen	direction
2	H:	Ein Loch	request for clarification
3	S:	Ein Loch	partial repetition of direction
4	H:	Was ist das	request for clarification
5	S:	Mit der Tum[+]	direction
6		Mit dem Daumen	repair
7	H:	Ich nicht verstehen nicht	metacomment
8	S:	Dein Daumen	direction
9		Dein Daumfinger[++]	repair
10	H:	Daum mit	request for clarification (implied in repetition)
11	S:	Mit der Daumfinger	direction
12	H:	das tykke der [+++]	request for clarification
13	S:	Ja	answer
14		Machst du ein Loch drein	direction
15	H:	(non-verbal)	execution
16	S:	Ein schönes Loch drein machen	direction
17	H:	(non-verbal)	execution
18	S:	Dein Daumen du nimmst	direction
19	H:	(non-verbal)	execution
20	S:	Ja	evaluation

(Text VII; [+] from English *thumb*; [++] from Danish *tommelfinger* (German: *Daumen*); [+++] Danish *tyk* (German: *dick*); Danish *der* (German: *da*)

Some preliminary linguistic considerations

Within the instruction pattern, the direction is particularly interesting from a linguistic point of view. It consists of at least a two-place predicate:

```
pred      (arg. , arg.)
do        (you , X )
```

and can be realized in various ways (as a semantic paraphrase):

(1)   Nimm eine weisse Platte.
       Zuerst nimmst du eine weisse Platte.
       Kannst du eine weisse Platte nehmen?
       Mit der weissen Platte . . .
         . . .

As a consequence of the highly structured nature of the communication, everything the instructor says is taken up as either an instructional move or an evaluation — depending on whether it occurs before or after an action performed by the instructee.

This functional determination of the utterances allows for considerable linguistic reduction while the communicative function is maintained. Utterances like

(2)   Weisse Platte
       Weisse Stein
       Weiss

are interpretable in the context of the instruction even though only the argument or a fragment thereof is verbalized:

```
pred      (arg. , arg.)
ø          ø     weisse platte
                 weisse ø
```

Analysis

Following Rehbein (1977) we conceive of the process of instruction as a complex action process. But as the type of communication we analyse is restricted and somewhat artificial, compared to the communicative situations described by Rehbein, we can simplify his model in some respects (see for instance Rehbein 1977, pp. 16f, 137f, 195f). Thus we can consider the 'plan' a constant, to mention but one example. In the following, we shall explain the communicative model contained in Figure 1 and discuss its adequacy for a description of the communicative processes involved in the verbal instructions.

The speaker (S) has to reach a prescribed *action goal* ('Handlungsziel') by following a pre-established plan of action. The plan

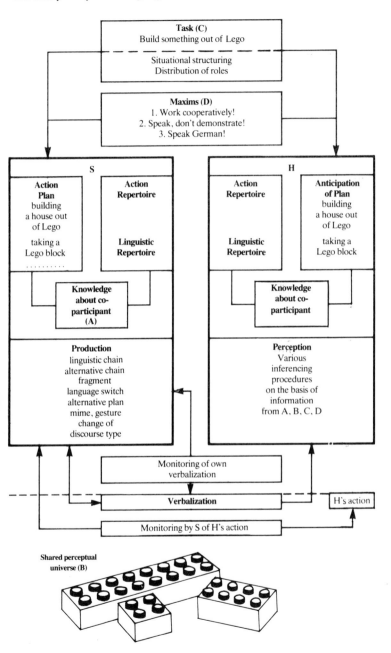

Figure 1

is broken down into a number of steps, each of which leads to a sub-goal. By taking these steps, the speaker reaches the overall goal. However, it is not clear to what extent the individual steps are fully specified in the overall plan. It is striking that in the instructions, the experimenter does not describe the action goal (house-building) just as he does not specify the function of the individual intermediate steps. He typically describes the action which the instructee has to perform without specifying the function of this action relative to the overall goal. This, on the contrary, is what the subjects do several times, as can be exemplified from Text VI (Appendix 2): build a house, make a roof, put a chimney on top. The instructor in this way guides the comprehension of the instructee in a goal-oriented way. Undoubtedly, what we have to do with here are strategies of communication which, however, are not immediately related to what is normally termed communication strategies in the literature. Similarly, the instructee has a certain previously established expectation regarding the speaker's utterance, a goal and plan expectation, which is formed by the *formulation of the task* (C) and information derived from the *shared perceptual universe* (B).

The subjects have linguistic repertoires in several languages at their disposal, which are incorporated into a comprehensive repertoire of actions. They know their interlocutor very well (knowledge of co-participant, (A)), and can take his linguistic knowledge into consideration in executing the plan. They share a perceptual universe, from which they primarily utilize visual information.

From the *formulation of the task* ('S instructs H how to build something out of Lego') one can expect a certain structuring of the situation, functionally distributed roles and, ideally, a specific discourse structure (see above). What is also prescribed through the specification of the discourse are certain maxims of action which the subjects observe:

D(1) Be cooperative

D(2) Explain, avoid non-verbal means of communication

D(3) Speak German, avoid using other languages

In his instruction, the speaker creates a plan relative to a sub-goal, for instance the sub-plan to shape the clay into a ball. In order to represent the plan interactionally (verbalization), he utilizes his repertoire of actions and his linguistic repertoire (we simplify our description at this point in so far as we do not go further into the actual execution plan, see Wagner 1983). Appropriate elements are selected from the repertoire of actions. Appropriacy is a term which can only be defined relative to the situation in its widest sense, i.e. including the interlocutor. By choosing those elements from his repertoire by means of which he can reach his goal in the most optimal way, relative to a specific situation, the speaker proceeds strategically from the very beginning. Communication strategies predetermine the verbal planning, they serve the function of adjusting the plan to the situation, i.e. each individual utterance is to be seen as strategic.

What is specific for IL users is that plans of action cannot be directly converted into verbal plans, because of gaps in the speaker's (and hearer's) linguistic repertoire. The primary function of communication strategies in the speech of IL users is to compensate for this deficit. This does not mean that we accept the emergency theory mentioned above, on the contrary, we want to insist on the interrelationship of all communicative behaviour and emphasize the similarity, but also the difference, between the communication of native speakers and that of IL users. The similarity is caused by the fact that all speakers employ strategies when communicating: native speakers also have gaps in their linguistic repertoires, and consequently there are no strategies which are specific for IL users. Normally, however, IL users have to improvise much more than native speakers and create solutions in their verbal plans in an ad hoc manner. This is particularly so in the area of vocabulary. In the following we shall analyse and describe some concrete manifestations of such strategic improvisations on the basis of the model (Figure 1). The subsequent stage in our research, which we cannot expand on within the limits of this article, will be to analyse whether such improvised solutions do not in fact derive from conventionalized procedures.

We can now demonstrate the ongoing communication process by a few examples from the learner texts. In this way, the adequacy of the model established above can be assessed.

The communicative model in Figure I is simplified in so far as only those components in the process are included which are relevant in the context of the present analysis. We have thus excluded from consideration H's perception apparatus, S's production apparatus, and the interdependence of these.

We have already given an example of a change of plan ('plan shift'): S starts off by giving the instruction for a sub-step which, however, she cannot execute. She therefore switches to an alternative plan by asking H a question.

In the following example, the verbal realization of the reference is insufficient: 'und dann nimmst du der lange gelbe' (Text VI, 8/9). For H, however, this reference is quite sufficient, as he can infer from C and B as well as from the actional context in which this step is located that it must be a Lego block. As there are two types of yellow blocks in his perceptive universe, he needs the specification *lang* in order to establish the correct reference.

In Text VIII, 5, S has established a reference (yellow blocks) without, however, performing a predication. On the basis of the location of the utterance in the discourse, H expects a direction, but S only utters a few hesitation signals (*und, öh*). He thus indicates that he cannot execute the plan due to production difficulties. H understands this and reacts by a tentative execution which, however, turns out to be wrong and is negatively evaluated by S. A similar procedure by S was already to be found in line 3. S had given the ambiguous direction 'bauen du einen mauer', which H misunderstands. S is not able to indicate verbally what H's mistake is, and uses hesitation signals. H has not yet completed the action and can infer from the discourse structure that S is trying to perform an evaluation. As an evaluation is redundant if H executes the action correctly, H can infer a negative evaluation, which he can then ask S to clarify, thereby taking A and D(1) into consideration.

In the example from Text VIII, 5/6, which has just been analysed, S makes a new start after his failed attempt at instruction, by again establishing a reference ('der rote mauer') without, however, specifying what H is supposed to do with the yellow blocks and the 'red wall'. H tries out a tentative action again which is positively evaluated by S (*ja*). But now H has become insecure and indicates this by means of a hesitation signal (*öh*). He verbalizes the predicate (*über*) and gets confirmation from S. (We disregard H's using *über* in his IL instead of *auf*, which would be in accordance with L2 norms.)

'und dann nimmst du das weisse platte . . . — und öh setz / eller macht ein dach' (Text VI, 13/14). S begins by a description of an action which, however, she is unable to execute. In contrast to the example given above, she does not shift to an alternative plan but verbalizes a different aspect of the sub-plan: she names the function ('roof') instead of the action, i.e. she uses a pragmatic paraphrase. This, in combination with the information from B, enables H to infer what he has to do in order to reach the sub-goal of his action. It becomes clear from this example that the individual steps in a plan should not be considered as given sets of information but as action knowledge which can be developed in an interaction. The example transcribed on page 163 above is also easier to understand in the framework of the model. S provides a linguistically complete direction which H, however, fails to understand. H repeats a fragment of utterance (2), the action goal *Loch* ('hole'). Interestingly enough, S responds at first with a mere repetition in (3) and later with an explanation of the tool which H is to use in order to reach the action goal (5, 6, 8, 9, 11). In doing so, S relies on H being able to infer the action goal from the information contained in B after a successful identification of the tool (— after all, what else can one do with one's thumb in a lump of clay but make a hole?). S's strategy proves to be successful: as soon as H, after several attempts, has identified the action instrument (12), he understands the direction 'ein loch machen', although he had wanted to ask for the meaning of *Loch* only a short time ago.

We can therefore conclude that S has a number of strategies at his disposal for executing the sub-plan of his action. In the model, some possibilities are mentioned in the block 'production'. These execution possibilities are to be regarded as alternatives and are not ordered in an empirically established hierarchy. This can only be the result of further investigations, which will then allow for deciding whether or not the following list of strategies is complete:

- the production of a *complete syntactic chain* in IL or L2;
- the production of a *reduced chain*, a fragmentary utterance, while anticipating possible inferences by H on the basis of available information from A, B, C and D. The fragment itself can consist of a predication or of one or several arguments. The necessary inferencing procedures on the part of H can be anticipated on the basis of maxim D(1);
- the production of an alternative (possibly reduced) syntactic chain in IL or L2 in terms of a *semantic paraphrase*;
- the production of an alternative (possibly reduced) chain in IL or L2 in terms of a *pragmatic paraphrase*;
- violation of maxim D(2) and *use of gesture and mime*;
- violation of maxim D(3) and *use of L1 or L3*;
- shift to an *alternative plan*, possibly to linguistically routinized alternative plans like 'asking questions';
- *handing over the verbalization* to H.

The last-mentioned strategy, which we have met in Text VIII in particular, results in a change of the discourse structure, and hence also of the task. The three-phase structure 'direction–execution–evaluation' tends to be converted into a two-phase structure 'attempt at execution–confirmation'. Thereby the action pattern of *instruction* is changed into one of *guessing*. The instructor in this way has a double advantage: the confirmation move involves considerably less linguistic effort than an instruction move, and he can leave the verbalization to his interlocutor. In Text VIII one of the weakest course participants instructs one of the linguistically best students. As the instructor knows that the linguistic potential of his interlocutor is larger than his own, the obvious thing for him to do is to leave the task of verbalization to the interlocutor.

Hesitation phenomena, which are extremely frequent in these text types, function as indicators of plan or strategy shifts. Under hesitation phenomena we include unfilled and filled pauses, false starts and non-phonemic lengthenings of speech sounds. In addition to these, L1 elements mark points at which the plan is changed: in our case, the learners primarily use *eller* ('or') or *nej* ('no') as metacommunicative signals.

In addition to marking plan shifts and to indicating problems in converting a plan into verbal or other modes of production, these elements indicate the effect of monitoring processes in speech production. The speaker in Text VIII corrects himself particularly often: the verbal product is seen as diverging from the norm of the foreign language and is repeated in a more correct form. In these cases of self-interruptions, hesitation phenomena or L1 elements occur frequently.

In the speech of IL speakers we can observe the following phenomena with a particularly high frequency, although the same phenomena also appear in the speech of native speakers:

- a frequent change of strategies in connection with the production of plans or sub-plans. The verbal strategies are of particular interest for IL research and should be analysed independently of other strategies.
- a change in the type of discourse, induced by the speaker's knowledge of his interlocutor. In this way the linguistically better-equipped interactant is charged with an increased load of verbalization;
- an emphasis on ensuring mutual comprehension, primarily on the part of the 'better' interactant (cf. Wunderlich 1976).

Appendix 1

Instructions

clay pot

1. Nimm eine gute Handvoll Tonmasse und forme daraus eine Kugel, indem du den Ton zwischen deinen Händen rollst.
2. Jetzt drückst du mit dem Daumen ein Loch in die Kugel, aber nur so tief, dass noch ein Boden erhalten bleibt. Das Loch darf nicht ganz durchgehen.
3. Versuche jetzt, die Öffnung auseinanderzuziehen, indem du den Daumen im Loch lässt und mit den übrigen Fingern deiner Hand drückst und ziehst.
4. Mit der anderen Hand drehst du die ganze Zeit den Tonkörper und machst auf diese Weise das Loch immer grösser.
5. Wenn das Loch gross genug ist, machst du die Innen- und Aussenwand mit den Fingern schön glatt.

house out of lego

1. Nimm eine weisse Platte und lege sie auf den Tisch.
2. Nimm die roten Klötze und baue am Rande der Platte eine geschlossene Mauer, so dass in der Mitte ein Loch entsteht.
3. Nimm einen gelben Klotz und setze ihn auf die lange Seite der roten Mauer. Nimm den anderen gelben Klotz und setze ihn auf die andere lange Seite. Auf den beiden kurzen Seiten sind jetzt zwei Öffnungen.
4. Nimm die zweite weisse Platte und lege sie oben auf das, was du gebaut hast, so dass sie passt.
5. Nimm den letzten Klotz und stelle ihn genau auf die Mitte der weissen Platte.

Appendix 2

ISAK Instruktion VI

1. s: Esther – öh – wir sollen ein – öh – ein haus bauen mit diese –
    H:

2. s: legosteine   und – öh – du nimmst – öh – die – grosse weisse
    H: ja

3. s: platte   ja (lachen)
    H: ja – es wird ein kleines haus sein   die weisse

4. s: ja und dann nimmst du – öh – allen die – roten steine –
    H: platte

5. s: ja   dann s/öh baust du ein – schönes
    H: die alle   was mach ich jetzt

6. s: mauer –   ja –– so es/ es ist / eller – das soll
    H: so hier rund

7. s: eine – kleines/öh was heisst das hier (lachen)
    H: ein kleines loch

8. s: ja   so und dann nimmst du – der
    H: ahja – das verstehe ich – so

9. s: lange gelbe – und   nur die eine ja   und setzt
    H: nur nur die eine   ja

10. s: auf die lange seite –   und dann nimmst du
    H: ja –   so

11. s: ja und dann nimmst du die andere – lange gelbe
    H: ja

12. s: und setzt auf die lange seite   ja
    H: auf die andere lange seite   ja

13. s: und dann nimmst du – das weisse – platte
    H: und was jetzt   aha

14. s: un öh – setz – / eller macht ein dach –   ja
    H: so

15. s: ah ah wir sind nicht fertig (lachen)
    H: ist das schön   naa

16. s: öh – und so sollen wir auch eineeeee – sorn/schorn/schornstein
    H: schornstein

17. s: (lachen) und öh das ist die gelbe da   ja   und das
    H: das ist die kleine

18. s: soll – öh – in die ganze mitte – sitzen
    H: ganze mitte dann muss

19. s: ja   ja   ja – ich bin zu
    H: ich öh zählen   ja – so   das gut

20. s: frieden (lachen)
    H: das ist gut danke

ISAK Instruktion VIII

1. s: du bist öh –/nej dann du tagen einee – weisse platte –
    H: ja
2. s: und – mit öh die rote – /die rote öh klössen öh bauen – du einen
    H:
3. s: mauer –– –9– ah – ähm   ja das ist falsch
    H: ja   ist es falsch
4. s: öh – ganz ganz   ja –6–
    H: mmh   ah – ganz herum   so
5. s: ja und dann tagen du – die lange gelbe klös/klodsten ––
    H:
6. s: und – öh – nej und der – raute/rot/rote mauer –
    H:
7. s: ja   ja   gut ja – sehr gut
    H: öh über   ja
8. s: –– und dann – öh – tagen öh du die/dann tagen du –öh – nej
    H:
9. s: (lachen) die weite –/ die weisse – plat   un öh legt
    H: ja ––
10. s: über – die gelbe – klöste ja   dann – tagen du die/öh
    H: ja
11. s: – der kei/kleine – öh – gelbe kloste – und öh setzen –
    H:
13. s: mit öh – on der weisse platte ––   ja
    H: so   dann wird es gemacht
14. s: sehr gut danke   ja
    H: ist das alles   ja – nich so viel

Notes

1. Here, and in the following utterance, segments are used in the analysis. The segmentation is based on the functional determination of the utterance. The examples are ordered according to: number of segment, indication of discourse participant (s or H), segment, function of segment.

References

Glahn, Esther (1980). 'Introspection as a Method of Elicitation in Interlanguage Studies', *Interlanguage Studies Bulletin Utrecht*, **5**, 119–128.

Palmberg, Rolf (1979). 'Engelska som målspråk — finska och finlandssvenska Kommunikationsstrategier', in Linnarud, Moira and Svartvik, Jan (eds.), *Kommunikativ kompetens och fackspråk*, Lund: Läromedelscentralen, 137–149.

Rehbein, Jochen (1977). *Komplexes Handeln*, Stuttgart; Metzler.

Tarone, Elaine, (1977). 'Conscious Communication Strategies in Inter-
. language', in Brown, H. Douglas, Yorio, Carlos and Crymes, Ruth H.
(eds.), *On TESOL '77*, Washington, D.C.: TESOL, 194–203.
Wagner, Johannes (1983). *Kommunikation und Spracherwerb im Fremdsprachenunterricht*, Tübingen: Narr.
Wunderlich, Dieter (1976). *Studien zur Sprechakttheorie*, Frankfurt:
Suhrkamp.

10 How a story is done in a second language

Hans W. Dechert

1 Introduction

The history of science, according to Thomas Kuhn (Kuhn 1970), is not a steady accumulation of knowledge. It is rather characterized by rapid changes which take place from time to time when an old paradigm is destroyed and replaced by a new one. Paradigm shifts reflect scientific revolutions. Just as is the case with political revolutions, they are initiated by only a few people who realize that the questions and methodology they have are no longer represented by the old paradigm. What may demand a revolution of scientific thought for one group of scientists may not be noticed at all by others. Yet revolutions are necessary so that new problems are seen and new solutions proposed.

In a well-known article with the title 'Toward a Third Metaphor for Psycholinguistics' (1974), George Miller has taken up this idea and outlined a short history of psycholinguistics. To him it comprises three successive stages each designated by a particular paradigm.

The first stage in the history of psycholinguistics is marked by the *association* paradigm. Until 1950 connections between words and things were sought. Psycholinguistics concentrated on the study of vocabulary and vocabulary growth. To learn a language was to learn associations between words and concepts.

But language is more than words. In the 1950s *communication* became the new paradigm. It signalled a shift of interest from words to sentences. A new grammar describing sets of syntactic rules had to be developed. These rules determine language in communication. To learn a language was to learn how to communicate according to grammatical rules.

Yet language is more than lexicon and syntax. The third paradigm which may announce a new stage in the development of psycholinguistics is the *computation* paradigm. As a result of the information processing revolution that has profoundly influenced the history of the language sciences, it stands for the procedures performed when language is used. Languages are processed in terms of programs which compute the linguistic data. To learn a language means to learn words and sentences, but also to learn the procedures to retrieve and process them. To know a language means to have both declarative and procedural knowledge.

Internal procedures of mental processing can of course not be observed directly. What can be observed are the temporal variables (pauses, hesitations, drawls) involved as well as the deficiencies (errors) in the linguistic output at the periphery of the system. Internal mental processes can moreover be simulated with the help of computers. The resulting models of computation can be used to model and explain the mental procedures possibly involved in producing language. This is the methodological implication of the computation paradigm.

The notion of *strategy*, widely used in different scientific contexts with quite different connotations (cf. Færch and Kasper, Part One, this volume; Raupach, 1981), to us basically refers to procedures (not associations, not rules) involved in using language. Procedures ('strategies') are means for 'performing a task as being composed of a fixed set of elementary information processes that are evoked by both aspects of the external environment and the internal representation of the problem' (Simon 1979, p. 85). On the following pages we shall mainly focus on the internal aspects of the problem.

In our analysis of a second-language speech sample from the Kassel corpus, we are interested in what procedures on what levels of representation are actually activated by a second-language speaker in the performance of a special task. What we would like to know is what this learner does when telling her story.

In order to analyse and understand such a complex phenomenon, it must be decomposed into a number of elementary operations or routines working on different levels.

Schemata or scripts, in spite of some criticism, are generally agreed to represent prototypical structures of knowledge within a certain culture. They are based on the experience of prior events and organize the perception, memorization and reconstruction of new events (and the episodes out of which they are formed). Schemata and scripts provide the material and the procedures for our expectations. They are plans for understanding, for acting, and for talking about events.

For reasons of distinction, we shall use the term *schema* for narrative schema only, the term *script* for a knowledge source in which knowledge of the world is organized.

The recent discussion on interlanguage (IL) communication has not only suffered from the fact that it has been dominated by the communication paradigm, but also that IL communication has been considered as an isolated phenomenon *sui generis* especially connected with the notion of erroneous behaviour (cf. Raupach, this volume). Of course there are, for instance, reduction strategies used in IL communication that help to reach communicative goals. But there certainly are reduction strategies in L1 production, too, indeed, primarily so. Since, from a psycholinguistic point of view, there is only one language processing system, the question of what insight into language production procedures we can get by looking at productions in various languages (L1 and L2) seems to be more interesting than concentrating on IL production only, as long as we know so little about language processing in general.

However, 'understanding is not an all-or-none affair. One can speak of degree, range, and depth of understanding' (Simon 1979, p. 472). It is our hope that the following analysis which tries to follow the computation paradigm will contribute to an understanding of the procedures ('strategies') involved in the production of interlanguage.

2 The speech sample

2.1 *Subject*

The following speech sample of Christa, at the time a twenty-two-year-old English major at the University of Kassel, was recorded in November 1978 as part of a student's assignment in a seminar on language production. This assignment aimed at the replication and possible improvement of elicitation tasks in the Goldman-Eisler vein, the verbalization of cartoons.

Before attending the University of Kassel, Christa had had nine years of English in high school (Gymnasium) and in the course of her language studies at university about one year of intensive language training by different English and American native speakers of English. This is important to know as most of the errors occurring in Christa's production seem to be of a very elementary nature, probably not expected by many people. There can be no doubt that it is the high level of complexity of such a task and the high processing load caused by it which are responsible for the tremendous planning problems and errors quite frequently to be found in such productions.

During her last two or three high school years, Christa had occasionally written reproductions of orally presented narratives. She had no experience in oral narrations elicited by pictures, nor had she taken any courses in text linguistics. In 1980 she passed her final examination with above average grades. Just recently she has begun her teacher training.

2.2 *Elicitation*

In our recent attempts to elicit second-language productions under conditions that come close to being natural and at the same time allow normal planning problems (which we are especially interested in) to occur, the dog-and-raven cartoon (cf. Text 2) has proved particularly useful in that it creates various processing problems for advanced second-language speakers of English.

The cartoon represents two scripts, the dog-eating-his-food script and the theft script. On the basis of all the data we have collected, it seems to offer the following difficulties:

- Since there is no verbal information such as title of story, keywords relating to meaning, captions translating the scenes, utterances of the characters involved, etc., the verbalization task is not prompted.
- The first scene (the *setting*) and the last scene (the *resolution*) in the cartoon clearly illustrate the beginning and end of the action. Scenes 2 to 5, based on exactly the same pattern, present in minute detail the slowly progressing *complication* of the action. They are overcomplete and thus more difficult to describe.
- The complication and resolution of the story as to the dog's entangling himself with the rope shown in scenes 5 and 6 of the cartoon is physically impossible. It is really a *deus ex machina* resolution!
- There are only three props involved in the story: the stump, the rope and the dog's food. All of them are obligatory; they are 'outstanding details' in Bartlett's sense of the term (Bartlett 1932). At least in two cases, however, the drawing is rather vague; one can hardly recognize what exactly the dog is

fastened to, and what it is he is fastened with. This situation causes search problems. The third prop, the dog's food, presents an additional problem. What's the word for 'dish', that the dog eats from (or out of)? Or is the object's real name the generic word 'food'? And if so, would that be the proper level of utility determined by this particular context (cf. Brown 1958)? The specific dog-eating-his-food script, and the vocabulary expressing it is, as we have learnt from our data, quite unfamiliar for an average non-native speaker of English who is not a dog lover.

– The second script is a very special case of the theft script concerning the pathway which leads to the exchange of property in the end. The bird's trick of using the dog's excitement and rage to make him unaware of what's going on around him until he is finally fixed to the pole, combined with his own ability to defer the badly desired gratification until the very end while not doing anything except walking around the dog, all this is perhaps easier to analyse than 'just' to tell from an onlooker's perspective.

– The two characters, the dog and the bird (raven), cause difficulties for German speakers from a linguistic point of view as far as the attribution of grammatical gender is concerned, not only because of possible interference from their L1, but also because of the problem of differentiating between the pronouns referring to dog and bird after their introduction and reintroduction in each episode.

– The animals' actions quite vividly resemble human behaviour and thus invite the narrator in a very special way to identify with one of them, the winner or the loser. The cartoon is likely to evoke projections, thereby adding a new dimension to language processing problems.

2.3 *Procedure*

The cartoon was presented to Christa (as well as to the other students taking part in the task) in printed form (18 cm × 24 cm, each picture representing each scene), all six scenes making up the story at once, so that before starting to speak she would understand it and plan her production as a whole. No additional information was given besides a standardized instruction that she should verbalize the cartoon. While speaking, she could look at the pictures in front of her. Everything was done to create as informal an atmosphere as possible, although she knew that we wanted as good productions as possible. There were no interruptions (pauses) during the recording except the ones listed in the transcript (cf. Text 3). The recordings were transcribed by an experienced student assistant and myself independently. The resulting transcripts were compared; discrepancies were discussed; mistakes and omissions were corrected.

The following is the non-segmented, edited version of Christa's production:

Text 1

a little dog is sitting in the garden and he's tied um on a piece of wood with a long rope and in front of the dog there is um food and a big bird is come flying down and it wants to eat the food but the little dog gets very angry and tries to catch the bird but the bird is very clever and runs around the piece of wood and the little dog is running after the bird and he's getting always angrier and while he's running around the wood his rope is becoming shorter and shorter and in the end he's bended to the wood and um he can't move any more and the bird eats his um it hit its food.

A synopsis of the corresponding passages in Christa's production with the six scenes in the cartoon reveals the close relationship between the pictures and the resulting verbalization (Text 2).

2.4 *Analysis*

2.4.1 *Schemata*   It is true that such a synoptic comparison between the cartoon and Christa's story, as suggested above, may disclose the correspondence between the pattern of the elicitation format and the pattern of the product. However, such a comparison does not say anything about the processing of the text. If we take the non-verbal boundary markers: falling intonation contours and pauses, as well as speech errors and their corrections, as indicators of units of planning — an approach which we have described elsewhere (Dechert 1980a, b; cf. also Chafe 1980a, b; Labov and Fanshel 1977) — we come to the following segmentation, quite different from the one suggested by the synopsis above (Text 3).[1]

Text 2

A little dog is sitting in the garden and he's tied on a piece of wood with a long rope. And in front of the dog there is food. And a big bird is flying down and it wants to eat the food.

But the little dog gets very angry and tries to catch the bird.

But the bird is very clever and runs around the piece of wood.

And the little dog is running after the bird and he's getting always angrier. And while he's running around the wood his rope is becoming shorter and shorter.

And in the end he is bended to the wood. And he can't move any more.

And the bird eats its food.

Text 3

1.1 A LITTLE DOG IS SITTING IN THE GARDEN
1.2 – AND HE'S TIE:D –– u:m ––––– ON A: – PIECE OF WOOD WITH A LONG ROPE //
2.1 ––– AND IN FRONT OF THE DOG ––– THERE IS u:m ––––– FOOD //
3.1 –––– AND A BIG BIRD IS ––– come FLYING DOWN
3.2 –––– A:ND ––––– IT WANTS TO: EAT THE FOOD
3.3 –––– BUT THE: LITTLE DOG GETS VERY ANGRY
3.4 ––– AND TRIES TO CATCH THE BIRD //
4.1 ––– BUT THE BIRD IS VERY CLEVER
4.2 –– AND RUNS AROUND THE PIECE OF WOOD
4.3 AND THE LITTLE DOG IS RUNNING AFTER THE BIRD
4.4 –––– AND HE'S GETTI:NG ––– ALWAYS ANGRIER //
5.1 –––– A:ND WHILE HE'S RUNNING AROUND THE WOOD
5.2 ––– HIS ROPE IS BECOMING ––– SHORTER AND SHORTER
5.3 –––– AND IN THE END ––– HE'S BENDED TO THE WOOD
5.4 ––– A:ND um HE CAN'T MOVE ANY MORE
5.5 AND THE BIRD EATS his um it – hit – ITS FOOD //

This narrative schema of Christa's production has five episodes. It is not identical with the schema of the cartoon, which consists of six scenes. In spite of the large number of deficiencies and elementary errors in Christa's production, the underlying narrative schema has an astonishingly concise and coherent structure, as Text 4 shows (cf. Rumelhart 1975, 1977; De Beaugrande and Colby 1979):

Text 4

Episode 1: Identification of setting

Identification of protagonist	A dog
Identification of location	In the garden
Identification of problem state	The dog is tied to a pole with a rope.

Episode 2: Identification of problem object

| Identification of object | The food |
| Identification of owner | The dog |

Episode 3: Creation of problem state: complication

Identification of antagonist	A bird
Identification of goal state	The bird wants to eat the food.
Reaction of protagonist	The dog gets angry and tries to catch the bird.

Episode 4: Transition from problem state to goal state

Identification of pathway to goal state	The bird is clever and runs around the pole.
Identification of preventing action	The dog runs after the bird.
Result of preventing action	The dog is getting angrier and angrier.

Episode 5: Achievement of goal state: resolution

Achievement of pathway to goal state	The rope is getting shorter and shorter. The dog is fixed to the pole and can't move.
Achievement of goal state	The bird eats the food.

It is our *first assumption* that second-language narrations such as Christa's, at least in those cases in which the narrator's L1 and L2 belong to the same or a similar narrative tradition such as German and English, are generated from an underlying meta-linguistic processing procedure that may be activated in L1 as well as in L2.

The narrative schema as revealed in Text 4 above is Christa's own contribution to the task. It enables her to reconstruct the rather difficult visual input quite well. The accessibility of such a narrative-processing schema gives her the necessary degree of freedom to deal with other, lower level, yet highly complicated second-language specific processing problems. Their solution demands the activation of special knowledge sources to deal with lexical search, interference mechanisms, pronominalization routines, etc.

2.4.2 *Islands of reliability* If one looks carefully at the seg-mented version of Christa's production (Text 3), one finds, generally speaking, two types of stretches of speech, those that are marked by hesitations, fillers, drawls, and corrections, and others which run smoothly and fluently. Native-like utterances such as:

SHORTER AND SHORTER (5.2) or
AND IN THE END (5.3) or
AND IN FRONT OF THE DOG (2.1) or
AND TRIES TO CATCH THE BIRD (3.4) or
BUT THE BIRD IS VERY CLEVER (4.1) or
A LITTLE DOG IS SITTING IN THE GARDEN (1.1), etc.

make up 'islands of reliability' in the flow of speech. This is a term that has been used by Lesser and Erman (1977, pp. 794f) in their retrospective description of the Hearsay-II system, a computer architecture to simulate speech-understanding processes. Understanding speech (just as producing speech) may be modelled in terms of hypothesize-and-test actions. According to this notion there must be points in the speech data to be analysed and understood to anchor this search. In the Hearsay-II system such 'islands of reliability' have successfully proved to initiate hypothesis testing procedures on the word level of processing and above.

The computation metaphor 'islands of reliability' exactly describes procedures of language production as well. One who sets out to plan and execute speech must try to anticipate and develop such islands. They may then become the basis for search processes necessary in the course of planning and executing speech, in L1 as well as in L2.

It is our *second assumption* that the production of any language, L1 or L2, is to a large degree based on such 'islands'. To speak a language competently means to have control over a large repertoire of such islands; to learn a language, to acquire an ever-increasing number of knowledge sources which may form such islands.

We would hesitate to call the kind of language used to build 'islands of reliability' 'prefabricated' or 'formulaic'. However, language production may be much less the result of creative construction processes than we have thought for a long time. If we did not have particular knowledge sources from which to retrieve formulae as anchoring points, we could not activate the procedures necessary to develop and test the hypotheses which are needed.

We are not taking up the association paradigm again; we are rather talking about knowledge structures that have been tentatively paraphrased with expressions like frames, scenes, clichés, etc. (cf. Fillmore 1979). At present we seem to know little about them and their function in the production of language. They will have to form an important chapter in a performance grammar of language not yet written (cf. Bates and MacWhinney 1981).

2.4.3 *Lower-level processes*   Other passages in Christa's production display deficiences. The troublesome search, development and testing of alternative or competing plans not easily accessible are obvious in utterances such as:

– AND HE'S TIE:D –– u:m ––––– ON A: – PIECE OF WOOD (1.2)
or ––– AND IN FRONT OF THE DOG ––– THERE IS u:m ––––– FOOD
(2.1).

Since there is planning in language production which is not re-vealed by pauses, errors, etc., we cannot say for sure what under-lying processes are actually taking place. Nor does one know what stage in their development from thought into speech these plans have reached. It is very likely — for reasons we have stated before — that the two examples above disclose lexical search pro-cesses. In the first case it is probably the concept finally para-phrased with the expression PIECE OF WOOD for which a word is needed. In the second example, the concept for which the generic term FOOD is at last chosen causes the search.
Only in:

line 3.1 AND A BIG BIRD IS ––– com[ing] FLYING DOWN

and in:

line 5.5 AND THE BIRD EATS his um it – hit – ITS FOOD

the false starts and their corrections reveal overtly competing plans, namely:

coming vs. FLYING

his vs. ITS

As the two cases of interlingual interference:

ON (German 'an') A PIECE OF WOOD (1.2)

and:

HE IS GETTING ALWAYS ANGRIER (German 'immer ärgerlicher) (4.4) nevertheless show, we may often observe the activation of plans (or at least the failure to suppress them) even in cases where there is no unequivocal evidence such as in lines 3.1 and 5.5. L1 and L2 knowledge sources quite often compete with each other, not only in the language of beginners, and certainly not only on lexical and syntactic, but also on 'strategic' levels (cf. Bates and MacWhinney 1981).

The competing plans hypothesis (CPH) (Baars 1980; cf. also Butterworth 1980; Garrett 1980; Dechert, in press) developed by Baars, provides a theoretical description of language processing which does not consider errors as deviations to be avoided but as a necessary ingredient in the system. According to the CPH, the competition of speech plans is responsible for the various disrup-tions, disfluencies and errors which occur not only in the speech of second-language learners but of any speaker whatsoever. This competition of speech plans is the result of the complex architecture of executive systems that 'work better if there are intelligent semi-autonomous sub-systems "with a will of their own" so that they can adapt flexibly to local changes' (Baars 1980, p. 49). We cannot avoid the errors and hesitations in our speech. They are the price we pay for the great flexibility and adaptability of the cognitive and linguistic system through which we master reality. The sub-systems on lower levels which cause the production problems we have help us at the same time to deal opportunistically with our processing problems on the way. Two examples from Christa's production illustrate this.

2.4.3.1 *Example 1*   The wrong grammatical structure ALWAYS ANGRIER in line 4.4, as mentioned before, is suggested by the L1 model *immer ärgerlicher*. It is not just a slip since it is preceded by a lot of hesitating and the prolongation in GETTI:NG, which provide a relatively long time to plan and to revise planning. Since Christa has used the adjective ANGRY before in line 3.3, she might want to avoid it for reasons of stylistic variation. If so, the result would indicate that she has not found an alternative plan or has turned it down if she had one. Alternatively, she might want to use it but not be able to retrieve it. As to the wrong grammatical construction ALWAYS ANGRIER, the fossilized form instead of the correct one breaks through, although Christa knows the rule, as shown in line 5.2: SHORTER AND SHORTER. Sub-routines successfully activated in one place need not necessarily be accessible in another place. There may be a third problem she has, although there is no overt indication for the validity of this argument. The comparison of the monosyllabic 'short–shorter' is quite in correspondence with Christa's L1 model. There is no internal competition between L1 and L2 concerning the model. However, the adjective ANGRY may be compared either way, *angrier* or *more angry*, and thus the choice between the two may present a production problem, especially in the particular context where it is not the simple compared form *more angry* but either the form *more and more angry* or the more common form *angrier and angrier* that is required.

As we have found in many other cases of L1–L2 interference, it is not just the simple linguistic overlapping of L1 and L2 forms which causes competition of speech plans and eventually errors but rather the overload of processing problems that makes fossilized forms break through. This explanation might also make Christa's error ON in line 1.2 plausible.

It is our *third assumption* that too high a processing load in the speaker, caused by too many sub-processes initiated in too short a time, without an island 'nearby' to jump on, may cause a breakdown in the sub-system involved, which will be the source of errors, such as interference errors. The system may be restored through the activation of other knowledge sources on the same or different level(s).

2.4.3.2 *Example 2*   Finally we would like to discuss the most interesting passage in Christa's text which particularly exemplifies the enormous complexity of decision-making during the processing of a story in a second language. It illustrates, as just mentioned, that data and concept-driven processes on various levels are occasionally necessary to solve problems which arise through the breakdown of sub-routines.

Throughout the text Christa makes a clear distinction between the two main characters of the story with respect to their grammatical gender:

    1.1–2 A LITTLE DOG ... HE'S TIED ON
    3.1–2 A BIG BIRD ..... IT WANTS TO EAT

This strategy of consistently contrasting referential choices, i.e. of keeping the two opposing characters linguistically apart with the help of gender attribution and pronominalization, can be observed in later episodes as well. Theoretically lines 4.3–4 would run easily with 'he' ellipted:

    AND THE LITTLE DOG IS RUNNING AFTER THE BIRD
    AND IS GETTING MORE AND MORE ANGRY ...

But after the mention of *bird* Christa seems to feel the necessity to reinstate the distinctive referent *he*:

    AND HE'S GETTING ...

For this reason the planning problems she has in the final line 5.5 of the text are quite surprising and incomprehensible at first:

    AND THE BIRD EATS his um it – hit – ITS FOOD.

Within the frame of reference set up by this line the following seven underlying plans are theoretically possible:

    Plan 1 The bird (it)   eats 'his (the dog's) food.
    Plan 2 The bird (it)   eats 'its (the dog's) food.
    Plan 3 The bird (he)   eats 'his (the dog's) food.
    Plan 4 The bird (he)   eats 'its (the dog's) food.
    Plan 5 The bird (he)   eats his (the bird's) 'food.
    Plan 6 The bird   'eats it   (the food).
    Plan 7 The bird (it)   eats its (the bird's) 'food.

The first four plans make sense only if the possessive pronoun in question carries contrastive stress. This does not seem to be the case. Therefore Plans 1 to 4 seem to be irrelevant, although we admit that because of the disruptions in our sample it is hard to trace the suprasegmental cues.

It is true that the subject's gender in Plan 5 (as well as in Plans 3 and 4) does not correspond with the gender attributed to *bird* in the preceding parts of the text. Since Plan 5, however, provides one plausible theoretical explanation for the alternative *his* tested in line 5.5 it should be discussed. Plans 6 and 7 stand for two other relevant options:

Text 5

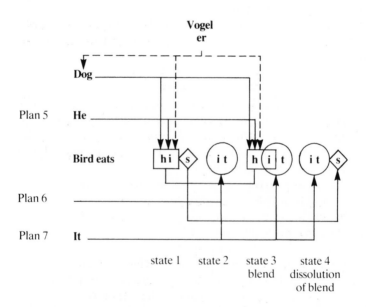

The early abandonment of the version *his*, which in the referential network of the preceding text clearly refers to *dogs*, demonstrates that Plan 5, from a semantic point of view is an irrelevant solution: this is not what Christa wants to say. But why is this plan developed and executed? And why does it reappear in the blended form *hit*?

Plan 6, because of being dropped, proves to be only a theoretical possibility. The second state therefore does not stand for the completed pronoun *it* referring to *food*. It rather represents an incomplete state of development on the way to the intended final form *its*, whose referent is *bird*.

The competition revealed in line 5.5 of Christa's text is therefore one between Plan 7 *The bird* (*it*) *eats its* (*the bird's*) *food*, and a plan with the pronoun '*his*' as the centre. We do not know if this plan is identical with Plan 5.

Unfortunately, very little is known about the mechanisms leading to blends, they 'are something of a puzzle' (Garrett 1980, p. 211). The only thing we may say about the blend *hit* in our example is that Plan 5 (or any other going along with the pronoun *his*) seems to be a strong one, hard to discard. Ambiguities such as the one in our sample are a well-known phenomenon in the speech-error literature (cf. Baars 1980, p. 46ff). They are considered to be the consequence of complexity in the language processing system. In any case, the speech sample in line 5.5 illustrates quite convincingly how 'sub-systems occasionally escape from executive control' (Baars 1980, p. 48). The following considerations are intended to give a number of hypothetical explanations for the breakdown and restoring of speech planning in Christa's production:

Text 6
1. The dog (*protagonist*)

Episode 1

| 1.1 | A little dog | Introduction |
| 1.2 | He | |

Episode 2

| 2.1 | The dog | Reintroduction |

Episode 3

| 3.3 | The little dog | Reintroduction |
| 3.4 | (He) | (Ellipsis) |

Episode 4

| 4.3 | The little dog | Reintroduction |
| 4.4 | He | |

Episode 5

5.1	He
5.2	His
5.3	He
5.4	He
5.5	his (?)

2. The bird (*antagonist*)

Episode 3

3.1	A big bird	Introduction
3.2	It	

Episode 4

4.1	The bird	Reintroduction
4.2	(It)	(Ellipsis)
4.3	The bird	

Episode 5

5.5	The bird	Reintroduction
5.5	Its	

3. The food (*problem object*)

Episode 2

2.1	Food	Introduction

Episode 3

3.2	The food	Reintroduction

Episode 5

5.5	Its food	Reintroduction

The preceding referential network discloses a number of interesting aspects illuminating the planning problems in line 5.5. Although the dog and the bird appear equally often in all six scenes of the cartoon, and although the bird is the true initiator of the action and the winner who teaches the dog a lesson, and although the dog is the affected party and the loser, Christa explicitly mentions the dog almost twice as often as the bird. Her production is rather a dog than a bird story, rather a tragedy than a comedy. This may be partly suggested by the cartoon itself. In the sequence of scenes the dog gets more and more into the centre of the action which is going on around him. The carefully worked out pattern of introduction and reintroduction through the use of the noun phrase with the indefinite or definite article at the beginning of the episodes is given up only once at the transition from episode 4 to episode 5. The use of the inexplicit referential pronoun in line 5.1 contrary to the previously established pattern presupposes an anticipated tacit understanding that it is *he* who by now has become the real hero who is talked about. The dog script is dominant throughout the production; it is particularly active in episodes 4 and 5. In the face of the fact that the bird in line 5.5 has not been mentioned during the preceding five lines, the prevailing predominance of the dog script offers one hypothesis for the occurrence of the slip *his* and the breakdown of planning.

Additional hypothetical evidence for a description and explanation of the processing difficulties in line 5.5 comes from a different point of view. The dog is obviously the character who Christa identifies with. She not only sees and tells the events of the story from his perspective but makes it quite clear whom she favours and whom she opposes.

It is true that the dog in the cartoon is a bit smaller and the bird a bit bigger than dogs and birds usually are in comparison with each other. However, it remains remarkable that Christa perceives the slight distortion and makes an issue of it. She uses her observation for the important purpose of differentiating between the two characters, in contrast with real life but corresponding to the role they play for her in the story:

A LITTLE DOG VS. A BIG BIRD.

The attribute *little* of course is more than a characterization of size and of function in the story-world. It is an expression of empathy for the dog that is robbed.

The long uninterrupted sequence of inexplicit pronominal reference in lines 4.4 to 5.4 furthermore creates an atmosphere of emotional warmth, after the referent *dog* has been talked about from the very beginning. There is little distance left between the story-world in which *he* suffers and the real world in which the narrator fondly talks about and suffers with *him*.

Our third hypothesis on the possible cause of the breakdown in the final line of Christa's production is derived from a collision of planning strategies that she might become aware of at precisely this point. As we have seen, from the very beginning she has adopted the masculine gender for dog and the neutral gender for bird. But can one really speak of the *little* he-dog and the *big* it-bird? Shouldn't it be the other way around? For this reason the slip-of-the-tongue *his* is·quite justified in spite of everything else that has been said before. The grounds for the dropping of that plan nevertheless remain unquestioned.

Our fourth hypothesis is based on the semantics of the cartoon story. In the end the bird is beginning to eat the dog's food. The bird has achieved the goal he has so intelligently and constantly pursued. Is this the message? Or is it rather to demonstrate the dirty tricks with which honest and decent people are cheated, however hard they try to resist them? And moreover, as to the story's moral, whose food is it in the end from a theoretical point of view? Does the bird's tricky action justify the exchange of food? Is it really its? Or does he just eat it, although it is still his? The answers to these questions are left open. The ambiguity necessarily connected with the open ending may be another reason for Christa's processing problems.

And finally, given that L1 knowledge sources have some potentially interfering effect in L2 narrative productions, even of advanced speakers such as Christa, it does not seem impossible that the L1 plan *der Vogel* might have some influence in line 5.5 in connection with the particular emotional and cognitive stress the narrator has to cope with here. This hypothesis gains some support from the fact that the correct use of the possessive pronouns in English on an advanced level presents a particular problem for speakers whose L1 is German. Already in line 2.1 the long hesitations and the filled pause might partially go back to the attempt to solve the problem just delineated. The solution that is found:

––– AND IN FRONT OF THE DOG ––– THERE IS u:m ––––– FOOD

does not seem to be one which proves full knowledge and control of the problem.

In line 5.5 there is no overt evidence for a competition between possessive pronoun and definite article preceding *food*. However, it seems to us quite plausible that the awareness of an editing problem potentially resulting from an L1 interference mechanism which may have been experienced in line 2.1 may contribute to the heavy load in line 5.5.

3 Conclusion

In order to identify, analyse and describe the processes and sub-processes contributing to the short narrative production of an advanced speaker of English, we have tried to decompose it on different levels of representation. Such an approach at present cannot avoid being approximative and tentative. There are passages of the production that have not been discussed, errors that have not been explained. There can be no doubt that the very small sample we are dealing with does not provide the grounds for making any generalized statements reaching beyond this sample. We hope, though, that we were able to demonstrate the theoretical relevance of the computation paradigm as well as its richness and explanatory power.

A first attempt to formulize our basic assumptions would look like this:

Processing levels

The fully elaborated narrative *schema* in our sample, which is not identical with the visually stimulated schema of the cartoon, stipulates the overall structural frame of reference for the production. It is most likely to represent a basic metalinguistic cognitive structure.

The two *scripts* comprise lower-level cognitive and linguistic knowledge structures through which knowledge of the world may be retrieved and activated.

Formula-like linguistic units of various lengths and syntactic structures provide the material for building islands of reliability. These may serve as anchoring points or the implementation of sub-processes which deal with left-over, lower-level processing problems such as *lexical* search, interference mechanisms, pronominalization routines, etc.

Partially independent knowledge sources or modules of knowledge sources take over the instantiation of these sub-processes, which have certain degrees of freedom. Eventually they are the cause of breakdowns of the sub-systems which must be restored (cf. Hayes-Roth and Hayes-Roth 1979).

Planning and telling a story for these reasons appears to be a multidirected top-down and bottom-up process. Because of its extreme complexity and difficulty it must necessarily be opportunistic, having the freedom to be creative as well as erroneous.

Notes

1. The symbols used stand for:
   pauses   –   up to 300 msec.
                – –   up to 500 msec.
                – – –   up to 1 sec.
                – – – – up to 1.5 sec.
                – – – – – longer than 1.5 sec.
   filled pauses   um
   drawls   :
   unit-final intonation contours   //
   small letters   fillers and abandoned plans

References

Baars, Bernard J. (1980). 'The Competing Plans Hypothesis: An Heuristic Viewpoint on the Causes of Errors in Speech', in Dechert and Raupach (1980) 39–49.

Bartlett, Frederic C. (1932). *Remembering: A Study in Experimental and Social Psychology*, Cambridge University Press.

Bates Elizabeth and MacWhinney, Brian (1981). 'Second Language Acquisition from a Functionalist Perspective: Pragmatic, Semantic and Perceptual Strategies', in Winitz, Harris (ed.), *Native Language and Foreign Language Acquisition,* New York: New York Academy of Sciences, 190–214.

Brown, Roger (1958). 'How Shall a Thing Be Called?', *Psychological Review*, **65**, 14–21.

Butterworth, Brian (1980). 'Introduction: a Brief Review of Methods of Studying Language Production', in Butterworth, Brian (ed.), *Language Production: Speech and Talk*, Vol. **1**, London, New York: Academic Press, 1–17.

Chafe, Wallace L. (ed.) (1980a). 'The Pear Stories: Cognitive, Cultural, and Linguistic Aspects of Narrative Production, in Freedle, Roy O. (ed.), *Advances in Discourse Processes*, Vol. **3**, Norwood, New Jersey: Ablex.

Chafe, Wallace L. (1980b). 'Some Reasons for Hesitating', in Dechert and Raupach (1980) 169–180.

De Beaugrande, Robert and Colby, Benjamin N. (1979). 'Narrative Models of Action and Interaction', *Cognitive Science*, **3**, 43–66.

Dechert, Hans W. (1980a). 'Pauses and Intonation as Indicators of Verbal Planning in Second-Language Speech Production: Two Examples from a Case Study', in Dechert and Raupach (1980), 271–285.

Dechert, Hans W. (1980b). 'Contextual Hypothesis Testing Procedures in Speech Production', in Dechert, Hans W. and Raupach, Manfred (eds.), *Towards a Cross-Linguistic Assessment of Speech Production*, Frankfurt: Lang, 101–121.

Dechert, Hans W. (in press). 'The Competing Plans Hypothesis (CPH) Extended to Second-Language Speech Production', in Di Pietro, Robert J. (ed.), *Selected Proceedings of the First Delaware Symposium on Language Studies*, Newark, Delaware: University of Delaware Press.

Dechert, Hans W. and Raupach, Manfred (eds.) (1980). *Temporal Variables in Speech: Studies in Honour of Frieda Goldman-Eisler*, The Hague: Mouton.

Fillmore, Charles J. (1979). 'On Fluency', in Fillmore, Charles J., Kempler, Daniel and Wang, William S.–Y. (eds.), *Individual Differences in Language Ability and Language Behavior*, London, New York: Academic Press, 85–101.

Garrett, Merrill F. (1980). 'Levels of Processing in Sentence Production', in Butterworth, Brian (ed.), *Language Production: Speech and Talk*, Vol. **1**, London, New York: Academic Press, 177–220.

Hayes-Roth, Barbara and Hayes-Roth, Frederick (1979). 'A Cognitive Model of Planning', *Cognitive Science*, **3**, 275–310.

Kuhn, Thomas S. (1970). *The Structure of Scientific Revolutions*, University of Chicago Press.

Labov, William and Fanshel, David (1977). *Therapeutic Discourse: Psychotherapy as Conversation*, New York: Academic Press.

Lesser, Victor R. and Erman, Lee D. (1977). 'A Retrospective View of the Hearsay-II Architecture', *Proceedings of the 5th International Joint Conference of Artificial Intelligence*, Vol. **2**, Cambridge, Mass.: Massachusetts Institute of Technology, 790–800.

Miller, George (1974). 'Toward a Third Metaphor for Psycholinguistics', in Weimer, Walter B. and Palermo, David S. (eds.), *Cognition and the Symbolic Processes*. Hillsdale, New Jersey: Lawrence Erlbaum, 397–413.

Raupach, Manfred (1981). 'Production Strategies in L2 Performance', in Dechert, Hans W. and Raupach, Manfred (eds.), *Psycholinguistic Models of Production*, Norwood, New Jersey: Ablex.

Rumelhart, David E. (1975). 'Notes on a Schema for Stories', in Bobrow, Daniel and Collins, Allan (eds.), *Representation and Understanding: Studies in Cognitive Science*, New York: Academic Press, 211–236.

Rumelhart, David E. (1977). 'Understanding and Summarizing Brief Stories', in LaBerge, David and Samuels S. Jay (eds.), *Basic Processes in Reading: Perception and Comprehension*, Hillsdale, New Jersey: Lawrence Erlbaum, 265–303.

Simon, Herbert A. (1979). *Models of Thought*, New Haven, London: Yale University Press.

Part Three
Problems in analysing communication strategies

The empirical studies reported on in the preceding section illustrate a wide range of procedures in analysing communication strategies. The two articles included in this section focus on the methodological aspects and discuss some of the problems which confront the IL researcher in his investigation of strategic IL speech production.

In the article 'Analysis and evaluation of communication strategies', Raupach demonstrates how difficult it can be to detect planning problems and to identify the specific nature of these on the basis of performance data only. The occurrence of temporal variables like unfilled and filled pauses, lengthening of syllables, false starts and repetitions can shed some light on where IL users experience planning problems and how they go about solving them by means of communication strategies, but such analyses of performance data are inevitably rather inconclusive. One reason for this is that temporal variables offer indirect, and not necessarily complete, evidence about the planning and execution of speech — hence the need to supplement analyses of performance data by introspective evidence. Another reason is that little is still known about the specific occurrence of temporal variables in IL speech production. To obtain more information about this specific question, Raupach advocates comparative studies of temporal variables in the learner's L1 and in his IL, in the L2 as used by native speakers, and in the IL as used by the same learner in different tasks and at different stages of learning.

The problem of how to identify communication strategies on the basis of performance features is also the main topic of our contribution 'On identifying communication strategies in interlanguage production'. We argue that the difficulty of the analyst's task varies with the stand one takes in defining communication strategies: if they are defined in interactional terms exclusively, the analytical problems are minor compared to a — broader — psycholinguistic concept: in the latter case, the analyst has to rely to a large extent on 'strategy markers', i.e. signals indicating that the IL user has adopted a communication strategy in order to solve a communicative problem. Starting off by a survey of how performance features like temporal variables, self-repairs and slips have been used as indicators of planning and execution in studies of L1 speech production, their potential function as strategy markers in IL production is discussed. It is suggested that it is not so much the type or the distribution of performance features as the increased frequency and co-occurrence of different features that indicate strategic IL use.

We conclude our contribution by a discussion of the interactional function of strategy markers, which are reinterpreted as 'signals of uncertainty'. For the interlocutor, these signals may function as more or less direct appeals for assistance, which explains why many communicative problems in interactional situations between a learner and a native speaker are often solved on a cooperative basis. We point out that in order to save 'face', learners may prefer to find solutions themselves to their problems and hence opt for non-cooperative strategies. This leads on to the hypothesis that advanced learners in particular will be able to predict communicative problems and find solutions at normal planning points in their discourse. A methodological consequence of this is that performance data will be increasingly unsuited for the analysis of communication strategies the higher the proficiency level of the learner. Hence the need, as also pointed out by Raupach, for the development of alternative methodologies.

11 Analysis and evaluation of communication strategies

Manfred Raupach

The concept of communication strategies in second-language (L2) performance implies at least two major difficulties for the analyst of textual data.

1.   In contrast to the notion of strategy as it is defined in cognitive psychology (Bruner, Goodnow and Austin 1956; Simon 1979), the concept of communication strategies in L2 is closely related to the idea of erroneous or non-native-like behaviour. Occasionally communication strategies are equated with errors, as can be seen by Richards' (1973) statement: 'Under communication strategies we may include errors which derive from the fact that heavy communication demands may be made on the second language...' (cf. also Selinker 1972).

   In any case, classifications like that presented by Færch and Kasper (this volume) suggest that communication strategies in L2 mostly lead to non-native-like performance — this is true for all reduction strategies — or to a change, if not to the abandonment, of the learner's original communicative goal.

   The relationship between communication strategies and errors reflects a fundamental problem the analyst has to face if he tries to elicit L2 performance: as the learner's activation of 'successful' strategies usually passes unnoticed, the best way to discover underlying mental processes consists of analysing deviant utterances, including hesitation phenomena and other signals of uncertainty (see further Færch and Kasper, Part Three, this volume). But a satisfactory interpretation of those indicators often requires some introspective comments made by the learner on his own performance.

2.   Whereas in cognitive psychology or in ongoing psycho-

linguistic research on L1 perception and production (cf. Bever 1970; Bierwisch 1975) strategies can be qualified according to their results, an evaluation of communication strategies in free L2 performance is much more delicate. Obviously, such an evaluation could have a great impact on the teaching of second languages; but it is difficult to see how the analyst can claim some strategies to be better than others. In the following, we want to discuss some textual data in view of these difficulties, basing our analysis on the current definition of communication strategies in L2 performance. We then propose to enlarge the given definition. Finally, we shall concentrate on the evaluation of communication strategies. The examples cited below belong to a corpus of learner language collected within the KAPPA-Project at the Gesamthochschule Kassel. They are taken from French (L2) productions of German undergraduate students, who had had French in school for several years and who had normally spent some months in France (for further specification see below). The given examples stem from two different types of L2 performance: from an interview the subjects had with a native speaker and from the re-telling of a story, the original French version having been presented to the subjects in written form.[1]

1 Analysis

In a first approach, we adopt the definition given by Færch and Kasper (Part One, this volume), according to which 'communication strategies are potentially conscious plans for solving what to an individual presents itself as a problem in reaching a particular communicative goal'.

The assumption of what the learner feels to be a problem in his planning a discourse is the central notion of this definition. So, there are at least two objectives in analysing communication strategies in language learner data: specifying the problems the learner faces, and describing the strategies he chooses.

As for the specification of the learner's planning problems, the analyst meets great methodological difficulties. Since the planning problems are not directly accessible, the analyst is dependent, in the first place, on the indicators that reflect the learner's attempts at problem-solving. It must be taken for granted that only a small part of the decision-making processes show up in the textual data in a way that allows an adequate interpretation. In

most cases the analyst must content himself with collecting hesitation phenomena and other implicit signals of uncertainty.

Here is one example taken from the corpus of story-tellings in
L2:

(1)   L²: *mais* elle n'a pas /0.8/ elle n'a pas réussi /0.5/ à /0.7/
         trouver euh /0.4/ la maison /1.9/ euh /0.7/ alors elle
         /0.6/ *euh* /0.8/ elle a /0.8/ pendant 1 . . . /0.4/ses /0.3/
         prochaines vacances ⁄ elle a essayé de n . . . elle est
         partie de nouveau ⁄ /1.4/ et /8.0/ elle est /1.1/ elle a
         cherché dans la région de Paris ⁄ /0.6/ (. . .) et /0.4/
         elle l'a trouvée ⁄ la /0.4/ la maison ⁄ /0.4/ (. . .)

This paragraph contains a number of hesitation phenomena
such as unfilled (= silent) pauses, filled pauses, lengthening of
syllables, false starts, self-corrections, repetitions, etc. It should
be mentioned that there are no generally accepted definitions of
those 'temporal variables' (cf. Dechert and Raupach 1980a), the
case of unfilled pauses being particularly instructive: up to now,
there has been a lively discussion about the cut-off point of unfilled pauses, that is to say what should be the minimum length of
a pause if it is to be regarded as such. The most relevant point at
issue concerns, however, the fact that most investigators have
studied the observed phenomena in isolation and mainly on the
sentence level (cf. Dechert and Raupach 1980b). Restrictions of
this kind necessarily lead to questionable descriptions of speech
performance. In addition, the temporal variables, which should
include suprasegmental and paralinguistic features and which
should be analysed in connection with non-verbal signals, can
only convey a sort of first impression that the learner was having
some problems in his verbal planning, but they do not give evidence of the kind of problem he had.

So, in example (1), the surprisingly long pause of /8.0/ seconds
leaves the analyst without information about the specific problem
the learner has experienced when planning and editing the passage in question. According to the learner's own interpretation,
this pause reflects the difficulty she was having, at this point of
her narration, in recalling the plot of the story. The reason for
this momentary lapse of memory must be seen in connection with
another major problem the learner had been preoccupied with
during the planning of the whole paragraph, namely to avoid, for
stylistic reasons, the repetition of the phrase *trouver la maison*
she had used several times before in her narration. In this case,

only the information given by the learner can enable the analyst to advance plausible arguments that may help to explain why this paragraph, compared with the rest of the learner's narration, shows so many signs of hesitancy. Obviously enough, the learner's communicative behaviour, that is her trying to meet certain stylistic standards and her taking the risk of making relatively long pauses, is strongly influenced by the specific task of re-telling a story.

As stated above, the description of a learner's planning problems, if at all possible, constitutes only the first part of an analysis of communication strategies in the given sense; it is the prerequisite for the ensuing identification of strategies. There are, of course, different ways of classifying them. If the analyst is primarily interested in the mental activities the learner displays in the presence of planning difficulties, examples like (2), (3) and (4), which give evidence of lexical search problems and their solving strategies, may be helpful:

(2)   L: euh /0.4/ non je veux /0.6/ je *veux* appuyer⟋sur euh /0.6/ le Sprachpraxis euh le /0.8/ euh pra... pratiquement de /0.3/ euh /0.4/ de language je *veux* me pratiquer beaucoup en français /0.8/ (...)

(3)   L: je trouve pas u...u.../1.0/ un très grand différence ⟋ mais /1.4/ peut-être les cartes les b⋮...les tickets⟋pour 1 ... pour le /0.3/ pour la RU (...)

(4)   L: et en plus les cartes les billets⟋/0.4/ les euh plutôt les tickets /0.6/ poure le RU⟋c'était pas tellement /0.3/ non plus cher /0.4/ c'était (...)

Examples (2), (3) and (4) are taken from the same interview. They reveal the learner's tendency to solve her retrieval problems under strong influence of her L1. In (2) she opens the series of different trials with a lexical borrowing from German (*Sprachpraxis*), in (3) and (4) her first proposal, *carte*, is a negative transfer from German (*Karte*). It is curious to note that the sequence of hypotheses tested in (3) and (4) is the same, although there is an interval of several minutes between the occurrence of the two passages in the interview. Examples of this kind may yield some insight into the organization of the learner's internal lexicon. Analyses carried out in such a psycholinguistic spirit must, of course, be integrated into a theory of speech production, the development of acceptable theories in this domain still being one of the most challenging tasks.

Another way of looking at communication strategies consists of describing them as a function of the interrelationship between the speakers. The classification then leads to a distinction between direct and indirect appeals which the learner addresses to his interlocutor (cf. Færch and Kasper. Part Three, this volume):

(5)   L: et je veux peut-être faire je sais pas la récolte ↗ou
            je ne sais pas comment ça s'appelle (. . .)
      NS: la vendange

(6)   L: je trouve que c'est plus strict /0.3/ dans les cours
            /0.6/ toujours le /0.4/ euh /0.8/ l'enseignement ↗
            frontal ↗/0.5/ je sais pas si on peut dire ça mais le
            professeur est en est avant ↗devant ↗(. . .)

(5) and (6) belong to the same interview as the preceding examples. In both cases, the learner's uncertainty, which is signalled through the rising intonation (*récolte ↗; l'enseignement ↗frontal ↗*), is verbalized in such a way that the interviewer may or may not feel the obligation of responding to it. Whether the learner's communicative behaviour has functioned as an appeal is only dependent on the interlocutor's reaction; thus, the distinction between implicit signals like hesitations, intonation contours, non-verbal signs, etc. and explicitly verbalized signals or appeals loses its importance. If the analyst accepts, for example, the well-attested existence of different types of L2 learners according to their hesitation and speech correction behaviour, he can easily think of describing these learner types as activating different communication strategies. Seliger (1980), for example, proposes a distinction between learners who appear to be primarily planners and others who seem to be correctors. He offers several examples showing that utterance planning and correction behaviour 'serve a communicative function for the L2 learner in his contact with native speakers'.

If a learner's excessive use of temporal variables, like making extremely long pauses, inserting a number of pause fillers, lengthening constantly one's syllables, etc., can be interpreted in a double way, namely in that it gives evidence of the learner's planning problems and, at the same time, may function as an appeal for help from the interlocutor, a similar approach would be valuable in connection with another group of speech phenomena. We want to follow this line of argument with an example from the same learner's data:

(7)   L: elle sonna /0.9/ et toujours elle était désapp . . euh
        /0.3/ frustée quoi /0.4/ (. . .)

The final particle *quoi*, added in a lower voice, reveals that the
learner has experienced some problems when planning the preceding part of her speech: according to her own comment she had
anticipated difficulties with the pronunciation of the form *désap-
pointée* and was looking for a substitute. But the final *quoi* may
also be taken as an appeal to the interlocutor to accept the given
version, although the learner herself does not seem to be fully
satisfied with it; this can be seen from the indistinct articulation of
the substitute *frustrée*.

Similar examples from the same learner are:

(8)   L: elle s'est demandée s'il y a encore des /0.4/ gens *en*
        euh Paris ⬈ /0.3/ dans les provinces ⬈ /0.9/ qui qui /0.4/
        croyaient encore à 1 . . . /1.6/ euh /0.8/ euh /0.4/ aux
        fan . . . fantômes ⬈ fantômes quoi ⬊ /0.5/ (. . .)

(9)   L: euh elle a voulu savoir qu'est-ce qui euh qui est qui
        c'est qui ⬈ /0.8/ euh *les* /0.9/ propriétaires et si elle
        pouvait /0.8/ visiter cette /0.3/ ce château quoi ⬊ /0.8/
        (. . .)

In both examples the final *quoi*, combined with a falling intonation, again reflects foregoing planning difficulties and indicates
simultaneously that the learner now regards the problem as being
solved, leaving it to the interlocutor to accept the final version or
not. If comparable phenomena occur with a certain regularity in a
learner's performance, as is the case here, the analyst is justified
in describing them as communication strategies.

This view leads us to introduce into the discussion additional
forms of communicative behaviour that we feel have been
neglected so far. Our data show that many of our learners prefer to
rely constantly on a limited number of communication patterns.
They manifest the learner's general attitude when communicating
in L2. We are inclined to assign to these forms of behaviour the
status of communication strategies. Before discussing this view in
more detail, let us look at some examples:

(10)   NS: oui mais sinon comment se passait le quotidien ⬈
        L: le quotidien ⬈
        NS: à l'intérieur de la cité /0.3/ les rapports avec les
            autres ⬈
        L: les rapports avec les autres ⬈

(11)   NS: oui est-ce que pendant ces trois mois tu as eu des dif-
               ficultés d'argent ⁄ par exemple
        L: des difficultés d'argent ⁄/0.5/ pff (. . .)

(12)   NS: qu'est-ce que tu as constaté là-bas
        L: là-bas ⁄
       NS: dans la réaction des gens là-bas
        L: des gens /0.4/ pff (. . .)

One of this learner's favourite responses is, in case of uncertainty, to repeat the final part of the interviewer's utterance.

(13)   L: parfois il y a des accidents ⁄ et c'est /0.3/ terrible ici
           mais en France ce n'est pas terrible /0.6/ s'il y a *un*
           petit peu cassé /0.4/ la voiture quelque chose comme
           ça /0.8/ ça lui est euh /0.9/ c'est égal pour eux (. . .)

(14)   L: et bon euh /1.0/ et je ne sais pas si je dois payer je
           crois pas /0.3/ que je dois payer (. . .)

This learner, identical with that of examples (2) to (9), prefers to repeat literally a preceding phrase (*ce n'est pas terrible*; *je dois payer*), thus avoiding the problems a possible variation — for example using a pronoun — might have brought about.

The frequent use of (*ou*) *quelque chose comme ça* (see example 13) is another characteristic feature of this learner's performance. Here are some more examples:

(15)   L: c'était tellement difficile de les convaincre ou quel-
           que chose comme ça

(16)   L: je vais pas exag . . . exagérer ou quelque chose
           comme ça

(17)   L: que je veux euh /0.6/ comprendre quelque chose sur
           la littérature ou quelque chose comme ça

There are, of course, still other frequently recurring strings in this learner's performance, like *je crois* (*pas*) with a falling intonation, indicating the end of an utterance, or (*ça*) *c'est vrai*, introducing several responses to the interviewer's contributions.

The analysis need not be restricted, however, to fixed expressions as they occur in the examples cited above. So, the same learner's story-telling becomes very monotonous owing to the overuse of a single linguistic structure: most of the sentences are introduced by (*euh*) (*et*) *elle a/est* + past participle, the pronoun *elle* referring to the central figure of the short story:

(18)   L: elle est entrée╱avec sa voiture (. . .)
              elle desc . . . elle est descendue de sa voiture (. . .)
              elle a commencé à parler (. . .)
              et cette femme elle elle demande elle a demandé
              (. . .)

These phenomena are not necessarily linked only to specific
planning problems nor can they be described as being mostly
erroneous. They belong to the learner's repertoire and are always
at his disposal. They ought not to be neglected in an analysis of
communication strategies.

2 Evaluation

Although it is generally accepted that analysing temporal variables
and other possible strategy markers is a promising approach for
understanding mental activities involved in language processing,
we are still in need of models of speech production that account
systematically for differences between L1 and L2 performance.
All we know is that, in general, free elicited L1 performance,
too, is anything but 'fluent' in the sense of 'ideal delivery of
speech'. The following examples, offered by two French students
re-telling the same story as our German learners, may serve as an
illustration:

(19)   NS: et ce serviteur lui dit que la mai . . . le le château que
              ce petit château est à vendre╱/0.6/ non à louer╱par-
              don /0.6/ le château est à louer╱/0.7/

(20)   NS: c'est que ses propriétaires sont qui l'ont quittée╱/0.4/
              parce qu'ils se sont aperçus qu'elle était hantée╱/1.8/
              et euh /2.8/ hantée euh /1.4/ hantée par cette fille le
              l'homme qu . . . à qui en f . . . en face de qui elle se
              trouve /0.8/ lui dit que /0.6/ l'en . . . la la maison était
              hantée par elle-même╱/3.3/ euh /8.8/ euh c'est tout //

A more detailed analysis of our data[3] leads to the following
assumptions: the distribution of possible strategy markers in L1
differs markedly from that in L2 performance. This may indicate
that, on a certain level of language processing, L1 speakers have
other units in planning their discourse than learners of that
language.

Not only the distribution, but also the nature of some hesitation phenomena and communication strategies does not seem to

be the same in L1 and L2 performance. Our learners usually do not master the language-specific use of phenomena like drawls, filled pauses, repetitions, etc. as they can be observed in L1 performance; this is true, above all, for non-verbal behaviour. In contrast to these phenomena, certain forms of communicative behaviour are mostly learner-specific and only exceptionally activated by native speakers; among these are code-switching, ruptures, certain types of word coinage and paraphrase, direct appeals, etc.

However, the results obtained by comparative descriptions of communication strategies must not too readily be generalized. The analyst can hardly account for the variety of factors, including variables, that may have influenced the communicative behaviour of the speakers. Hence, a detailed description, based on a large corpus of a single learner's data, may yield more valuable information, especially when the analyst can rely on several types of text produced by the same learner. Thus it is surprising to note how much an individual learner changes his planning and communicative behaviour with a given task. Instead of illustrating this observation by comparing in some detail the story-telling and interview data of an individual learner, we prefer to draw attention to two other types of comparative analyses. Our data allow us to compare L2 productions of learners at the beginning and at the end of their one-term study at a university in France. Whereas the interviews following the stay abroad showed no appreciable progress in the learners' command of grammatical structures, there generally was a considerable change in the use of communication strategies. We shall confine ourselves to a collection of expressions and forms of verbal behaviour one of the learners seems to have newly acquired during her stay in France. In cases of uncertainty she now was able to insert time-gaining fillers like *si on veut*, her reactions to the interviewer were much more spontaneous and idiomatic (frequent use of *ça c'est sûr; oui c'est ça; je trouve que*...), and she made use of devices that were helpful in structuring her discourse (*donc*; *oui*...*mais*; *en ce qui concerne*), etc.

The last form of analysis we want to mention is the comparison of a learner's L1 and L2 performance. We believe that some forms of communicative behaviour in a learner's L2 performance can be adequately interpreted only in light of his L1 behaviour. The correspondence between these two modes of communication often is quite considerable. This holds not only for the kind and the distribution of temporal variables indicating that the learner's planning processes in L1 and L2 are, in some way, comparable, but is also true for the use of certain expressions that serve communicative functions. This means that many factors that constitute a learner's fluency in his L1 (cf. Fillmore 1979) are liable to occur, in one form or another, in the learner's L2 performance.

To summarize in short our proposals concerning the analysis and evaluation of communication strategies in L2 performance: The analysis should be based not only on the learner's erroneous or non-native-like behaviour, but should account for the activation of 'successful' strategies as well. The analysis should be carried out with reference to other relevant data, the learner's own L1 behaviour being one of the most valuable sources of information.

Notes

1. The short story to be retold was 'La maison' by A. Maurois; it appeared in 1946 in Paris in the collection *Toujours l'inattendu arrive*.
2. In the examples, the following conventions are used: L = learner; NS = native speaker; / = unfilled pause, the figures between two dashes indicating pause length in seconds; euh = filled pause; italicized syllables = lengthening, drawl; ↗ ↘ = intonation contour.
3. The corpus consists of language productions of 15 French students and 30 German students of French.

References

Bever, Thomas G. (1970). 'The Cognitive Basis for Linguistic Structures', in Hayes, John R. (ed.), *Cognition and the Development of Language*. New York: John Wiley, 279–352.

Bierwisch, Manfred (1975). 'Psycholinguistik: Interdependenz kognitiver Prozesse und linguistischer Strukturen', *Zeitschrift für Psychologie*, **183**, 1–52.

Bruner, Jerome S., Goodnow, Jacqueline J. and Austin, George A. (1956). *A Study of Thinking*, New York: John Wiley.

Dechert, Hans W. and Raupach, Manfred (eds.) (1980a). *Towards a Cross-Linguistic Assessment of Speech Production*, Frankfurt: Lang.

Dechert, Hans W. and Raupach, Manfred (eds.) (1980b). *Temporal Variables in Speech. Studies in Honour of Frieda Goldman-Eisler*, The Hague: Mouton.

Fillmore, Charles J. (1979). 'On Fluency', in Fillmore, Charles J., Kempler, Daniel and Wang, William S.-Y. (eds.), *Individual Differences in Language Ability and Language Behavior*, New York, London: Academic Press, 85–101.

Richards, Jack C. (1973). 'Error Analysis and Second Language

Strategies', in Oller, John W. Jnr. and Richards, Jack C. (eds.), *Focus on the Learner*, Rowley, Massachussetts: Newbury House, 114–135.

Seliger, Herbert W. (1980). 'Utterance Planning and Correction Behavior: Its Function in the Grammar Construction Process for Second Language Learners', in Dechert and Raupach (1980a) 87–99.

Selinker, Larry (1972). 'Interlanguage', *IRAL*, **10**, 209–231.

Simon, Herbert A. (1979). *Models of Thought*, New Haven, London: Yale University Press.

12 On identifying communication strategies in interlanguage production

Claus Færch and Gabriele Kasper

The following samples of learner language[1] contain words which it can be difficult to explain within an IL analysis: *babysitter* in (1), *durance* in (2), *men* in (3), and *sprog* in (4):

(1)   L: every Monday I erm – er I'm *baby –– sitter* –
      NS: aha
      L: babysitter
      NS: yer –
      L: is that right –
      NS: yer you er – you're a babysitter and you go
           babysitting –
      (PIF)

(2)   NS: I don't know if you can learn much in three days
      L: why not –– just I think it's not a a a question of the –
           durance ––
      (BO)

(3)   L: I think I better like to maybe (laugh) I really don't
           know *men* maybe I better like to live there than er –
      (PIF)

(4)   L: I think that erm when you are going to speak a erm –
           erm – erm – a *sprog*
      NS: yeah a language yeah
      (PIF)

As the word *babysitter* is a correct English word, it would be fairly obvious to consider it part of learners' IL vocabulary if it occurs in their IL performance. This, however, is not necessarily the case, as illustrated by (1): the learner appeals to her interlocutor for information about the word — which happens to be the most widely used Danish word for *babysitter*. Consequently, there exists the possibility that the learner in (1) does not have *babysitter* as part of her *IL* vocabulary but uses it as a strategy in order to communicate her intended meaning.

In (2), one might be tempted to establish a (non-existing as seen from a L2 point of view) lexeme 'durance' (meaning *duration*) as part of the learner's IL. But the word could also be described as an ad hoc form, created by the learner in order to fill a perceived gap in her IL vocabulary (cf. the pauses before and after the word).

The word *men* (Danish for *but*) in (3) occurs without any indication of the learner being uncertain about using the word, in contradistinction to *sprog* (Danish for *language*) in (4), which is preceded by a series of hesitations and pauses. One would therefore be more ready to characterize *men* as automatic rule application than *sprog*, the usage of which seems to be connected with some uncertainty by the learner. But this does not mean that *men* is necessarily part of the learner's IL system — an alternative (and more likely) explanation is that *men* is a 'slip', produced because of it being highly automatized within the learner's L1.

On the basis of these examples, we obtain the following possibilities for analysing language learner data:

(a) the data have been produced on the basis of the learner's IL system;

(b) the data have been produced on the basis of a system different from the relevant IL system and more highly automatized than this (typically the L1 system);

(c) the data have been produced as a result of the learner having made use of a communication strategy.

As the learner's IL system is the result of various learning strategies, one of which is interlingual transfer, it may contain elements which are similar to the learner's L1 system. Observing a distinction when analysing IL performance data between such elements (a) and elements which are brought about by the spontaneous transfer of highly automatized L1 rules (b) is no easy matter. Although this is an important, and still largely unresolved, issue in contemporary IL research we shall largely ignore it in this paper and concentrate on the distinction between on the one hand (a) and (b), on the other hand (c).

Two ways of defining communication strategies

The two following definitions of communication strategies have been offered by Tarone and the present authors:

1. 'the term [communication strategy, Færch and Kasper] relates to a mutual attempt of two interlocutors to agree on a meaning in situations where requisite meaning structures do not seem to be shared' (Tarone, Part One, this volume)

2. 'Communication strategies are potentially conscious plans for solving what to an individual presents itself as a problem in reaching a particular communicative goal' (Færch and Kasper, Part One, this volume)

According to the 'interactional' definition offered by Tarone, communication strategies are cooperative in nature: the different linguistic codes (in a wide sense) of the interlocutors necessitate a negotiation of the message as intended by one and perceived by the other discourse participant; the learner and his interlocutor are aware of there being a communication problem which they then attempt to solve on a cooperative basis. This implies that both the problem and its solution must somehow surface in the performance, which enables the analyst to identify communication strategies directly in performance data.

The second, 'psycholinguistic', definition relates to the learner, more precisely, to the problems experienced by the learner in speech reception and in the planning and execution of speech production. The definition makes no claims about the cooperative nature of communication strategies: the strategy adopted by the learner *may* be cooperative, i.e. the learner may try to solve his communicative problem by appealing for assistance from his interlocutor, but this is not a *necessary* condition: the learner may also decide to find a solution himself, without the cooperative assistance of the interlocutor. This implies that the learner may make use of a communication strategy (as defined by the present authors) without signalling to his interlocutor that he is experiencing a communication problem and, consequently, that the presence of a repair on the part of the interlocutor is no necessary condition for the identification of a communication strategy.

One significant difference between the two definitions of communication strategies is hence that communication strategies can be directly identified in performance data according to the interactional definition, whereas this is not always the case with strategies defined on the basis of the psycholinguistic definition. In the latter case, the analyst is forced to rely on indirect evidence to a very large extent. In the following, we take the 'broader' psycholinguistic definition as our point of departure and discuss the problem of indirect identification in some detail. The identification of communication strategies on the basis of the interactional definition will be further discussed below in the final section of the article.

Strategic and non-strategic planning/execution

The psycholinguistic definition enables us to specify the conditions for a particular IL item to be classified as the result of a communication strategy rather than of IL rule application: (1) that the learner has experienced a problem in reaching his communicative goal by means of his available linguistic resources; (2) that the learner has attempted to solve this problem by setting up a strategic plan which may or may not be conscious in the given situation; and (3) that the data in question have been produced on the basis of this plan. Central to the definition is the notion of *problem*. In our article in Part One of this volume we specified *problem* as referring to the situation in which the existing resources are insufficient to reach a desired goal, and this is the way we shall use the term throughout this article.

Problems may crop up both in the planning and in the execution of speech (as discussed below). Whenever we want to refer explicitly to planning or execution in which a problem is involved, we shall use the terms *strategic planning/execution*. The most central task within a psycholinguistic approach to the identification of communication strategies is to find out whether there are specific features of performance which unambiguously indicate that the planning/execution process leading to this performance has been strategic. As a prerequisite for discussing this problem we need to take a look at the related question of what features of performance can be used as indicators of (non-strategic) planning/execution processes in general. This question has been quite extensively investigated in relation to L1 speech production, and we shall summarize those results we consider most relevant for our subsequent discussion of performance features indicating strategic planning/execution.

Performance features as indicators of planning/execution in L1

Speakers pause to breathe — but they also pause to plan what to say next and how to do so. An analysis of the location, frequency and length of pauses might therefore shed light on the planning process leading to speech production. This is the methodological assumption behind psycholinguistically oriented analyses of speech: that certain performance features like pauses and hesitation phenomena can be used as evidence of how planning and execution take place.

The performance features we want to consider in the following fall into three classes: *temporal variables*, i.e. modifications of speech along the temporal dimension; *self-repairs*, i.e. speaker-initiated modifications of already produced speech segments; and finally *speech slips*, usually caused by one speech element affecting another speech element.

1. Temporal variables

Rate of articulation

The rate of articulation is an aspect of, but not identical with, the speed of delivery: the latter comprises the total speaking time including linguistic items and pauses, whereas the former refers to the vocal speech utterances only, excluding pauses. It has been shown that the rate of articulation is unaffected by the complexity of the speaker's intended message but varies according to the degree of automatization of the employed linguistic items: highly automatized items involving less creative activity like set phrases and routine formulae are articulated at a higher speed than items which are not prefabricated but newly organized for a specific communicative intention (Goldman-Eisler 1961a).

Pauses

The effect of pauses on the speed of delivery is considerably stronger than that of the articulation rate. One can roughly distinguish between four types of pauses according to their various functions: articulatory pauses due to stop consonants, inhalatory pauses used for breathing, conventional pauses which are necessary for the correct linguistic interpretation of an utterance, and hesitation pauses. Only the last-mentioned pause type is indicative of underlying speech planning. It has been demonstrated in quite a few studies (see in particular Goldman-Eisler 1968, 1972; Rochester 1973) that hesitation pauses tend to occur both at constituent boundaries and at lexical selection points. This evidence has been taken to indicate two different levels of verbal planning: a syntactic level whose planning units are sentence constituents, and a lexical level on which the formerly unspecified content words are chosen. A distinction is normally made between un-filled (silent) pauses and filled pauses, i.e. pauses which involve some non-lexical vocal cord activity like *er*, *erm*, *uh*, or gambits like turn-internally used starters (*well*) or cajolers (*I mean, you know*) (see Edmondson and House 1981; Færch and Kasper 1982a). Goldman-Eisler (1961b) suggests that filled and unfilled pauses reflect different internal processes: unfilled pauses in-crease with the cognitive difficulty of the task involved, whereas non-lexicalized filled pauses reflect affective states like situational anxiety. However, the exact functions of the various types of pauses are still far from being well-described, as pointed out by Dalton and Hardcastle (1977, p. 37).

Drawls

Like pauses, drawls, i.e. the lengthening of a syllable relative to a speaker's normal syllable length, can be used as time-gaining de-vices for the planning of a subsequent speech unit. We do not know of any investigation into this temporal variable in English, but our hunch would be that drawls typically occur in function words in order for the speaker to gain time for the selection of the next lexical item.

Repeats

Repeats are repetitions which can stretch from a single phoneme up to several words. According to Maclay and Osgood's study (1959), repeats involve function words rather than content words. They thus seem to serve the same function as pauses before con-tent words and drawls: gaining the speaker time at a lexical selec-tion point.

2. Self-repairs

Whereas the temporal variables discussed above primarily indi-cate where planning takes place, self-repairs (including 'correc-tions', cf. Schegloff, Jefferson and Sacks 1977) reveal that the speaker runs into some difficulty in executing his plan, or that he considers the already executed plan insufficient as a means of communicating his intended meaning.

A self-repair (or more precisely, a self-initiated self-completed repair, cf. Schegloff, Jefferson and Sacks 1977) can be placed immediately next to the item to be repaired (the 'trouble source'), or it can be placed at a later point in the same speaker's turn, normally at a 'possible completion point'. In the former case, the self-repair is usually referred to as a *false start*, whereas no generally accepted term exists for the latter type of self-repairs. For lack of a better term we shall refer to these self-repairs which are separated from the problem source as *new starts*. False starts — and to some extent new starts — divide into two classes, dependent on whether the speaker repeats (some of) the context in which the problem source was embedded when correcting it (*I saw a beautiful* A FANTASTIC *film*) or just corrects the item without providing any context (*they sold newspapers* MAGAZINES *in the street*). With false starts, the repeat always involves one or more of the *preceding* words (*I missed the bus* THE TRAIN *this morning*), whereas new starts may involve a repetition of items both preceding and following the problem source (*I hate pea-soup* I LIKE PEA-SOUP *I mean*). In studies on false starts, the terms *retraced* and *unretraced* false starts are normally used with reference to contextualized/non-contextualized repairs, respectively.

Self-repairs are often preceded by filled pauses, the psycholinguistic function of which is to gain time for planning. Lexicalized filled pauses like *I mean, that is* (*gambits*) which occur in connection with self-repairs also have the *interactional* function of being *repair signals* — they communicate to the interlocutor that what follows or what precedes is to be interpreted as a repair on previously communicated information and not as additional information. This is particularly important in connection with new starts as these are typically placed at a possible completion point, i.e. where a new move might begin.

The best-analysed types of self-repairs from a psycholinguistic point of view are the retraced and unretraced false starts. In their study of hesitation phenomena in English, Maclay and Osgood (1959) found that false starts tend to occur more often with lexical words than with function words (i.e. the opposite of what was found to hold true for repeats). Furthermore, they found that the false start is typically unretraced if it occurs with a function word and retraced in connection with a lexical word. This finding can be used an indication of the syntactic constituent not only being a psychologically relevant unit in the planning of speech but also of speakers trying to *execute* syntactic constituents as wholes.

False starts, together with repeats and pauses at lexical selection points, indicate disruptions in the execution of constituent plans. This raises the interesting question in what ways lexical items are represented in these plans. Whereas repeats and pre-lexical pauses indicate that the speaker needs time to establish an articulatory plan for the intended lexical item, false starts could be interpreted as indications of speakers executing articulatory plans which are both highly automatized and semantically related to the intended concept.

One might hypothesize that new starts indicate that the speaker has second thoughts about the adequacy of his syntactic/lexical plan as a means of communicating his intended meaning. This may be a result of a post-execution monitoring process in which the speaker so to speak places himself in the role of his interlocutor and tries to assess whether his already completed utterance will in fact convey what he intended. This brings new starts close to other-initiated self-repairs, where the repair is brought about by interactional feedback (for instance an explicit repair request or a missing uptaking gambit; cf. Færch and Kasper 1982b for further discussion of this point).

3. Slips

Slips of the tongue (*lapses, speech errors*) have been defined as 'an involuntary deviation in performance from the speaker's current phonological, grammatical or lexical intention' (Boomer and Laver 1973, p. 123). Among the most commonly observed slips are anticipations (*particle shift → farticle shift*), perseverations (*a phonological rule → a phonological fool*), reversals (phonemic: *Hockett or Lamb → locket or ham*, lexical: *a tank of gas → a gas of tank*), blends (*dealer/salesman → dealsman, terrible/horrible → herrible*), word substitutions (*my boss's wife → my boss's husband*), and grammatical errors (*the last I knew about it → the last I knowed about it*) (all examples from Fromkin 1973, pp. 243ff).

For almost a century, slips have been considered *the* performance evidence for both the psychological reality of linguistic assumptions and for unobservable planning and execution processes (see Fromkin 1973, pp. 11ff). For instance, the quoted slips of anticipation, perseveration and phonemic reversal indicate that the smallest unit in the articulatory programme cannot be the individual 'word' but must (at least) be the phonemic segment: otherwise the phonemic substitution slips cannot be accounted for. Lexical reversals like *a gas of tank* are evidence that the articulatory programme also contains units larger than individual words: both the lexical items *tank* and *gas* must have been incorporated into the articulatory programme before their reversal (the countable *tank* preceding the uncountable *gas*, as indicated by the indefinite article in the first position of the sequence). From data like this, the psychological reality of the syntactic constituent as a planning unit has been further confirmed (see Clark and Clark 1977, p. 278). Furthermore, the blends mentioned above (*dealsman*, *herrible*) suggest that before the actual selection of a lexical item, alternative realizations for a particular 'slot' are primed (see Laver 1973). Similarly, word substitution slips like *husband* for *wife* indicate that instead of the immediate selection of a specific semantic content, a larger semantic field is activated in the first place from which the speaker then makes his specific lexical choice. Finally, grammatical errors like the regular tense marking of an irregular verb (*knowed*) suggest that lexical and morphological information is stored separately from each other (see also Fromkin 1973, p. 29).

All the performance features listed above occur with high frequency in the spontaneous production of normal L1 speakers. As Goldman-Eisler puts it: spontaneous speech is 'a highly fragmented and discontinuous activity. When even at its most fluent, two-thirds of spoken language comes in chunks of less than six words, the attributes of flow and fluency in spontaneous speech must be judged an illusion' (1968, p. 31). This warning implies that 'fluency', which can be described as the 'transition smoothness' at different linguistic levels (e.g. at the phonetic level between sounds or syllables, see Dalton and Hardcastle 1977, pp. 26ff), is regularly affected by performance features. Precisely to what extent the presence of such features in L1 speech is considered acceptable would be necessary information for establishing a criterion for 'fluency' in IL performance. At present, such information is scarce. It will therefore be difficult to specify which occurrences of performance features in IL production are identical with or similar to L1 production, and which are IL specific. Nevertheless, some investigation into this area has been conducted recently (see in particular the contributions in Dechert and Raupach 1980), which we shall report on in the following section.

Performance features in IL production

It has been shown — and a look at any stretch of spontaneous IL speech will confirm this — that all the performance features mentioned above also occur in IL production. The most comprehensive attempt at matching performance features with the various levels of planning in IL production has been provided by Seliger (1980b). However, as it is not clear from this study to what extent the use of performance features and the planning processes they indicate are learner-specific, we shall not go into it here.

From the perspective of the present article, some relevant questions to ask in connection with the analysis of IL data are:

(a) Does the occurrence of specific performance features in IL differ from their occurrence in L1 speech?

(b) Which IL-specific planning processes can be identified on the basis of performance features?

(c) Which performance features allow for singling out strategic from non-strategic planning?

(a) IL-specific use of performance features

In a study of the performance of Finnish–Finnish, Swedish–Finnish and Swedish learners of English, it was found that their *rate of articulation* in English was slower than that of native speakers of English (Sajavaara and Lehtonen 1980). On the surface of it, this result reflects the fairly obvious fact that learners normally have a lower degree of automatization of their IL than native speakers — thus the rate of articulation is likely to vary with the learner's proficiency level. However, the learner's rate of articulation also seems to vary according to his L1: thus even the most advanced Finnish–Finnish learners of English had a slower rate of articulation than the less advanced Swedish–Finnish learners (Sajavaara and Lehtonen 1980), a finding we interpret as reflecting differences in the rate of articulation of Swedish and Finnish.

Furthermore, it has been established that the frequency and location of *unfilled pauses* differs in IL speech from native speaker production. The distribution of unfilled pauses in German learners' English (Pürschel 1975) and French learners' German (Raupach 1980) followed the pause patterns of the learners' native languages. This is in line with a more general observation made by Grosjean (1980) who concluded from a comparison of the pause patterns in the productions of English and French native speakers that pauses are language-specifically distributed and reflect the structure of an individual language. An interesting case of partial transfer of unfilled pauses is reported by Sajavaara and Lehtonen (1980): they found that Finnish learners of English transferred the *frequency* of unfilled pauses from Finnish into their IL performance. The intraconstituental *placing* of their pauses, however, was an IL-specific feature which could not be attributed to L1 transfer.

We have not found any reports on IL-specific use of *filled pauses* in the literature, but one can hypothesize from casual observation that the 'noises' learners use are likely to be highly automatized elements from their L1 which get transferred into IL production. Thus French learners of English may use the French pause filler [ɜ:] instead of the English equivalents [ə], [əm] or [ɑ] (cf. Landschultz and Stage 1977).

Finally, Raupach observes that French learners of German use *drawls* more frequently in their German thån native speakers do, which is again in accordance with their L1 (1980)

Even though one cannot conclude from the literature that learners always rely on their L1 in using temporal variables in IL, there is certainly a tendency to that effect which can be explained by the high degree of automatization these elements have in speakers' L1. For the analyst, this implies that he/she has to be careful not to overhastily attribute any non-native-like use of temporal variables to specific planning or execution problems the learner experiences when performing in IL: he might simply be transferring his L1 performance behaviour to IL production (see also Raupach, this volume).

Another area of performance features which specifically reflects the situation of the IL speaker is the one of speech *slips*.

In contradistinction to the adult L1 speaker, the IL user's linguistic repertoire at the time of speaking is characterized by (a) the psychological presence of more than one linguistic system; (b) different degrees of availability of rules and items belonging to the IL system. The first characteristic is evidenced by the occurrence of items from another, generally more automatized, language (typically the learner's L1) in the speaker's performance, as the occurrence of the Danish conjunction *men* in the utterance of a Danish learner of English, quoted above (example 3). In contradistinction to L1 slips of content words (see Fathman 1980 for examples), slips in the area of L1 gambits and exclamations often remain uncorrected: they seem to escape the speaker's attention

in self-monitoring. This indicates different degrees of 'habitu-
alization' of L1 elements, as mentioned in connection with performance features in L1 production, and thus a different likeli-
hood for them to 'interfere' with IL production.

Apart from automatic language switch, the learner's L1 might
function as a basis for the spontaneous selection of IL elements
which the learner, when monitoring, can self-correct. This is illustrated in example (5):

(5)   L: I only know Simon was asked to *bring* er to to take
            along some good records
        (BO)

The verb *bring* is likely to be selected on the basis of German
bringen, which would be the obvious word to use in a German
context. Its formal similarity and partial functional equivalence
makes the item *bring* highly salient so that the learner produces it
'involuntarily'. The second major class of IL-specific slips, namely
those due to differently automatized IL rules or items, can be
illustrated by examples: (6) and (7):

(6)   L: do you *wanna* – to drink a beer with me
        (BO)

(7)   L: and so we could go – alone and say afterwards er that
            we had *forget* forgotten it to meet him
        (BO)

In (6), the (advanced) learner uses the phrase *do you wanna*,
followed by an infinitive with *to*, thereby producing what might
be called a syntactic blend. One possible explanation of this could
be that her use of *do you wanna* reflects an earlier learning stage
when this expression was learned and used as a prefabricated pattern. In the present case, however, it seems more likely that the
fixed expression belongs to an informally acquired repertoire of
the IL user which is activated simultaneously with her formally
learned IL rule. This interpretation is in line with the 'competing
plans hypothesis' discussed by Dechert (this volume).

Example (7) is similar to the 'grammatical errors' committed by
L1 speakers as collected by Fromkin (1973): the verb is first produced as 'lexical entry', with its contextually correct morphological form only added later. According to Fromkin, this can be
taken as evidence for the separate storage of lexical and morphological information. However, in the case of the foreign language

learner, it can also indicate the higher automatization of the morphologically unmarked form *forget*.

Our discussion of slips in IL production cannot but be sketchy in the present context. But in spite of its obvious limits, it has some implications for more general issues in IL theory and analysis.

First of all, it sheds light on which aspects of IL production qualify for the 'psychologically relevant data' in IL research. We agree with Seliger (1980a, b) that *all* aspects of IL performance are of potential value for an understanding of the processes underlying L2 learning and communication, including all of the performance features mentioned above. This implies a fundamental criticism of a position held in error analysis some ten years ago, when it was maintained that the 'relevant data' were *competence errors* only, as they were assumed to reflect the learner's current stage of proficiency. *Performance errors* like slips, on the other hand, were discarded as purely accidental and unin-. teresting from a theoretical point of view (see in particular Corder 1967, 1973). It is certainly not accidental that the analytical problem of how to distinguish between competence and performance errors in learner data has never been solved: the learner's IL competence is typically transitional (unstable); it comprises components of a hypothetical nature and of different degrees of automatization. Its complex structure is reflected in the performance data, and it is therefore neither possible nor desirable to determine *a priori* the analytical relevance of various IL phenomena (see Raabe 1979; Seliger 1980a, b).

Secondly, the slips mentioned above provide a possibility for taking up a long-standing problem in second-language acquisition research, namely that of IL products being caused by 'interference' or 'transfer'. The concept of *interference* is heavily marked by belonging to the behaviourist paradigm of learning, and as such, it was perhaps *the* key concept in behaviourist language acquisition studies. As all language capacities were considered habits, errors which had traces of the learner's L1 or of already learned L2 rules or items were regarded as due to the (inter- or intralingual) interference of a previously learned habit with the formation of a new habit (see, for instance, Osgood 1953; Lado 1964). After the behaviourist paradigm had been substituted by the cognitive model, the concept of interference rapidly lost its popularity, as it was not compatible with viewing language learning as a creative cognitive activity. The influence of the learner's already existing linguistic capacities was therefore no longer seen as the effect of prior established habits but as the learner's active use of his linguistic knowledge for problem-solving tasks in L2 learning or communication, which has been referred to as *transfer* (see, for instance, Sharwood Smith 1979).

The shortcoming of both learning models is that they view the language-learning process, the storage of linguistic information and the ways in which it is used in communication as guided by *either* behavioural *or* cognitive principles. The aspects of IL use under discussion in this article indicate, however, that language learning and use are more adequately seen as comprising both aspects: the concept of (communication) strategy implies a potentially conscious problem-solving activity, whereas the speech slips evidence the existence of habitualized components of linguistic capacity. To the extent that prior inter- or intralingual experience is involved in these phenomena, we see no harm in referring to the slips as being brought about by interference, and to the communication strategy in question as transfer, thus taking account of their different psychological bases (see Kielhöfer 1975, pp. 100 ff; Vogel 1976, p. 56 for observing a similar distinction between transfer and interference). On a more general level, this implies the need for a comprehensive model of L2 learning and use, which comprises both cognitive and behavioural aspects.

(b) *Performance features as indicating IL-specific planning*

Little is known about verbal planning which could be characterized as being *typical* for IL use. Seliger (1980a) suggests a categorization of L2 learners according to their planning behaviour into 'planners' versus 'correctors'. Planners — learners who carefully plan their utterances before they start talking — can be identified by their extensive use of unfilled and filled pauses, whereas correctors — learners who start on the execution of their utterances before they have established a complete plan — typically use a lot of repeats and self-repairs in order to improve on their executed utterances.

That the scope of planning in IL is often more limited than in L1, even in the case of advanced learners, has been shown in the performance of German learners of English who were conversing with English native speakers: the intonation contours used by the learners were considerably shorter than those of the native speakers, which indicates shorter planning units (Kasper 1981, p. 418). Similarly, in a task involving reported speech, German learners of French were found to repeat the reporting verb more frequently during the indirect discourse than a French native speaker control group, which also suggests shorter planning units in IL use (Raupach 1980; see also Raupach, this volume).

(c) *Performance features as strategy markers*

In the preceding sections, no distinction was made between what we referred to above as strategic vs. non-strategic planning. No studies of performance features in IL production have so far addressed themselves to this issue specifically (see, however, the article by Raupach in this volume), although some of the evidence reported in the literature can be interpreted as indicating strategic planning in our sense, i.e. the learner trying to cope with a communicative problem.

No performance feature can itself be taken as unambiguous evidence for strategic planning — what indicates a communicative problem is the increased frequency and the co-occurrence of performance features, making it likely that the subsequent utterance is the result of a communication strategy. This can be illustrated from the study of German learners of French, mentioned above, in which Raupach found an increase in filled pauses, repeats, false starts and corrections immediately before or at the beginning of an indirect discourse, thus indicating a 'trouble source'. In most cases, the learners proceeded with indirect speech, occasionally they shifted to direct speech. In the former case, one can assume that the strategy adopted was one of retrieval, the learners having difficulty retrieving the appropriate verb form. In the latter case, the strategy might be identified as one of formal reduction, the learner avoiding the appropriate past tense form of the verb by using a present tense form instead.

Retrieval problems may be identified on the basis of performance features which indicate that the speaker is searching for a linguistic rule/item (or perhaps testing out various possibilities internally before executing any of them, as suggested by Dechert 1980 and Seliger 1980a). In the following example, the retrieval problem is indicated by a drawl, followed by a series of false starts:

(8)   NS: what did you say you need this for
       L: for the: univers- vers- – for the university of Bochum
            – you know – I want to study
       (BO)

Occasionally, the retrieval strategy itself surfaces in the performance, as in the following example, in which the learner retrieves the word *examination* via his L1:

(9)   NS: whăt did you say you do with this form – you take it
             băck to the university in Germany
      L: yes well – I think I neĕd it for my erm – Examĕn
             [German pronunciation] – examĭnation you know
      (BO)

The retrieval process can be explained by the learner first activating the semantic concept 'exam' without its specific lexicalization in IL. In order to get access to the IL word, he uses the more easily accessible L1 word as a prime. With respect to verbal planning in general, this example has a similar indicative function as some blends and word substitution slips in L1 speech which also evidence the activation of a semantic field prior to the choice of a particular lexical item.

The following excerpt illustrates co-occurrences of different performance features which can be used as strategy markers by the analyst:

(10)   NS: do you learn German – at school –
      L: not me – *I'm st I'm stop – stopped*[a] to learn Germany
           er *then I gi – er then I was*[b] – in seven – ten class – be-
           cause – I'm *no er very*[c] bad to English – and my my
           teacher said – if I – er learn Germany also – er will I
           – when I speak with the Englænder – will I er speak
           German Germany – and English – the same time
      (PIF)

In (a) there is an unfilled pause followed by two false starts, both of which are retraced (though to different degrees). The learner's problem is caused by her starting off with a L1-based form of the verb phrase (Danish present perfect *jeg er holdt op*, literally 'I'm stopped'). The learner manages to find the necessary verb form, and we would classify the strategy used as one of retrieval.

In (b), the problem is again caused by the learner starting off on a Danish-based form of the verb phrase (*da jeg* GIK *i syvende klasse* — 'when I went to seventh class'). After an unfilled pause followed by a filled pause the learner retraces the conjunction

and the subject and corrects the verb to *was*. We can imagine two
reasons why the learner did not use *went* (the formal equivalent
to Danish *gik*): (1) she had difficulty finding the correct form; (2)
she did not feel confident enough transferring the Danish verb
because she considered the expression *gå i x klasse* ('go to x
class') specifically Danish. Whichever is the case, the learner
makes use of a formal reduction strategy.

The restructuring in (c) is less clearly marked by performance
features than is the case with (a) and (b): after one filled pause
the learner exchanges the negation (*no = not*, Danish *ikke*) for
the modifier *very*, and continues with a negative adjective (instead of the positive adjective which would have had to follow
no). Apparently the learner found it easy in this case to come up
with an appropriate strategy for finishing her sentence.

Examples of strategy markers in connection with other achievement strategies are contained in the following excerpt:

(11)   NS: how do you go to school – [. . .]
        L: [. . .] sometimes I take my er – er – what's it called –
            er – er – my cykel – er (laugh) knallert – [knælə] – er
            (laugh)
        NS: what does it look like –
        L: you know er Puch – kn Puch – (laugh) you know so –
            er some people – er have er a cykel –– (laugh) er ––
            no I can't explain it – you know some people have
            a car – and some people have a er bicycle – and
            some people have a er – erm – a cykel there is a m
            motor
        NS: oh a bicycle – with a motor –
        (PIF; *knallert* Danish for 'moped')

The example contains most of the performance features discussed in the previous sections: unfilled and filled pauses, gambits
(*what's it called*, *you know*), and self-repairs, retraced and unretraced. The sequence of strategies adopted by the learner is one
frequently found among beginning learners: L1-based strategies
(borrowing, interlingual transfer), followed by IL-based
strategies (description, exemplification) (cf. the contribution by
Haastrup and Phillipson in this volume).

That learners repair on a communication strategy by means of
another communication strategy, as illustrated by (11), can often
be observed in IL data: in fact, co-occurrences of what may be interpreted as the product of communication strategies aimed at

solving one and the same problem may be used as one way of identifying strategic planning on the basis of performance data. This is also seen in the following example:

(12)   L: you give me – I think the medicine you gave me was too strong or the erm – you gave me too much of the medicine – because now I have some pimples they are reddish and they itch very much

(BO)

The fact that the learner tries to communicate almost the same meaning twice (*I think the medicine you gave me was too strong, you gave me too much of the medicine* — for *the dosage was too high*) can be taken to indicate that she is experiencing a problem and is not entirely satisfied with her first attempt at solving it (by means of a paraphrase). She therefore tries again with a different paraphrase — and then goes on, apparently believing that she has succeeded in communicating to the doctor what she intended.

In (11), the learner uses rising intonation throughout the extract, hereby appealing to her interlocutor to signal whether she has understood what the learner is trying to say. This appealing for uptaking is also signalled paralinguistically, the learner frequently looking at her interlocutor in an enquiring manner.

A different pattern of stress and intonation is seen in the following examples:

(13)   L: I need – I need this money which I would – I would get if if I could – could care for him

(BO)

(14)   L: give me your hand I am very (laugh) very angry to cross the street

(BO)

In (13) and (14), the lexical items which are produced as a result of the learner using a communication strategy receive main stress and falling intonation. As there is a general tendency in the Bochum data for learners to overuse rising intonation (possibly in order to mark for uncertainty, cf. Kasper 1981, pp. 387f, 425ff), it is rather surprising at first sight to find heavy falls on several items which are otherwise marked as the product of communication strategies. One possible interpretation of this is that the learner believes that he reaches a solution to his problem and marks this by falling intonation, without appealing to his interlocutor for

228 *Claus Færch and Gabriele Kasper*

uptaking (see also Seliger 1980a; Raupach in this volume).

In the examples quoted there are no instances of speech slips in combination with communication strategies. This is not accidental, as speech slips reflect the direct opposite of strategic planning, namely the execution of already planned — and possibly highly automatized — speech segments. To the extent slips can be identified as such in the IL performance (see the discussion of this above), they can probably be used as indicators of *non-strategic* performance. The segment(s) following the slips, however, may be the result of a communication strategy if the learner experiences a problem in repairing on the slip, in particular in the case of L1-based slips, as in the following example:

(15) NS: what is your job at the library
      L: I shall put *eller* er *hvad hedder det* (giggles) I shall put the books on the *hill er hvad hedder det*
      NS: on the shelves
      L: er yeah shelve
      (PIF; *eller*, Danish for 'or'; *hvad hedder det*, Danish for 'what's it called'; *hill = hylde*, Danish for 'shelf')

In our discussion of performance features in L1/IL speech production, we have paid little attention to how these features are influenced by sociolinguistic factors like type of task and type of communicative situation. That the distribution of performance features is subjected to such factors has been convincingly demonstrated for both L1 (Grosjean and Deschamps 1975, p. 152) and for IL (Raupach 1980 and in this volume; Sajavaara and Lehtonen 1980). It is therefore necessary to emphasize that with very few exceptions, our discussion of IL speech production has been based on interactional data in which a learner converses with a native speaker of English.

Communication strategies and strategy markers: interactional functions

In the preceding section, we discussed how the analyst can use performance features in learner discourse for the identification of communication strategies. In this section, we shall go into the implications of these and other problem indicators for the interlocutor, which links up with a discussion of the interactional definition of communication strategies by Tarone (this volume).

In the literature on the pragmatics of language use, one is often referred to the 'cooperative principle' as stated by Grice:

'Make your conversational contribution such as is required, at the stage at which it occurs, by the accepted purpose or direction of the talk exchange in which you are engaged.' (1975, p. 45).

This formulation focusses on the *productive* aspect of interlocutors' contributions. However, in order for verbal interaction to flow smoothly, there must also be conversational rules which regulate the *receptive* aspect of communication, i.e. rules which specify general principles of how to respond to one's interlocutor's contribution in a cooperative way. One such principle could be that the recipient of a message ought to interpret it as a meaningful and relevant contribution, no matter how superficially unrelated it seems to be. It is by participants generally following this principle that the use of indirect speech acts can function (see, for instance, Searle 1975; Candlin 1981). Observing the 'receptive' cooperative principle is a necessary condition for any successful verbal interaction. However, in certain types of interaction it is not sufficient for ensuring understanding. The situations we have in mind are those where the participants have unequal access to the code they use. Although such situations occasionally occur between native speakers of a language — for instance because one of the interlocutors is having retrieval problems, or because he is not familiar with a specific occupational register — the typical role constellation is that of a learner conversing with a native speaker of a given language. In this case, the native interlocutor's behaviour is governed by the principle 'if the learner signals that he has problems formulating himself, help out'. This cooperative principle for learner-native speaker interaction, however, does not hold unrestrictedly. In fact, it might conflict with another interactional principle, namely that of face-saving (see Goffman 1967; Brown and Levinson 1978): treating the other person as inferior in any respect counts as a potentially face-threatening act which cooperative interactants try to avoid. Consequently, in order not to treat the other person as being linguistically inferior, the native speaker might decide not to assist even though the learner shows signs of verbalizing problems, thus giving the principle of face-saving priority to the principle of linguistic cooperation. The factors which might influence the native speaker's option for one or the other principle are manifold, among others, the learner's level of proficiency in L2, the relative social status of the participants and the urgency of the content matter to be communicated. That native speakers do in fact often give priority to the principle of linguistic cooperation is a function of the foreigner role which allows for treating the other person as linguistically handicapped without this being intended or perceived as a face-threatening act.

When the learner is faced with a problem in establishing or carrying out a verbal plan, this is usually indicated in (at least) one of the following ways:

1. by an implicit signal of uncertainty like the performance features discussed above;
2. by an explicit signal of uncertainty like the 'handicap signals' mentioned by Beneke (1975), e.g. *I don't know how to say this, I can't say/explain that*;
3. by the learner addressing his interlocutor directly, as in example (16):

(16)   L: I wanted to improve my knowledge of −− what is
             Kunst

        NS: art

        L: art − in England

        (BO)

The last alternative is co-extensive with the cooperative communication strategy *appeal*. How do these three types of problem indicators differ in interactional terms? From the hearer's point of view, they *can* all be interpreted as appeals for assistance. However, they vary in the degree of obligation to assist imposed on the interlocutor, which can be indicated schematically:

Problem indicator	Obligation for interlocutor to assist
strategy markers = signals of uncertainty performance features: implicit signals of uncertainty	weak
handicap signals: explicit signals of uncertainty	
Communication strategy: appeal	strong

From the analyst's point of view, the ambiguity of the problem indicators varies relatively to the degree of obligation for assistance: the more ambiguous the problem indicator (e.g. few instances of performance features), the weaker the obligation to assist; the less ambiguous the problem indicator (e.g. an appeal), the stronger the obligation imposed on the interlocutor. This parallelism of ambiguity for the analyst and obligation for the interlocutor can be explained in analogy to the interactional implications of direct versus indirect speech acts (cf. Brown and Levinson 1978; House and Kasper 1981). If addressed, for instance, by the direct version of a request (*get that bottle of akvavit from the fridge*), the hearer is confronted by an imposition on the part of the speaker which leaves him no 'escape routes' but to either comply or refuse: the 'conditional relevance' (see Sacks 1972 for the original definition of this term), i.e. the degree to which a speech activity predetermines socially acceptable responding behaviour, is high in the case of a direct request. On the other hand, if addressed by an indirect version of the same speech act, for instance, a 'mild hint' (*we had this fantastic akvavit at Gitte's dinner last Wednesday*), the hearer's reaction possibilities are much more varied: he can 'take the hint', ignore it, engage in a discussion of the relative merits of various types of akvavit, of the party in question, etc. In other words, the conditional relevance of this type of indirect speech act is very low, as it allows for a wide range of socially acceptable responding behaviour. Similarly, an interlocutor who is faced by a direct appeal (see example (15)) from a learner is obliged to 'help out' if he does not wish to behave in a markedly uncooperative way: the conditional relevance for assistance is high. If the learner uses a signal of uncertainty, however, the interlocutor's range of acceptable reactions is wider, as can be illustrated by the following data:

(17)   L: he is in – [kəʊ'li:ʒə]–['kəʊlidʃ] – I don't know what –
         NS: college
         L: yes
         (PIF)

(18)   L: after my school I'll start erm (sigh) er – I learn erm shirts and er (laugh) can't explain that –
         NS: no –
         L: er – sy – [sy:] I I can't say that –
         (PIF; *sy* Danish for 'sew')

In (17), the native speaker takes up the learner's handicap signal (*I don't know what*) in a cooperative way, providing the correct pronunciation. In (18), on the other hand, she only confirms the learner's explicitly marked formulation problem (*can't explain that*) without any attempt to provide the needed word or to find out what the learner is trying to communicate. Both the 'cooperative' and the 'uncooperative' alternative are socially acceptable responses due to the relatively low conditional relevance of the handicap signals used.

The interlocutor's reaction potential becomes even larger in cases where the learner uses performance features as implicit signals of uncertainty, of which (19) and (20) are examples.

(19)   NS: but you like reading books about history –
         L: not about hist er this history –
         NS: aha –
         L: you know – er er young histories – er not not with this old things you know kings [NS: aha] or – all that – but er (laughs)
         NS: (laughs) in er in er for example – what – 1930 – or so – do you mean – recent – [. . .]
         (PIF)

(20)   NS: [. . .] what er colour is it –
         L: er skim – (laughs) [NS: laughs] er – er –– what's – colour is this – (points)
         NS: er grey –
         (PIF; *skimlet* Danish for 'grey' with reference to animals)

(19) shows that the native speaker is trying to make sense of the learner's fragmentary hints and attempts at paraphrase by offering herself an approximation to what the learner might mean ('more recent history'). She starts on her feedback precisely after the learner's last attempt at paraphrase (*kings or all that*) which is accompanied by an increased use of filled and unfilled pauses and a laugh, thus taking up the learner's signals of uncertainty cooperatively. In (20), however, the native speaker does not even take up on the learner's unambiguously marked problem (use of language switch to Danish, filled and unfilled pauses), but responds only after a direct appeal, the conditional relevance of which is even more strengthened by the learner's deictic gesture.

So far, we have focussed on the (para-)linguistic means which can serve as problem indicators without as yet going into the various ways in which the learner might use them. Quite often, the learner indicates through his kinetic behaviour whether he is just expressing having a communication problem or whether he is appealing to his interlocutor for assistance. Thus, by using a lot of hesitation phenomena while looking appealingly at his interlocutor, the learner's communicative activity might exert as strong a conditional relevance as a verbalized direct appeal. Conversely, what without an extraverbal specification functions as an appeal might be used as a purely expressive problem indicator without any appealing force:

(21)   NS: ... how do you get on with girls –
           L: oh (giggles) I'm very oh – what do you call it – you know (laughs) I get a red in my head – (giggles)
         NS: yes shy
           L: shy yer (giggles)
       (PIF)

That the learner, in his first turn, does *not* appeal for assistance, even though using what superficially looks like an appeal (*what do you call it*), becomes clear from his interrupting the eye contact with the native speaker and looking concentratedly away. The 'appeal' functions here as an *aside* (Edmondson and House 1981, p. 82), a gambit which allows the learner to keep his turn before using a paraphrase as a communication strategy (see also Færch and Kasper 1982a for the turnkeeping function of gambits).

From the preceding discussion follows that from an interactional perspective, problem indicators can function in various ways: the learner might or might not call for assistance, and the native speaker might or might not help out — depending on the conditional relevance of the (para-)linguistic problem indicator used and the contextual specification it receives through extraverbal behaviour.

Having specified the interactional function of strategies and strategy markers as defined according to the 'psycholinguistic' definition, we can now return to the alternative, 'interactional', definition as proposed by Tarone and clarify how the two definitions differ. Communication strategies defined according to Tarone's definition form a subset of what is considered strategies on the basis of the psycholinguistic definition. This can be illustrated by the following diagram, in which the hatched area is identical with strategies in Tarone's sense.

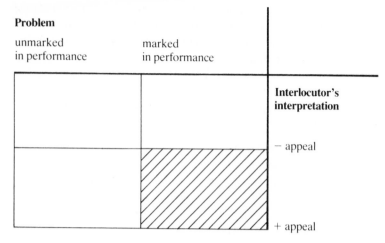

The hatched subset has the following characteristics:
(a) the learner's problem is marked in his performance, either by an implicit/explicit signal of uncertainty or by a direct appeal;
(b) the signal is interpreted by the interlocutor as an appeal;
(c) the interlocutor acts in a cooperative manner and helps the learner communicate his intended message.

One obvious advantage of adopting the interactional definition is that it is easy to apply to performance data: if there is no indication of the learner experiencing a communicative problem and if the interlocutor does not act cooperatively, no communication strategy will be identified. Although we certainly consider the subset delimited by the interactional definition a highly significant aspect of IL communication, worth specific investigation, we would like to maintain that the other, non-hatched, parts of the diagram also represent important aspects of what we consider strategic performance.

First of all it is clear from (videotaped) conversations between learners and native speakers that (1) the native speaker does not always help the learner out even when it is clear that he is having a communicative problem — hence the learner has to find a solution himself; (2) the learner sometimes marks that he is at the same time having a problem and that he wants to solve it himself. We see no reason for excluding such non-cooperative behaviour from the area of communication strategies, in particular as the consequence of this would be that learners could not make use of communication strategies in non-interactional situations.

Second, it is a fairly well-known fact that advanced learners, who are capable of planning longer units, can often predict a communicative problem within the following constituent and attempt to solve it beforehand, i.e. as part of the normal planning process. This means that the problem need not surface at all in connection with the problem spot itself but results in a lengthening of the regular planning pause. The speech of such learners will be characterized by a higher degree of 'transition smoothness' at the articulatory phonetic level within constituent boundaries, whereas the transition smoothness between constituents or clauses will depend on the learner's pause pattern: if he makes use of filled, in particular lexicalized, pauses which are in accordance with the target language norm and which help him hold the floor, his overall fluency may be high in spite of his being a 'planner' (cf. Seliger 1980a) and in spite of his making use of communication strategies. It might therefore be highly appropriate to teach learners at the advanced levels how to use floor-holding gambits, as suggested by Edmondson and House (1981, pp. 69ff).

Even advanced learners are likely to experience communication problems in their IL — not least because their communicative aspiration level often increases with their developing IL proficiency, but because of their less clearly marked foreigner roles their need for face-saving is greater than is the case with less advanced learners. 'Covertly' used communication strategies are ideally suited for such learners, and we feel that a definition of communication strategies which will be of relevance for learners beyond the more elementary levels should be comprehensive enough to incorporate these. Unfortunately, what is good for the learner is not always good for the analyst: if learners are able to plan ahead and conceal their use of strategies it is next to impossible for the analyst to identify such strategies in performance data. The identification of communication strategies on the basis of the occurrence of strategy markers in performance data therefore has to be supplemented by other techniques, for instance by introspection.

Notes

1. The language learner data used throughout this article are taken from two collections of such: data collected within the PIF project, Department of English, University of Copenhagen (marked PIF in the text); and data from the project 'Kommunikative Kompetenz als realisierbares Lernziel', Seminar für Sprachlehrforschung, Ruhr-Universität

Bochum (marked BO in the text). The PIF project is supported in part by a grant from the Danish Research Council for the Humanities. For further information about the projects and the data, cf. p. 56, footnote 1.

The following conventions are used in the transcriptions of the data:

″primary stress

↘fall

↗rise

↘↗fall-rise

— pause relative to speaker's speed of delivery

(. . .) extraverbal activity

References

Beneke, Jürgen (1975). 'Verstehen und Missverstehen im Englischunterricht', *Praxis des neusprachlichen Unterrichts*, **22**, 351–362.

Boomer, Donald S. and Laver, John D. M. (1973). 'Slips of the Tongue, in Fromkin (1973), 120–131.

Brown, Penelope and Levinson, Stephen (1978). 'Universals in Language Usage: Politeness Phenomena', in Goody, Esther N. (ed.), *Questions and Politeness. Strategies in Social Interaction*, Cambridge University Press, 56–289.

Candlin, Christopher N. (1981). 'Discoursal Patterning and the Equalizing of Interpretive Opportunity', in Smith, L. (ed.), *English for Cross-Cultural Communication*, London: Macmillan, 166–198.

Clark, Herbert H. and Clark, Eve V. (1977). *Psychology and Language*, New York: Harcourt Brace Jovanovich.

Cole, Peter and Morgan, Jerry L. (eds.) (1975). *Syntax and Semantics*. Vol. **3**: *Speech Acts*, New York: Academic Press.

Corder, S. Pit (1967). 'The Significance of Learners' Errors', *IRAL*, **5**, 161–170.

Corder, S. Pit (1973). *Introducing Applied Linguistics*, Harmondsworth: Penguin.

Dalton, Peggy and Hardcastle, W. J. (1977). *Disorders of Fluency and Their Effects on Communication*, London: Arnold.

Dechert, Hans W. (1980). 'Contextual Hypothesis Testing Procedures in Speech Production', in Dechert and Raupach (1980), 101–121.

Dechert, Hans W. and Raupach, Manfred (eds.) (1980). *Towards a Cross-Linguistic Assessment of Speech Production*, Frankfurt: Lang.

Edmondson, Willis and House, Juliane (1981). *Let's Talk and Talk about It. A Pedagogic Interactional Grammar of English*, München: Urban und Schwarzenberg.

Færch, Claus and Kasper, Gabriele (1982a). 'Ja und — og hvad så? A Contrastive Discourse Analysis of Gambits in German and Danish', in Fisiak, Jazek (ed.), *Contrastive Linguistics*, The Hague: Mouton.

Færch, Claus and Kasper, Gabriele (1982b). 'Phatic Metalingual and Metacommunicative Functions in Discourse: Gambits and Repairs', in Enkvist, Nils Erik (ed.), *Impromptu Speech*, Åbo: Åbo Akademi.

Fathman, Ann K. (1980). 'Repetition and Correction as an Indication of Speech Planning and Execution Processes among Second Language Learners', in Dechert and Raupach (1980), 77–85.

Fromkin, Victoria A. (ed.) (1973). *Speech Errors as Linguistic Evidence*, The Hague: Mouton.

Goffman, Erving (1967). *Interaction Ritual. Essays on Face-to-Face Behavior*, New York: Anchor Books.

Goldman-Eisler, Frieda (1961a). 'The Significance of Changes in the Rate of Articulation', *Language and Speech*, **4**, 171–174.

Goldman-Eisler, Frieda (1961b). 'A Comparative Study of Two Hesitation Phenomena', *Language and Speech*, **4**, 18–26.

Goldman-Eisler, Frieda (1968). *Psycholinguistics: Experiments in Spontaneous Speech*, London, New York: Academic Press.

Goldman-Eisler, Frieda (1972). 'Pauses, Clauses, Sentences', *Language and Speech*, **15**, 103–113.

Grice, H. Paul (1975). 'Logic and Conversation', in Cole and Morgan (1975), 41–58.

Grosjean, François (1980). 'Temporal Variables within and between Languages', in Dechert and Raupach (1980), 39–54.

Grosjean, François and Deschamps, Alain (1975). 'Analyse contrastive des variables temporelles de l'anglais et du français: vitesse de parole et variables composantes, phénomènes d'hésitation', *Phonetica*, **31**, 144–184.

House, Juliane and Kasper, Gabriele (1981). 'Politeness Markers in English and German', in Coulmas, Florian (ed.), *Conversational Routine*, The Hague: Mouton, 157–185.

Kasper, Gabriele (1981). *Pragmatische Aspekte in der Interimsprache.* Eine Untersuchung des Englischen fortgeschrittener deutscher Lerner, Tübingen: Narr.

Kielhöfer, Bernd (1975). *Fehlerlinguistik des Fremdsprachenerwerbs*, Kronberg/Ts.: Scriptor.

Lado, Robert (1964). *Language Teaching. A Scientific Approach*, New York: McGraw-Hill.

Landschultz, Karen and Stage, Lilian (1977). 'Tøvemekanismer i fransk', *RIDS*, **52**, University of Copenhagen: Romansk Institut.

Laver, John D. M. (1973). 'The Detection and Correction of Slips of the Tongue', in Fromkin (1973), 132–143.

Maclay, Howard and Osgood, Charles E. (1959). 'Hesitation Phenomena in Spontaneous English Speech', *Word*, **15**, 19–44.

Osgood, Charles E. (1953). *Method and Theory in Experimental Psychology*, Oxford University Press.

Pürschel, Heiner (1975). *Pause und Kadenz. Interferenzerscheinungen bei der englischen Intonation deutscher Sprecher*, Tübingen: Niemeyer.

Raabe, Horst (1979). 'Zur Bedeutung des Performanzfehlers', in Kühlwein, Wolfgang and Raasch, Albert (eds.), *Kongressbericht der 9. Jahrestagung der Gesellschaft für Angewandte Linguistik GAL e.v.* Bd. III, Heidelberg: Groos, 61–69.

Raupach, Manfred (1980). 'Cross-Linguistic Descriptions of Speech Performance as a Contribution to "Contrastive Psycholinguistics"', in Dechert and Raupach (1980), 9–22.

238   *Claus Færch and Gabriele Kasper*

Rochester, S. R. (1973). 'The Significance of Pauses in Spontaneous Speech', *Journal of Psycholinguistic Research*, **2**, 51–81.

Sacks, Harvey (1972). 'An Initial Investigation of the Usability of Conversational Data for Doing Sociology', in Sudnow, David (ed.), *Studies in Social Interaction*, New York: Free Press, 31–74.

Sajavaara, Kari and Lehtonen, Jaakko (1980). 'The Analysis of Cross-Language Communication: Prolegomena to the Theory and Methodology', in Dechert and Raupach (1980), 55–76.

Schegloff, Emanuel A., Jefferson, Gail and Sacks, Harvey (1977). 'The Preference for Self-Correction in the Organization of Repair in Conversation', *Language*, **53**, 361–382.

Searle, John (1975). 'Indirect Speech Acts', in Cole and Morgan (1975), 59–82.

Seliger, Herbert W. (1980a). 'Utterance Planning and Correction Behavior: Its Function in the Grammar Construction Process for Second Language Learners', in Dechert and Raupach (1980), 87–99.

Seliger, Herbert W. (1980b). 'Data Sources and the Study of L2 Speech Performance: Some Theoretical Issues', *Interlanguage Studies Bulletin Utrecht*, **5**, 31–46.

Sharwood Smith, Michael (1979). 'Strategies, Language Transfer and the Simulation of the Second Language Learner's Mental Operations', *Interlanguage Studies Bulletin Utrecht*, **4**, 66–83.

Vogel, Klaus (1976). 'Transfer und Fremdsprachenunterricht', in Börner, Wolfgang, Kielhöfer, Bernd and Vogel, Klaus (eds.), *Französisch lehren und lernen*, Kronberg: Scriptor, 40–58.

The Contributors

Ellen Bialystok (now, Associate Professor, Department of Psychology, York University, Toronto) received her Ph.D. in Cognitive Psychology from the University of Toronto. Her most recent research has examined second-language learning by adolescents and adults in an attempt to discover some of the processes involved and to describe aspects of the proficiency which results. She is currently directing a large-scale study entitled 'The development of bilingual proficiency'.

Shoshana Blum-Kulka received her Ph.D. from the Hebrew University, Jerusalem in 1974. Between 1965 and 1975 she served as Director of the Intensive Hebrew Language Program at the Hebrew University. In 1975 she joined the faculty of the Center for Applied Linguistics at the Hebrew University, where she taught second-language acquisition and translation. Currently she has a joint appointment at the Communications Institute and the School of Education. Her publications include papers on second-language pedagogy, second-language acquisition, translation and a comparative study of speech act performance in English and Hebrew. Her current research interests are: discourse processing in first and second language, discourse structure of the language of the media and the speech act performance of second-language learners.

Andrew D. Cohen is Associate Professor of Applied Linguistics in the School of Education at the Hebrew University of Jerusalem, Israel. He is currently Chairman of the Israeli Association for Applied Linguistics and Chairman of the TESOL Research Committee. His current research interests are in easifying second-language learning and in language testing. His publications include *A Sociolinguistic Approach to Bilingual Education* (Newbury House, 1975) and *Testing Language Ability in the Classroom* (Newbury House, 1980).

S. Pit Corder received his first degree from Oxford University in the field of Modern Languages. After war service he spent seventeen years working for the British Council teaching English in a number of countries overseas. He joined the staff at Leeds University in 1961 and moved to head the Department of Applied Linguistics in the University of Edinburgh in 1964. He is at present Professor of Applied Linguistics in that University. His research interests in the field of Applied Linguistics are in Interlanguage and Second-Language Acquisition.

Hans W. Dechert received his Ph. D. from the Johann-Wolfgang-Goethe University at Frankfurt in 1954. He has taught at Rutgers University, New Brunswick, NJ, USA and the Justus-Liebig-University at Giessen, Federal Republic of Germany. At present he is Professor in the University of Kassel, Federal Republic of Germany. Together with Manfred Raupach he has been particularly interested in temporal variables in speech and the psycholinguistics of second-language speech production of advanced speakers of English and German within the context of a research project of the Kassel Psycho- and Pragmalinguistic Research Group (KAPPA).

Guy Dumas is presently responsible for second-language research (English and French) for the Ministry of Education of Quebec (Canada).

Claus Færch has been employed in the Department of English, University of Copenhagen since 1975, first as assistant professor and, since 1980, as associate professor. Since 1977 he has been Director of Project in Foreign Language Pedagogy (PIF) in the same department, a project which is aimed at describing the interlanguage development of Danish learners of English. He has published both within theoretical linguistics and interlanguage studies. His present research interests comprise analyses of the relationship between interlanguage competence, classroom interaction and non-school communication, in particular with respect to procedural aspects of competence.

Kirsten Haastrup is currently lecturer in English at Haderslev College of Education, Denmark. From 1972 to 1979 she was associated to the Royal Danish School of Educational Studies, first as a post-graduate student (1972–75), and later as a lecturer in the Department of English (1976–79). From 1976 to 1981 she was also a part-time lecturer in the Department of English at the University of Copenhagen. Her publications are mainly in the areas of language testing. Over the last four years she has done research within the PIF project where she has been particularly interested in the role studies of learner language can play in degree courses of foreign language pedagogy.

Gabriele Kasper received her Ph.D. in language pedagogy ('Sprachlehrforschung') from Ruhr-Universität Bochum, Federal Republic of Germany. Between 1973 and 1980, she collaborated in research projects on pedagogic grammar and communicative competence in foreign language learning and teaching at the same university. Since 1981 she has been associate professor of applied linguistics at the University of Aarhus, Denmark. Her current research interests focus on psycholinguistic and interactional aspects of foreign language learning and communication in pedagogic and non-pedagogic contexts.

Eddie A. Levenston is associate professor in the Department of English, the Hebrew University of Jerusalem. He received his Ph.D. from the University of London in 1966. Since 1953, he has lived in Israel, where he has taught at the Hebrew University since 1958. His research interests include: contrastive analysis, second-language acquisition (especially lexis), language testing, linguistic approaches to literary texts (especially poetry).

Robert Phillipson is a graduate of Cambridge and Leeds Universities, England. In British Council posts he taught English in Algeria and worked in teacher re-training in Yugoslavia. Since 1973 he has been associate professor of English and language pedagogy at Roskilde University Centre, Denmark. Among his professional interests are pronunciation, error analysis, English grammar and lexicology, and learner-centred project studies, particularly at higher education level.

Manfred Raupach is Professor in the Department of English and Romance Languages and Literatures at the University of Kassel. He is a collaborator in the Kassel Psycho- and Pragmalinguistic Research Group (KAPPA) with special interest in second-language speech production of advanced learners. His publications include: *A Selected Bibliography on Temporal Variables in Speech* (Tübingen: Narr, 1980) (with G. Appel and H.W. Dechert); *Temporal Variables in Speech. Studies in Honour of Frieda Goldman-Eisler* (The Hague, Paris and New York: Mouton, 1980) (edited with H.W. Dechert); *Towards a Cross-Linguistic Assessment of Speech Production* (Frankfurt, Bern and Cirencester: Lang, 1980) (edited with H.W. Dechert); *Psycholinguistic Models of Production* (Norwood, New Jersey: Ablex, 1981) (edited with H.W. Dechert).

Elaine Tarone is Director of the Program in English as a Second Language, in the Linguistics Department of the University of Minnesota. She received her Ph.D. at the University of Washington in 1972, and has published extensively in the field of second-language acquisition since that time. Her current research interests include communication strategies, interlanguage phonology, code-switching, and English for special purposes.

Tamás Váradi has been a collaborator on the English–Hungarian Contrastive Linguistics Project since 1972, where he has been responsible for a large-scale error analysis. He is currently lecturer in the Department of English at the College for Foreign Trade, Budapest. His present research interests include methodological questions of contrastive linguistics, error analysis, approximative systems/interlanguage analysis, communication strategies and English grammar.

Johannes Wagner studied at the universities of Tübingen and Uppsala. Since 1975, he has been a lecturer at the University of Odense, Denmark where he received his doctorate in 1982. His research interests include language institutions and interlanguage communication. Special interests: dry red wine and bagpipe music.

Bibliography

Adjemian, Christian (1976). 'On the Nature of Interlanguage Systems', *Language Learning*, **26**, 297–320.

Albrechtsen, Dorte, Henriksen, Birgit and Færch, Claus (1980). 'Native Speaker Reactions to Learners' Spoken Interlanguage', *Language Learning*, **30**, 365–396.

Bates, Elizabeth and MacWhinney, Brian (1981). 'Second Language Acquisition from a Functionalist Perspective: Pragmatic, Semantic and Perceptual Strategies', in Winitz, Harris (ed.), *Native and Foreign Language Acquisition*, New York: Academy of Sciences, 190–214.

Bausch, Karl-Richard and Kasper, Gabriele (1979). 'Der Zweitsprachenerwerb: Möglichkeiten und Grenzen der 'grossen' Hypothesen', *Linguistische Berichte*, **64**, 3–35.

Beebe, Leslie M. (1980). 'Measuring the Use of Communication Strategies', in Scarcella, Robin and Krashen, Stephen D. (eds.), *Research in Second-Language Acquisition*, Rowley, Massachusetts: Newbury House, 173–181.

Beebe, Leslie M. (forthcoming). 'Risk-Taking and the Language Learner', in Seliger and Long (forthcoming).

Bialystok, Ellen (1978). 'A Theoretical Model of Second Language Learning', *Language Learning*, **28**, 69–84.

Bialystok, Ellen, (1979). 'The Role of Conscious Strategies in Second Language Proficiency', *The Canadian Modern Language Review*, **35**, 372–394.

Bialystok, Ellen (forthcoming). 'Inferencing: Testing the "Hypothesis Testing" Hypothesis', in Seliger and Long (forthcoming).

Bialystok, Ellen and Fröhlich, Maria (1980). 'Oral Communication Strategies for Lexical Difficulties', *Interlanguage Studies Bulletin Utrecht*, **5**, 3–30.

Bialystok, Ellen, Fröhlich, Maria and Howard, John (1979). *Studies in Second Language Teaching and Learning in Classroom Settings: Strategies, Processes and Functions*, Toronto: OISE.

Blatchford, Charles H. and Schachter, Jacquelyne (eds.) (1978). *On TESOL '78*, Washington, D.C.: TESOL.

Blum, Shoshana and Levenston, Eddie A., (1978a). 'Lexical Simplification in Second-Language Acquisition', *Studies in Second Language Acquisition*, **2/2**, 43–64.

Blum, Shoshana and Levenston, Eddie A. (1978b). 'Universals of Lexical Simplification', *Language Learning*, **28**, 399–416.

Brown, H. Douglas, Yorio, Carlos A. and Crymes, Ruth C. (eds.) (1977). *On TESOL '77*, Washington D.C.: TESOL.

Burmeister, Hartmut and Ufert, Detlef (1980). 'Strategy Switching?', in Felix, Sascha W. (ed.), *Second Language Development*, Tübingen: Narr, 109–122.

Canale, Michael and Swain, Merrill (1980). 'Theoretical Bases of Communicative Approaches to Second Language Teaching and Testing', *Applied Linguistics*, **1**, 1–47.

Candlin, Christopher N. (1981), 'Discoursal Patterning and the Equalizing of Interpretive Opportunity', in Smith, L. (ed.), *English for Cross-Cultural Communication*, London: Macmillan, 166–198.

Candlin, Christopher N. and Breen, Michael P. (eds.) (forthcoming). *Interpretive Strategies in Language Learning*, Oxford University Press.

Carton, Aaron S. (1971). 'Inferencing: a Process in Using and Learning Language', in Pimsleur, Paul and Quinn, Terence (eds.), *The Psychology of Second Language Learning*, Cambridge University Press, 45–58.

Cathcart, R. W., Strong, M. A. and Fillmore, L. W. (1979). 'The Social and Linguistic Behavior of Good Language Learners', in Yorio, Perkins and Schachter (1979), 267–273.

Clahsen, Harald (1978). 'Syntax oder Produktionsstrategien? Zum natürlichen Zweitsprachenerwerb der "Gastarbeiter"' *Wuppertaler Arbeitspapiere zur Sprachwissenschaft*, **1**, 62–79.

Corder, S. Pit (1978). 'Language-Learner Language', in Richards, Jack C. (ed.), *Understanding Second and Foreign Language Learning*. Rowley, Massachusetts: Newbury House, 71–93.

Corder, S. Pit and Roulet, Eddie (eds.) (1977). *The Notions of Simplification, Interlanguages and Pidgins and Their Relation to Second Language Pedagogy* (= Actes du 5ème colloque de linguistique appliquée de Neuchâtel 20–22 Mai 1976), Genève: Droz and Neuchâtel: Faculté des Lettres.

Dechert, Hans W. (1980a). 'Contextual Hypothesis-Testing-Procedures in Speech Production', in Dechert and Raupach (1980b), 101–121.

Dechert, Hans W. (1980b). 'Pauses and Intonation as Indicators of Verbal Planning in Second-Language Speech Productions: Two Examples from a Case Study', in Dechert and Raupach (1980a), 271–285.

Dechert, Hans W. (in press). 'The Competing Plans Hypothesis (CPH) Extended to Second-Language Speech Production', in Di Pietro, Robert J. (ed.), *Selected Proceedings of the First Delaware Symposium on Language Studies*, Newark, Delaware: University of Delaware Press.

Dechert, Hans W. and Raupach, Manfred (eds.) (1980a). *Temporal Variables of Speech. Studies in Honour of Frieda Goldman-Eisler*, The Hague: Mouton.

Dechert, Hans W. and Raupach, Manfred (eds.) (1980b). *Towards a Cross-Linguistic Assessment of Speech Production*, Frankfurt: Lang.

Færch, Claus (forthcoming). 'Inferencing Procedures and Communication Strategies in Lexical Comprehension', in Candlin and Breen (forthcoming).

Færch, Claus and Kasper, Gabriele (1980a). 'Processes and Strategies in

Foreign Language Learning and Communication', *Interlanguage Studies Bulletin Utrecht*, **5**, 47–118.

Færch, Claus and Kasper, Gabriele (1980b). 'Stratégies de communication et marqueurs de stratégies', in Arditty, Jo and Mittner, Michèle (eds.), *Acquisition d'une langue étrangère* (= Encrages, numéro spécial), Université Paris VIII — Vincennes à Saint-Denis, 17–24.

Færch, Claus and Kasper, Gabriele (1982a). 'Phatic, Metalingual and Metacommunicative Functions in Discourse: Gambits and Repairs', in Enkvist, Nils Erik (ed.), *Impromptu Speech*, Åbo: Åbo Akademi.

Færch, Claus and Kasper, Gabriele (1982b). 'Procedural Knowledge as a Component of Learners' Communicative Competence', in Bolte, Henning and Herrlitz, Wolfgang (eds.), *Kommunikation im (Sprach-) Unterricht*, Utrecht: Instituut 'Frantzen'.

Fathman, Ann K. (1980). 'Repetition and Correction as an Indication of Speech Planning and Execution Processes among Second Language Learners', in Dechert and Raupach (1980b), 77–85.

Fillmore, Lily Wong (1976). *The Second Time Around: Cognitive and Social Strategies in Second Language Acquisition.* Unpublished doctoral dissertation, Stanford University.

Fillmore, Lily Wong (1979). 'Individual Differences in Second Language Acquisition', in Fillmore, Charles J., Kempler, Daniel and Wang, William S.-Y. (eds.), *Individual Differences in Language Ability and Language Behavior*, London, New York: Academic Press, 203–228.

Gaies, Stephen J. (1977). 'The Nature of Linguistic Input in Formal Second Language Learning: Linguistic and Communicative Strategies in ESL Teachers' Classroom Language', in Brown, Yorio and Crymes (1977).

Gaskill, William H. (1980). 'Correction in Native Speaker-Non-native Speaker Conversation', in Larsen-Freeman (1980), 125–137.

Glahn, Esther (1980). 'Introspection as a Method of Elicitation in Interlanguage Studies', *Interlanguage Studies Bulletin Utrecht*, **5**, 119–128.

Hamayan, Else V. and Tucker, G. Richard (1979). 'Strategies of Communication Used by Native and Non-native Speakers of French', *Working Papers on Bilingualism*, **17**, 83–96.

Ickenroth, Jacques (1975). *On the Elusiveness of Interlanguage*, Progress Report, Utrecht.

Jordens, Peter (1977). 'Rules, Grammatical Intuitions and Strategies in Foreign Language Learning', *Interlanguage Studies Bulletin Utrecht*, **2/2**, 6–76.

Kasper, Gabriele (1979). 'Communication Strategies: Modality Reduction', *Interlanguage Studies Bulletin Utrecht*, **4**, 266–283.

Kasper, Gabriele (1981). *Pragmatische Aspekte in der Interimsprache.* Eine Untersuchung des Englischen fortgeschrittener deutscher Lerner, Tübingen: Narr.

Kasper, Gabriele (1982). 'Kommunikationsstrategien in der interimsprachlichen Produktion', *Die Neueren Sprachen* **81/6**.

Kasper, Gabriele (forthcoming). 'Pragmatic Comprehension in Learner-Native Speaker Discourse', in Candlin and Breen (forthcoming).

Kellerman, Eric (1977). 'Towards a Characterization of the Strategy of Transfer in Second Language Learning', *Interlanguage Studies Bulletin Utrecht*, **2/1**, 58–145.

Kleinmann, Howard H. (1977). 'Avoidance Behavior in Adult Second Language Acquisition', *Language Learning*, **27**, 93–108.

Knapp, Karlfried (1980). 'Weiterlernen', *Linguistik und Didaktik*, **43/44**, 257–271.

Larsen-Freeman, Diane (ed.) (1980). *Discourse Analysis in Second Language Research*, Rowley, Massachusetts: Newbury House.

Levenston, Eddie A. and Blum, Shoshana (1977). 'Aspects of Lexical Simplification in the Speech and Writing of Advanced Adult Learners', in Corder and Roulet (1977), 51–71.

Meisel, Jürgen (1977). 'Linguistic Simplification: A Study of Immigrant Workers' Speech and Foreigner Talk', in Corder and Roulet (1977), 88–113.

Naiman, Neil, Fröhlich, Maria, Stern, H. H. and Todesco, Angela (1978). *The Good Language Learner*, Toronto: The Modern Language Centre, OISE.

Nemonianu, A. M. (1980). 'The Boat's Gonna Leave: A Study of Children Learning a Second Language from Conversation with Other Children', in *Pragmatics and Beyond*, **1**, Amsterdam: John Benjamin.

Palmberg, Rolf (1979a). 'Investigating Communication Strategies', in Palmberg (1979b), 53–75.

Palmberg, Rolf (1979b). *Perception and Production of English: Papers on Interlanguage*, AFTIL vol. **6**, Åbo: Åbo Akademi.

Raupach, Manfred (1980). 'Cross-Linguistic Description of Speech Performance as a Contribution to "Constrastive Psycholinguistics"', in Dechert and Raupach (1980b), 9–22.

Raupach, Manfred (1981). 'Production Strategies in L2 Performance', in Dechert, Hans W. and Raupach, Manfred (eds.), *Psycholinguistic Models of Production*, Norwood, New Jersey: Ablex.

Richards, Jack (1973). 'Error Analysis and Second Language Strategies', in Oller, John W. Jr. and Richards, Jack C. (eds.), *Focus on the Learner*, Rowley, Massachusetts: Newbury House, 114–135.

Richards, Jack (1975). 'Simplification: A Strategy in the Adult Acquisition of a Foreign Language: An Example from Indonesian/Malay', *Language Learning*, **25**, 115–126.

Riley, Philip (forthcoming). ' "Strategy": Collaboration or Conflict? System Constraints, Deictic Reference and Disambiguation', in Candlin and Breen (forthcoming).

Rivero, Guillermo Alcalá and Best, Margaret (1978). 'Strategies for Solving Lexical Problems Through Discourse and Context', in Blatchford and Schachter (1978), 191–198.

Schachter, Jacquelyne (1974). 'An Error in Error Analysis', *Language Learning*, **24**, 205–214.

Schwartz, Joan (1980). 'The Negotiation of Meaning: Repair in Conversations between Second Language Learners of English', in Larsen-Freeman (1980), 138–153.

Seliger, Herbert W. (1980a). 'Data Sources and the Study of L2 Speech

Performance: Some Theoretical Issues', *Interlanguage Studies Bulletin Utrecht*, **5**, 31–46.

Seliger, Herbert W. (1980b). 'Utterance Planning and Correction Behavior: Its Function in the Grammar Construction Process for Second Language Learners', in Dechert and Raupach (1980b), 87–99

Seliger, Herbert W. (forthcoming). 'Strategy and Tactic: Universal Categories of Language Acquisition', in Candlin and Breen (forthcoming).

Seliger, Herbert W. and Long, Michael (eds.) (forthcoming). *Classroom Oriented Research in Second Language Acquisition*, Rowley, Massachusetts: Newbury House.

Selinker, Larry (1972). 'Interlanguage', *IRAL*, **10**, 209–231.

Selinker, Larry, Swain, Merrill and Dumas, Guy (1975). 'The Interlanguage Hypothesis Extended to Children', *Language Learning*, **25**, 139–152.

Sharwood Smith, Michael (1979). 'Strategies, Language Transfer and the Simulation of the Second Language Learner's Mental Operations', *Interlanguage Studies Bulletin Utrecht*, **4**, 66–83.

Sjöholm, Kaj (1979). 'Do Finns and Swedish-Speaking Finns Use Different Strategies in the Learning of English as a Foreign Language?', in Palmberg (1979b), 89–119.

Stern, H. H. (1975). 'What Can We Learn from the Good Language Learner?' *The Canadian Modern Language Review*, **31**, 304–318.

Stovall, Margaret (1977, 'Strategies of Communication in ESL Learners', in Henning, Carol Alice (ed.), *Proceedings of the Los Angeles Second Language Research Forum*, 76–84.

Tarone, Elaine (1977). 'Conscious Communication Strategies in Interlanguage', in Brown, Yorio, and Crymes (1977), 194–203.

Tarone, Elaine (1980). 'Communication Strategies, Foreigner Talk, and Repair in Interlanguage', *Language Learning*, **30**, 417–431.

Tarone, Elaine (forthcoming). 'Decoding a Nonprimary Language: The Crucial Role of Strategic Competence', in Candlin and Breen (forthcoming).

Tarone, Elaine, Frauenfelder, Uli and Selinker, Larry (1976). 'Systematicity/Variability and Stability/Instability in Interlanguage Systems', in Brown, H. Douglas (ed.), *Papers in Second Language Acquisition* (= Language Learning Special Issue No. 4), Ann Arbor, Michigan: Language Learning, 93–134.

Taylor, Barry P. (1975a). 'Adult Learning Strategies and Their Pedagogical Implications', *TESOL Quarterly*, **9**, 391–407.

Taylor, Barry P. (1975b). 'The Use of Overgeneralization and Transfer Learning Strategies by Elementary and Intermediate Students of ESL', *Language Learning*, **25**, 73–107.

Vogel, Klaus (1976). 'Transfer und Fremdsprachenunterricht', in Börner, Wolfgang, Kielhöfer, Bernd and Vogel, Klaus (eds.), *Französisch lehren und lernen*, Kronberg: Scriptor, 40–58.

Wagner, Johannes (1981). 'Pasch: Rule and Term Explanation in a Game with Speakers of Interlanguage', in *Proceedings of the 2nd Scandinavian-German Symposium On the Language and Speech of Immigrants and Their Children*.

Wagner, Johannes (1983). *Kommunikation und Spracherwerb im Fremd-sprachenunterricht*, Tübingen: Narr.

Widdowson, Henry G. (1978). 'The Significance of Simplification', *Studies in Second Language Acquisition*, **1**, 11–20.

Yorio, Carlos A., Perkins, Kyle and Schachter, Jacquelyne (eds.) (1979). *On TESOL '79*, Washington D.C.: TESOL.

Index